Dean Johnson

MARRIAGE COUNSELING:

THEORY AND PRACTICE

PRENTICE-HALL, INC.
Englewood Cliffs, N.J.
1961

PRENTICE-HALL, INC.
ENGLEWOOD CLIFFS, N.J.

LIBRARY OF CONGRESS CATALOG CARD NO.: 61-11988

Printed in the United States of America

55932—C

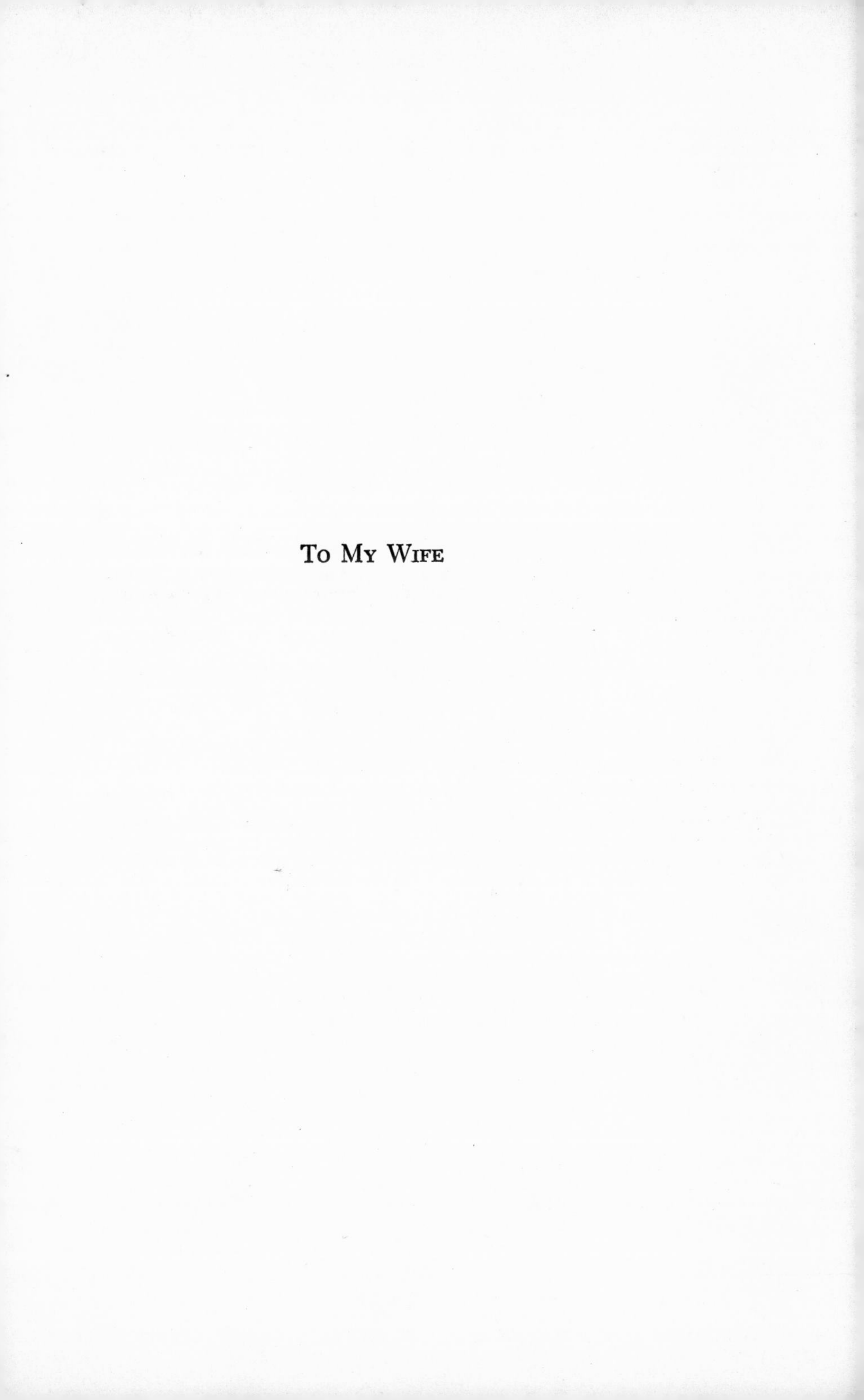

To My Wife

PREFACE

Like all books, this volume has certain specific aims and points of view. The aims are related to needs students have expressed in counseling seminars, case conferences, and supervision sessions over a period of several years devoted to the training of marriage counselors. The aims of this book are also related to the frequently expressed needs of a number of professional counselors. The points of view have evolved through many years of training and experience in the professional practice of counseling and while training and supervising student counselors.

This book is addressed to counselors-in-training, professional counselors, clinical psychologists, sociologists, clergymen, social workers, and others whose work includes counseling with individuals and couples who are experiencing difficulty in marital or premarital relationships. The primary aim, then, is to provide for these counselors certain operational definitions, theoretical formulations, and practical illustrations applicable to the practice of marriage counseling.

One of the first needs in counseling is to acquire a clear conception of what actually is done and why. In counseling interviews a counselor and a client engage in a process of communication which (hopefully) leads the client to adequate solutions to his problems. Counseling is not an exact science (however scientific its bases may be) but a practical art, in which principles are empirically derived. Thus, the beginner in counseling finds himself in a difficult situation. He has not yet acquired the *art* of counseling and, therefore, cannot adequately visualize the application of established principles. Nor can he find very much help in the present literature devoted to the field of counseling.

The professional counselor, on the other hand, may have acquired the art of counseling through experience, only to find his artistry ineffective in many cases because he lacks a clear idea of what needs to be done and why. Hit and miss *art* is scarcely more effective in counseling than *scientific knowledge* without artful application.

This book has been written in an attempt to overcome some of these lacks. Obviously, counseling cannot be learned by reading books. In the first place, experience in counseling cannot possibly be accurately or fully reproduced in writing. But even if that were possible, the most intent reader could not assimilate such experiences from reading about them. Counseling is best learned by working closely under constant case supervision with a well-trained and experienced counselor. This book is offered as an accompaniment to such experience.

Most books reflect the background of the author. Basic concepts revealed in this volume are the result of broad, eclectic training in the fields of psychology, sociology, social psychiatry, religion, and philosophy. Subsequent intensive studies in counseling, social casework, and psychotherapeutic principles and techniques, specialized training in marriage counseling, and several years of experience in professional practice and in training and supervising student counselors have served as a means for the experimental testing and revision of concepts.

I am deeply grateful to Karl A. Menninger, M.D., whose tireless efforts to bring light into darkness, faith into despair, and love into hate-dominated and impoverished life has been an inspiration; to Robert G. Foster, Ph.D., who was my colleague in the Menninger Foundation Training Program in Marriage Counseling and who read the manuscript and provided helpful suggestions; to William C. Menninger, M.D., who encouraged me in this writing task and whose interest and friendship over the years has greatly enriched my life and influenced my thinking; and to my students and counselors-in-training who, through their rigorously critical, though generously hospitable scrutiny of my basic concepts, have helped me to clarify and sharpen my ideas and convictions about helping people who are in trouble.

And what of the "people in trouble"? They have been the best teachers. Their striving and longing, loving and hating, admiring and despising, believing and doubting, hoping and despairing all belong to humanity and can be understood. Basically they sought some one who would try to understand. And this, more than anything else, they taught me—whatever else may be needed to help a person who is in trouble, his first and most pressing need is to be understood.

I owe a special debt to the late Dr. C. F. Menninger whose love of nature and its beauty was contagious and whose presence carried into any group an inspirational atmosphere of hope and certainty. Regretfully, he never knew it, but as I listened and observed this man who spent his life helping people, I knew fully that of far more importance in the helping process than his medical knowledge was the man himself and his total attitude toward people and things—an attitude that conveyed faith, hope, and love. That theme pervades this book. Counseling is not merely the use of certain techniques. It is first of all the counselor's use of himself in a manner that helps the counseled to do something constructive about his trouble. The key is not so much the techniques employed, important as they are, as it is the total attitude of the counselor, how he feels about people, what he believes about them and about himself.

DEAN JOHNSON

TABLE OF CONTENTS

1. Marriage Counseling: Its Aim and Development 1

2. Who Seeks Marriage Counseling 10

Who Comes for Counseling. Why the Client Seeks Counseling. Who Refers Clients. What the Client Expects. What the Client Fears.

3. The Client 21

What He Is. How He Functions. What He Needs.

4. The Counselor 34

The Counselor as a Person. The Counselor as a Professionally Trained Person.

5. Creating an Effective Counseling Relationship 51

Utilizing the Counseling Environment. The Counseling Relationship.

6. The Beginning Interview 61

The Initial Interview. The Joint Initial Interview.

7. Early Phases of Counseling 83

Accepting the Client for Continued Counseling. Rapport. The Client Talks: The Counselor Learns. Deterrents in Counseling.

8. Counseling on a Continuing Basis 99

The Initial Period of Testing. The Continuing Relationship: The Client's Viewpoint. Referent Reactions. The Use of Structure. The Metaphor in Counseling. Withheld Information. Quiet Stages in Counseling. Counseling with Both Spouses. Ending the Counseling.

9. COUNSELING SKILLS AND TECHNIQUES 128

Relations of Principles and Techniques of Counseling. Listening. Asking Questions. Making Comments. Silence.

10. CASE RECORDING 152

Taking Notes in the Interview Hour. The Interview Summary. The Verbatim Record. Marriage Assessment Summary. Progress Notes. Learning Through Studying Case Records. Problems of Isolated Practice. Ethical Considerations in the Use of Case Records.

11. THE USE OF PSYCHIATRIC CONSULTATION 171

Counseling as a Preventive Measure. The Purpose of Psychiatric Consultation. The Structure and Methods of Consultation. Referral for Psychiatric Consultation.

12. THE USE OF REFERRAL RESOURCES 182

The Counselor's Role and Function. Understanding the Client and his Problems. Referral Resources. Helping Clients to Accept Referral.

13. PROFESSIONAL TRAINING IN MARRIAGE COUNSELING 194

Didactic Training. Clinical Aspects of Training. Integration of Didactic and Clinical Training.

BIBLIOGRAPHY 233

INDEX 239

1 MARRIAGE COUNSELING: Its Aim and Development

Marriage counseling, in its current stage of development, is not a distinct profession. It is, rather, a professional activity practiced by persons whose basic training and affiliation center in one of the well-established professions such as medicine, sociology, theology, psychology, law, and social work.

For many years some form of counseling in the field of marriage and family relationships has been carried on, not only by professional persons but also by friends, parents, and other relatives of men and women whose maladjustments, disappointments, and sometimes desperation drove them to seek assistance with their marital or premarital difficulties. Usually only advice, admonition, or direct suggestion was offered. While this approach to marriage counseling was helpful in some instances, it was quite ineffective in many others. Today, more effective methods based upon new insight into human personality and motivation have been developed.

Marriage counseling is often referred to as an *eclectic* professional field. The meaning of eclecticism in this connection is derived from the historical development of marriage counseling.[1] Since the turn of the century we have become increasingly aware of pathological manifestations in many areas of human life. With the recognition of pathology have come many and varied attempts to determine causal factors. These endeavors have led to intensive studies in the field of both the normal and the pathological development of human personality. So much interest has been elicited in the study of the growth and development of personality that Smuts (1926) introduced

---

[1] For a comprehensive discussion of the historical development of marriage counseling, see Emily H. Mudd, *The Practice of Marriage Counseling* (New York: Association Press, 1951), pp. 1-72.

the term *personology* to designate systematic study in this field. Today it is recognized that the personologist must utilize concepts and data from an increasing number of disciplines. He must draw upon all the fields of psychology (experimental, genetic, general, clinical, social, abnormal, and the like), as well as upon such social sciences as economics, sociology, and cultural anthropology. He must also take into account concepts and data from the fields of psychiatry, neurology, physiology, and general semantics.

Because professional persons representing many different disciplines have contributed to the study of personality, today a large number of persons in all of these varied fields are intensely interested in the utilization of personality studies.

The marriage counselor must have an adequate working knowledge of the several fields devoted to aspects of personality study. Not only must he be familiar with the findings of the various professional groups with regard to the growth and development of the individual, but also with the accumulating data regarding human behavior being supplied by sociologists, psychiatrists, social workers, clinical psychologists, and others who work closely with people in a helping relationship.

Marriage counseling is one of the "helping" professional endeavors. It is concerned with helping individuals and couples to prepare adequately *for* marriage and to make satisfactory adjustments *during* marriage. According to the definition provided by the secretary of The American Association of Marriage Counselors, Inc., "Marriage counseling—marital and premarital—is here considered a specialized field of family counseling, concerned with the interpersonal relations of the two partners, in which the client is aided to a self-determined resolution of his problem." [2]

One well-known marriage counseling agency describes its work in these terms: "Counseling before and after marriage

---

[2] Janet Fowler Nelson, "Current Trends in Marriage Counseling," *Journal of Home Economics,* XLIV, 3, (April, 1952), 253.

consists of confidential interviews which provide an opportunity to talk over questions or problems with a well-trained and understanding person. Primarily people gain perspective on whatever situations they are facing, and counseling aims to help people deal with these situations in the manner best fitted to their particular needs."[3]

These definitions are broad and general and provide only a very vague knowledge concerning the actual practice of marriage counseling. Indeed, a definitive description acceptable to all persons engaged in marriage counseling is almost impossible, owing to the many disciplines represented and the variations in the training and experience of individual counselors.

However, whatever one's field of major emphasis may be, medicine, psychology, social work, religion, and so forth, it is generally agreed that the counselor should be trained in the psychology of personality development and interpersonal relations, elements of psychiatry, human biology, physiology and genetics, the sociology of marriage and the family, legal aspects of marriage and the family, and counseling techniques.

Marriage counseling as a professional activity is indebted for much of its development to the rise of marriage education which, in its turn, arose from an emerging emphasis upon the prevention of social and emotional maladjustment. It is also indebted to the increasing awareness in many disciplines of the importance of man's complex emotional nature and his unconscious motivations and strivings.

In terms of its development, therefore, the professional field of marriage counseling may be said to have threads of interconnection with at least a dozen disciplines. The modern conception of the complexities of human nature and the influence of early childhood experiences upon emotional reactions is certainly rooted in Freud's contributions to the knowledge of human behavior. Although marriage counseling has

---

[3] Mudd, *The Practice of Marriage Counseling,* p. 178.

developed with a different focus and along different lines than the psychotherapeutic views of the Menningers, Sullivan, Horney, Alexander and French, Rank, or Rogers, it is nonetheless indebted to the formulations by these individuals of psychoanalytic and psychotherapeutic concepts. It is also indebted to Gestalt psychology in its emphasis on "wholeness" and to cultural anthropology in its comparisons of interpersonal relationships in various cultures and subcultures.

The influence of psychology will probably become increasingly important as persons engaged in marriage counseling strive for objective measurement and operative definitions, and for disproving or verifying the assumptions of counseling. The contributions of experimental, educational, comparative, and other fields of psychology have provided counselors with greater understanding of the complex nature of learning and comprehension so essential to the development of effective counseling skills and techniques. In one sense, personality formation may be thought of as a lifetime process of learning. Interpersonal and intrapersonal adaptations or maladaptations may be understood largely in terms of the effectiveness or the ineffectiveness of the learning processes which involve perception, emotions, motivation, imagination, and remembering.

Supplementing the studies on feelings and emotions being conducted by experimental and physiological psychologists are the psychogenetic studies of the individual's emotions, including his feelings of dominance or dependence, anxieties, sentiments, phobias, traumatic experiences, and the like. These studies in abnormal and clinical psychology, together with the detailed studies of group interaction being conducted by social psychologists, have been of tremendous value in the search for adequate knowledge concerning the etiology of human behavior. The understanding of motivational processes in personality has been enhanced by the comparative psychologists' investigations of the functioning of basic drives, by the developmental and child psychologists' studies of acquired drives, and by the sociologists' and psychiatrists' studies in the field of motivation.

Sociologists have rightly emphasized the variations in value systems among different ethnic, religious, and occupational groups as well as among socio-economic classes. If a marriage counselor considers marriage only in terms of his own values, he will be in danger of attempting to impose the values of his social class upon his clients. Since most counselors in this country are of the middle class, the counselor's value system tends to be that of the middle-class society. Nimkoff (1952) points out the counselor's need to understand the values of the various social classes:

> The middle class places more emphasis on the visible expressions of romantic love, on duty, on ambition, on thrift, and on good manners than does the lower class. The lower class permits the freer expression of the aggressive and sexual impulses, as in fighting and extramarital intercourse, whereas the middle class encourages the inhibition of aggression and its sublimation in forms like ambition and economic competition.[4]

Sociological studies have also revealed the importance of social influences on marital behavior which are related to one's ethnic group. Values and standards of conduct vary from one ethnic group to another.

Desirable husband-wife roles are variously defined by different cultures. For example, the employment of married women in the United States has been widely accepted, whereas in Holland the employment of a married woman outside the home has not been considered socially desirable. Marital adjustment is dependent, in part at least, upon the cultural definition of desirable domestic roles.

Not less significant are the contributions of sociologists in the matter of the effect of religion upon one's values. Different religious groups define the husband-wife relationship in dif-

---

[4] Meyer F. Nimkoff, "Contributions to a Therapeutic Solution to the Divorce Problem: Sociology," *The University of Chicago Law School Conference on Divorce,* No. 9 (February 29, 1952), p. 58.

fering ways. The counselor who is not aware of these variations may be in danger of interpreting as maladjustment what in the definition of that particular religious group constitutes desirable adjustment. Marital conflict can be understood only when the various influences which have contributed to the concepts of husband-wife roles and marital expectations are understood.

In short, marriage counseling is not a matter merely of advice-giving and situational adjustment. If it were, any person with ordinary common sense could probably be an adequate counselor without much training. But the history of the advice-giving, information-providing, superficial type of counseling reveals its ineffectiveness in the large majority of cases. The bio-psycho-social organization of the total self is far too complex for such superficial measures to be beneficial in the majority of cases involving interpersonal conflict.

In the early development of marriage counseling a great deal of emphasis was placed upon the giving of information which was considered essential for the married couple and for persons preparing for marriage. But, just as in the field of marriage education, the discovery was soon made that information did not guarantee a change in an individual's attitudes. Information did not always help maladjusted marital partners to find solutions to their problems. This does not mean that providing information cannot, at times, be helpful. However, agreement is now general on the counselor's need for a basic understanding of the dynamics underlying human behavior, for some recognition of his own motivations, and for the acquisition of counseling skills and techniques derived largely from social casework and psychotherapy but applied to marriage counseling.

One of the important fields now coming under the close scrutiny of psychologists, namely, the relationship between learning and psychotherapy, will probably contribute greatly to the field of marriage counseling. If individual maladjustment occurs through the process of learning in social interaction, good reason exists to believe that any counseling aimed at helping an individual or couple to effect a more satisfactory adjustment should be based upon adequate learning theories. If counseling has as its goal helping individuals to replace attitudes contributing to maladjustments with attitudes better suited to successful interpersonal relationships, the counselor needs to be aware of the processes by which social learning takes place. Our modern understanding of the growth and development of personality indicates that the replacement of maladaptive reactions occurs in much the same manner that the unsuccessful reactions came into being —through social learning.

What, then, is marriage counseling? Aside from the previously quoted general definition provided by the American Association of Marriage Counselors, the answer to this question will vary according to the philosophy, training, and experience of the person replying. Obviously if a marriage counselor's training and experience have been largely in the field of social work, his definition of marriage counseling will not be the same as that of the person whose training and experience took place in the field of psychiatry. These two counselors would agree, though, that the very term "marriage counseling" implies a focus upon interpersonal relationships within the marriage or in the premarital state.

Considerable difference in the actual practice of counseling exists. For example, the marriage counselor who is also a psychiatrist would be more inclined to make interpretations to the client concerning his reactions and his underlying motivations, whereas interpretations probably would be used much more sparingly and perhaps more indirectly by the social worker engaged in the practice of marriage counseling. Nevertheless, the similarities in viewpoints are much more striking than are the differences among counselors whose training and experience vary. There is general agreement that marriage counseling is concerned with helping persons to make more adequate adjustments in marital and premarital situations. Such adjustments inevitably are concerned with what the client wishes to gain through the marital relationship, what he expects from marriage, how he uses himself (including his self-concept and how he feels about himself as a person), how he views the marital partner, how he feels about the partner, and how he conceives his (and his spouse's) roles in marriage and his interaction with the marital partner.

Although marriage counseling is focused on the interpersonal relationships in the marriage, the counselor should be aware of the personality functioning of each spouse. Such understanding is important because how one reacts in the interpersonal field is dependent in part at least upon the methods he has learned to use to fulfill his needs for love, appreciation, self-expression, and self-respect. Personality functioning is also dependent upon the methods one has learned to utilize in handling resentments and hostilities.

The goal of effective counseling, then, is not only to assist the client in clarifying his own thoughts and feelings concerning his situation and to aid him in finding solutions to his problems, but also to enhance his understanding of himself and his marriage partner so that each may thereby be better enabled to meet his own and his partner's personality needs. In short, the goal of counseling is to assist the client in gaining a realistic view of the situation in which he finds himself and to enhance his understanding of himself and his partner so that a more satisfactory adaptation to his marital environment may be made.

The points of view that are discussed and illustrated in this book follow a definition of marriage counseling as a method of helping individuals and couples to resolve their interpersonal relationship problems in marriage or in the premarriage state by using psycho-social material which is readily available to the client's consciousness. The material to be worked with may not always be completely in the main stream of the client's awareness but it is *readily available* to him through skillful help from the counselor. Clearly, then, the definition here espoused takes counseling out of the superficiality of mere advice giving and at the same time does not equate counseling and psychotherapy. The latter may deal with the *unconscious* whereas the former does not.

From this writer's point of view the marriage counselor should refrain from attempting to deal with the unconscious mental life of the client: He does not need to do so in employing the techniques described in this book. Furthermore, since these counseling techniques utilize the client's ego strengths, counseling would suffer from any attempts to deal with unconscious material. For example, a client began her first interview with the statement that a former counselor from whom she had sought help had told her that she was still in love with her father. "But what good did that do?" she asked. "How does that help me to get along with my husband?" As a result, her second approach to counseling was defensive and lacking in trust.

Obviously, this interpretation did little to solve the woman's problem. Nothing is more futile than to tell a person what is wrong with him if he cannot hear (in the sense of understanding) what is being said. Yet, this woman possessed good ego strength that was later called upon to help her to resolve her difficulties.[5]

---

[5] For a concise contrast between counseling and psychotherapy, see Robert G. Foster, "A Point of View on Marriage Counseling," *Journal of Counseling Psychology,* Vol. III, no. 3 (1956), pp. 212-15.

2 WHO SEEKS MARRIAGE COUNSELING

In a young professional field statistical information concerning clients is not readily available. One reason for this lack is that at the present time most marriage counseling is being done by persons who operate within the framework of a well-established profession, such as the ministry, social work, medicine, psychology, or education. As a result, correlation of data between fields is often lacking.

Who Comes for Counseling

A survey of those counseling services across the country whose directors were on the 1950 membership list of the American Association of Marriage Counselors revealed a wide variation in the proportion of men and women who sought marriage counseling.[1] Also considerable diversity existed with regard to auspices under which the services were sponsored, their means of support, length of client contact, and method and philosophy of counseling. Similarities were observed in the age range of clients, problems presented, sources of referral, length of interview, and in some other characteristics of the cases. In most of the services surveyed, about one third of the clients were men and two-thirds were women. Services sponsored by universities more nearly approximated an even distribution between men and women. The age range was from 18 to about 55 but, as would be expected, university services tended to attract a larger proportion of clients under the age of 25 than did most community services.

---

[1] Emily H. Mudd, *The Practice of Marriage Counseling* (New York: Association Press, 1951), pp. 42-72.

The nature of the client population in marriage counseling services may be expected to vary according to the name by which the service is known, the stated purpose and emphasis of the service, its sponsorship, and perhaps even its location. Although it will be several years before adequate data with regard to client age, sex, religion, occupation, and social and economic status can be accumulated to warrant generalizations, present observations indicate that the person who seeks marriage counseling is, for the most part, somewhat younger and somewhat better educated than the general population.

Persons from the lower socio-economic and educational groups seem less likely to seek marriage counseling than those from the middle and higher educational groups. Persons who are accustomed to thinking about ideas, thoughts, and behavior seem more often to seek, of their own accord, the aid of psychiatrists and psychotherapists. This is the tendency in counseling also. These individuals are usually found in the middle and upper socio-economic groups. They (in contrast to members of the lower groups) are not constantly confronted with immediate problems related to maintaining life. They can, therefore, devote more time to ideas concerned with the intricacies of interpersonal relationships. Also in our culture more is demanded of them in the way of aspirations and standards.

Why the Client Seeks Counseling

The client comes because either he or someone else thinks that he should have help for his difficulties. Inasmuch as he comes to an agency or office which utilizes the term "marriage counseling," either he or some other person believes that his problems lie somewhere in the area of the marital or premarital relationships.

Most of the agencies that function under the name of marriage counseling services make known the fact that they offer help to persons with premarital or marital problems.

Some agencies carry the title "Marriage and Premarriage Counseling Service." *Premarital counseling* is the term ordinarily applied to counseling an unmarried client concerning situations or problems prior to but anticipating the marital state. Some counselors speak of "postmarital" counseling to refer to counseling with married persons, but such terms are used merely to designate the person's status with regard to marriage. Usually the client seeks help in a marriage counseling service because his focus in thinking of his difficulties is on the marriage or premarriage situation.

The premarital client may seek aid in one or more of a large number of areas. He may think that he is in love but is not quite sure, and he wants to know how he can be certain that what he feels is love. He may feel that he loves someone who is not interested in him and may want to find some way of making an adjustment to this reality. He may be shy and withdrawn and seek help in overcoming these hindrances to social interaction and opportunities for more associations with the opposite sex. If he is considering marriage, he may have some reservations with regard to the personality characteristics of the person he wishes to marry; if he is planning to marry a person of a different religion, socio-economic or educational status, or of a different family background than his own, he may be concerned about the chances of success for such a union.

Frequently a couple who are planning marriage seek counseling together because they have specific questions on which they have been unable to reach agreement. Or they may simply want to be certain that they are doing all within their power to insure the success of their coming marriage. Many times they desire specific information which will contribute to their knowledge of just what is involved in the husband-wife relationship in marriage. They may want to know something more about the various roles of the husband and wife, what they can expect, and what they should prepare for in the area of parent-child relationships; they may have questions about the handling of finances, of relationships with in-laws, sex factors in marriage, or about various other matters which are of specific concern to them.

Occasionally the premarital client is a person who is doubtful of his ability to succeed in marriage. For example:

> A 24-year-old woman sought counseling because she was unable to carry through plans for her wedding. On three different occasions, under pressure from her fiancé, she had agreed to a wedding date but each time had postponed the date because she grew more tense and anxious and felt that she could not possibly go through with the marriage.

Problems presented by married clients vary widely in the specific meanings these problems have for the individuals seeking help. Some clients come because they are considering separation or divorce; some because they are thinking about a reconciliation following separation from the spouse; still others want to find ways of adequately adjusting to their life situation after divorce has taken place. Some may be troubled by in-law relationships, financial problems, or by difficulties resulting from the housing situation. Still others have problems in connection with necessary separation from the marriage partner in time of war or in periods of military training. Clients who have made adequate adjustment in the husband-wife relationships may seek help for specific needs, such as preparation for parenthood.

Marriage counselors frequently see persons whose difficulties are connected with personality immaturities and disturbances; for example:

> A 21-year-old man whose wife had been referred for counseling by her physician sought an appointment for himself and stated abruptly, "Well, I guess you know some of the difficulties my wife and I are having, but it is really all my fault. The trouble is in me. Although I have fought it for a long time, I can see now that I have got to have some help."

However, clients rarely come with a single or simple problem. For example:

A 24-year-old woman referred by her physician stated that she had been quite nervous recently and her physician had placed her in the hospital for rest. The physician had deduced from his conversations with her that her marital situation had a great deal to do with her physical problems. She agreed with the physician and accepted referral to the counselor. "My marital trouble is something that has been building up over a period of many months. It really has not been right since we married. There has always been too much tension. My husband has never shown any affection or emotion, and I have never understood him. Our sex life was never harmonious. My husband never thought there was anything wrong, but I was living something that was not true, thinking that the adjustment would be made after a while."

A client may complain of activities on the part of the marriage partner which are unacceptable to the client. Such complaints are usually related to the discrepancy between anticipated or desired self and spouse roles and actual roles in the marriage:

When my husband drinks he always drinks too much, whether this is at home alone or out with friends. Then he does anything to hurt me or make me unhappy. Sometimes he gets drunk and hits things such as the car or a chair with his fists. I am afraid he is going to hurt himself or me. Then, too, when he is drinking the sexual matter becomes an extreme problem. And that causes me not to want him to touch me at all at any time.

Many married clients express specific dissatisfactions with the marital partner and hope that the counselor will be able to change the spouse:

A 44-year-old husband sought counseling as a last resort and with considerable doubt that counseling would help his situation. "Maybe I really should just go ahead and get a divorce. I have thought of it for years. I don't see how we can ever work out our problems because I don't think my wife will ever change unless you people can do it. There is just no reasoning possible with her. Let me tell you what it has been like to live with her for twenty years. She has always been insanely jealous, even in the first week we were married. She saw me talking with a girl and jumped to the conclusion that I was having some sort of affair with her. She is always imagining that things are different than they really are. I have found out that it is just no use to talk with her. You can't reason with her."

At times the client's statement of purpose in seeking counseling is rather vague and indefinite:

A 27-year-old man telephoned for an appointment for himself and his 26-year-old wife. They came to the interview hour together. When, in the joint interview, the counselor asked what had led them to seek help, the husband stated that he and his wife had been married eight years "and things just don't seem to be working out." The wife added: "I have had one series of illnesses after another. Lately I have been losing weight. I have lost fifteen pounds, and I am not interested in anything or anybody. It is just an effort to live, and I don't think my husband is happy, either." The husband agreed that the marriage was not working out well: "Yet I feel we have too much together not to keep our marriage. I think I was happy at the beginning of our marriage but now she tells me that she was not." At this point the wife stated that in the past two years she had become more and more "emotional," in contrast to her previous reactions. "The reason we have got to do something about it is our son. When I start losing interest in him, I am failing as a mother. He is getting high-strung and nervous."

However vague the original statement of the client concerning the circumstances which prompted him to seek counseling, as soon as a good working relationship is established between counselor and client, the problem can be seen more clearly, and the real reasons underlying the client's wish to receive help for his marriage can more adequately be grasped.

Who Refers Clients

Out of his own feeling of need, a person may seek counseling because he has heard of the counselor or the counseling service or agency through other clients, relatives, or acquaintances, or through a pamphlet, book, or newspaper article concerning the agency. If the counseling service is well recognized in the community, other professional persons may refer clients to it. An attorney, referring a couple who have come to him about securing a divorce, may write or telephone the counseling service to say that he has referred the couple because he can see no very great reason for the marriage to be dissolved. A distraught, pregnant, unmarried girl may consult a physician and be referred to the agency for counseling. Physicians may refer married patients for counseling which will progress concurrently with the medical treatment being provided by the physician. Overburdened psychiatrists sometimes refer for counseling those patients whose difficulties seem to be focused within the marital relationship and whose psychopathology is not of such nature that counseling is contraindicated.

Since some clients seek counseling not because they really want this kind of help for themselves but because someone else wants help for them, often hostile feelings exist on the part of clients who do not welcome such referral. This is particularly true of the client whose husband or wife urges him to seek help. A client thus referred may explain in the first interview that he came only because he was told to do so and he was afraid his spouse would leave him if he did not comply.

In a few "psychologically sophisticated" communities, counseling is so widely accepted that clients proudly inform their friends that they are "in counseling" at the clinic or agency. In other communities, clients may carefully conceal from friends and relatives the fact that they have sought counseling for their difficulties. Such clients usually fear that other persons may believe that to seek counseling concerning one's marriage is to admit failure or near-failure. Extremely wide variations exist among communities and groups with regard to status values in seeking counseling.

What the Client Expects

Almost all clients who come to a counseling service hope that they will obtain help in their attempt to solve the problems confronting them. Frequently the client has little, if any, conception of what marriage counseling actually involves. He may expect that he will be advised or told just what he should do. He may hope that after he explains the situation the counselor will, in the first interview, provide him with an objective appraisal of the problem and a ready-made solution to it. Or he may expect that when he has explained why he is so dissatisfied and unhappy the counselor will "take sides" with him to such an extent that the client will be able to return home and report to his marriage partner, "You see, I was right all the time, the counselor says so." Or a lonely, discouraged person may hope to find encouragement and support, or at least to discover some ray of hope in his visits to the counselor. If he is dissatisfied with himself and senses his own inability to meet his life situations adequately, he may expect that some change will occur instantaneously, that *something will be done for him* to effect a sudden and spontaneous change in him without effort on his part. This wish is similar to the popular wish of the patient who consults his physician with the expectation that a prescription will be written for a drug specifically indicated for his physical disability.

All that we have said thus far refers to the client's conscious expectations. Unconsciously he may carry into the counseling situation a rather unrealistic and naive kind of belief in the counselor's "magical" ability to provide help. Frequently clients hope to impress the counselor favorably and so gain his respect, admiration, or friendship. Some unconsciously hope that the counseling process will not be successful because of their unconscious wish for punishment. The wished-for punishment could be realized if counseling (undertaken as a last resort) fails, because the client can thereby prove to himself that there is no hope for him.

Experienced counselors can recall numerous instances in which counseling proceeded very slowly over a period of months until finally one day the client, facing the fact that he must now either realistically work on his problems or discontinue the interviews, declares, "All this time I suppose I have really just been trying to impress you as I have always tried to impress other people." Following such recognition, movement in the case is greatly accelerated.

What the Client Fears

In seeking help for his marital difficulties, the client may feel that the very fact that he has reached the point of having to obtain counseling constitutes an admission of failure. Having such feelings, he may disguise his reasons for coming to the agency. Some clients cannot directly ask for help; instead they explain that they want to find the answer to some relatively innocuous question, or that they would like to borrow a book or pamphlet. Or a client may ostensibly seek help in the matter of disciplining a child and thus avoid the feeling of failure he would have if he were to state his real marital dissatisfactions and inadequacies.

Not infrequently clients feel that the counselor may substantiate their vague uneasy suspicions concerning their inability to measure up in a mature fashion to their marital roles:

> A 37-year-old wife was referred for marriage counseling by her gynecologist. She had gone to the physician with a complaint of insomnia and apathy. Following a complete medical examination the physician had frankly told her that he could find no organic reason for her difficulty and said that he wondered if something in her life situation could be bothering her. She at first reacted with denial, but eventually she indicated that her marital relationship was causing her some concern. The gynecologist promptly urged her to see a marriage counselor and offered to facilitate matters by making the appointment with the counselor immediately. She began to find many reasons for delaying the appointment, but the physician insisted that she should see the counselor at once.
>
> When first interviewed by the counselor, the client stated that

she really did not know why she was there, that she had come only because her doctor had insisted upon it. Eventually, however, she complained that sexual relations were not satisfactory to her and that she really wished they were not a part of marriage. Shortly before the hour set for her second interview, the client called to cancel the appointment, saying that she did not feel that she needed to continue and that she found it was somewhat upsetting to talk about herself.

Among the fears a client may have regarding counseling is the fear of being told that what he needs is psychiatric treatment or that he is mentally ill. This is quite understandable in view of the fact that some clients find their life situations so unsatisfactory and frustrating that tremendous tensions are built up.

Many female clients fear that they will not be able to talk about their intimate problems, particularly if the counselor happens to be a man. Some are afraid that they will be asked embarrassing questions or that the counselor will probe too deeply into the past. Others fear that they will be reprimanded or that the counselor may assume the same attitude the marriage partner has. Some clients are fearful of becoming too dependent upon the counselor, thereby allowing him to gain power over them. Others are afraid of becoming emotionally attached to the counselor. Although unrecognized by the client, he may also fear that counseling will change him. The unconscious fear of being changed is probably more prevalent than we have imagined because even if one's old familiar ways of meeting life situations have been unsuccessful they are at least familiar and provide some satisfaction.

A 21-year-old man sought counseling saying, "I have tried to work this out within myself and with my wife, and I just cannot seem to be able to do it. I have got to have help." At the close of the first interview, as the client was leaving, he turned to the counselor and said with a short laugh, "You know I am really a little afraid of what I might find. It is not that I am afraid of talking with someone like you. It is just that I know that somewhere there must be answers to the reasons why I do what I do, and I guess I am just afraid of finding the answers. I am afraid of what they might be."

What the client fears, then, depends upon the particular meaning counseling has for him. And this is always an individual matter.

3 THE CLIENT

After considering the client as one who seeks aid, we need now to discuss who the client is in the sense of what it is that makes him what he is.

What He Is

The client is essentially a bio-psycho-social organism attempting to adapt to a culture. He brings to the counseling situation more than just his problems: he brings himself, as he exists and interacts in a relationship. And what he is depends upon what he has become through the interaction of many forces. The human organism begins with a biological nucleus consisting of a certain set of inheritances or "givens." No two human beings ever have exactly the same heritage. The newborn infant has arrived in the world with his particular congenital nucleus, which is specifically influenced by a tremendous number of forces within his total social and physical environment, but he is always born into a specific culture. His very conception is brought about as a result of social and biological interaction, and his total life must be lived in interaction with other persons.

Relationships, then, among the culture into which he is born, his own biological inheritance and nature, and his group life determine what he eventually becomes as a person. Just as genetic and acquired biological factors have set limits within which one develops personality traits so, too, cultural patterns into which one is born and develops influence personality.

We have defined man as a bio-psycho-social organism. Thus far we have considered only the biological and social factors which influence the personality development of the client. Since man is a total organism, social, biological, and psychological phenomena are interrelated and interacting. We, therefore, cannot understand individuals unless we can know what their desires are, how these desires came about and how they change, and how the person attempts to satisfy them. The interrelations we have mentioned are inextricably woven into human needs and their satisfactions.

How He Functions

Basic to our thinking concerning the client is the concept that the human organism, like all other living organisms, has a fundamental tendency toward self-maintenance and that this tendency operates on biological, psychological, and sociological levels. Fundamental to the life of the individual is his constant attempt to maintain his equilibrium and to develop his potentialities. Cannon (1932) applied this principle (which he called *homeostasis*) to the field of biology:

> Organisms composed of material which is characterized by the utmost inconstancy and unsteadiness have somehow learned the method of maintaining constancy and keeping steady in the presence of conditions which might reasonably be expected to prove profoundly disturbing.[1]

The human organism, although constantly having its biological equilibrium disturbed, tends constantly to reestablish it. Disturbance of equilibrium is believed to occur when external stimulation brings about tension. The homeostatic function is to reestablish the energy state that was effective prior to the stimulation and thus to maintain the body in a state conducive to survival. On the biological level, then, we may think of homeostasis as providing for the organism's adjustive behavior.

When we attempt to apply the principle of homeostasis to the organism's psychological functions we cannot be as con-

---

[1] Walter B. Cannon, *The Wisdom of the Body* (New York: W. W. Norton, 1932), pp. 21-22.

fident that we know the precise nature of the needs involved because, unlike biological needs, psychological needs seem to be capable of extreme variations. However, ever since Fechner [2] spoke of the "principle of constancy" and Freud [3] indicated belief in the tendency of the human organism to maintain a certain level of excitation, this basic principle has found increasing acceptance among students of personality. "Homeostasis is a principle at the root of all instinctual behavior; the frequent 'counterhomeostatic' behavior must be explained as a secondary complication, imposed upon the organism by external forces.[4]

In contemporary behavior science, the old dichotomy between body and mind is gone. We now recognize that the human organism operates as a totality. If we wish to do so we may make certain distinctions among the various facets of the organism's functional operations, such as the psychological, the biological, and the social aspects of personality. But such divisions are arbitrarily made for the sake of concentrating study upon each facet of personality functioning, and they are made in the full awareness that the human organism actually *unifies* its functions.

The term "homeostasis" today refers to the force or principle that maintains a *dynamic* (in contradistinction to *static*) equilibrium within the organism in the interest of preserving the integrity and intactness of the organism as it attempts to cope with threats or pressures from within the organism itself and from its environment. As Ackerman points out, homeostasis "regulates response to experience not in order to maintain sameness, but rather to preserve a resilient capacity for change while preventing change from becoming too

---

[2] Vide Sigmund Freud, *Collected Papers,* (London: Hogarth Press, 1950), II, 255-256.

[3] Vide Ernest Jones, *The Life and Work of Sigmund Freud* (New York: Basic Books, Inc., 1953), I, 365-404.

[4] Otto Fenichel, *The Psychoanalytic Theory of Neuroses* (New York: W. W. Norton, 1935), p. 13.

rapid—so rapid as to disintegrate resources for adaptation and growth."[5]

What He Needs

Although there are many individual and group variations in psychological motives, certain general psychological needs are relatively common in socio-cultural environments. Admittedly some of these needs are stronger in one culture than in another or among the individuals within a group. But in most individuals in our society the inability to secure satisfactions of the need for security, self-adequacy, affection, social approval, and self-esteem tends to propel them toward unhappiness, a vague uneasiness about life, and in some cases mental illness.

Note, however, that the individual very quickly learns to strive toward securing and maintaining conditions which are likely to satisfy his needs. Moreover, through many reward-punishment experiences he learns to postpone the satisfaction of some of his wishes, to moderate some, and to displace or channelize still others. This is true because the growing individual very early learns that his needs must be integrated with the needs of his environment which, of course, includes other persons.

In his attempt to find gratification for his needs, a person may obtain a total gratification which discharges the tension that produced the stimulus toward fulfillment of the desire. On the other hand, he may only partially gratify and partially deny the wish with the result that the tension is partially bound and partially discharged. In psychoanalytic terms the ego defenses serve the binding process.

We may assume, then, that the client is a person who, like all other human beings, is striving basically toward self-preservation and the maintaining of an equilibrium of his bio-

---

[5] Nathan W. Ackerman, *The Psychodynamics of Family Life* (New York: Basic Books, Inc., 1958), p. 71.

psycho-social self. Long before he seeks counseling, the client —through his learning and growth experiences in childhood— has established characteristic ways of attempting to satisfy his needs. The interacting wish-defense systems which serve to harmonize his internal strivings with his external world have become the basis for habitual reactions. Such systems have been successful insofar as they have enabled the client to secure sufficient gratification for his impulses, to tolerate his frustrations adequately, and to form realistic judgments concerning his behavior.

The client who, out of his own feeling of need, seeks marriage counseling obviously has some dissatisfactions with that relationship. Some of his needs are not being met, or for some reason his life pattern is not providing adequate satisfaction. The counselor cannot know what all of the needs of the client may be, but he may be reasonably certain that in some respects this particular client is like all other persons he knows. That is, this individual is endeavoring in one way or another to find adequate satisfaction for deeply rooted wishes and needs.

Adequate understanding of the client and his problems is important if a counselor is to be of assistance in aiding the client to move forward in a problem-solving process or (if necessary) to move toward acceptance of referral for a different kind of help.

A complete understanding of the client's total personality is not required, however. In the first place, that is an impossibility, and, second, it is not necessary. What must be assessed is whether the kind of help the client wants, needs, and can utilize falls within the range of the counselor's competencies and his agency's function. In addition, if a counselor is to be of assistance, not only will he need to know the nature of the problems for which help is asked, but he will also need to know enough about the client's social background and social functioning to decide whether to refer the client or to continue counseling with him.

When a client's need is financial assistance or legal counsel, the issues involved in the decision to refer are ordinarily far clearer than they are when the emotional impact of a client's problem is so great that he has become almost immobilized. Under the latter circumstances a counselor is faced with the problem of estimating the ego strength of his client. If the client has sufficient ego strength to utilize counseling (*i.e.*, with the counselor's help, to apply his reasoning powers in a problem-solving way), the counselor may proceed to work with him if no other factors indicate referral (for example, medical problems that may seriously contribute to the problem).

To this point the client has been discussed as a bio-psycho-social being who is in the process of adaptation to his environment. Now our attention needs to focus upon the factors that are involved in adaptation. For it is basically adaptive functioning with which a client who is experiencing difficulty in his marital or premarital interpersonal relationships has trouble. What he really asks is that someone help him to regain or enhance his ability to operate effectively as a social being. If he is to find the help he seeks, someone will have to be skillful enough and patient enough to understand and to help the client to understand why he is experiencing difficulty, what he has tried to do about it, how and why his attempts have been insufficient, and what else might be done. This is, in essence, the way people are helped in counseling.

This implies that the client is able to bring to bear upon the problems his conscious reasoning, problem-solving powers. It also implies an ability to scrutinize his own attitudes and behavior, wishes and fears, and, with help, to modify them in the interests of his own welfare and that of others. Inability to use one's reasoning, reflective, integrative powers in this manner may be indicative of emotional illness.

The counselor's task, then, involves making some assessment of his client's ego strength. For if the counseling process cannot be utilized by the client, referral for a different kind of help more suited to the client's abilities may be necessary. There are few exceptions to this principle. The exception most frequently seen is that of the person with organic brain damage who may need to have direct suggestions and advice. In collaboration with the client's physician, such direction may be undertaken. This kind of counseling is not, however, in the main stream of marriage counseling and should be approached with caution.

A counselor's skill in assessing ego strength necessarily involves certain basic understandings concerning an individual's functioning as a social being. Among them are the following: (a) What are the client's habitual methods of handling his aggressive and sexual drives? (b) What is his censor system like; how does it function? (c) What is his organizing and governing system like; what are the major forces in its operation? Freud called these factors of personality functioning the "id," the "superego" and the "ego." By whatever name one chooses to call them, they must be considered in any assessment of ego strength, for when these three facets of personality operate harmoniously, one's actions tend to promote personal and interpersonal satisfaction. Conversely, when these forces do not operate as a combined unit and are disruptive and discordant, one's actions tend to promote personal and interpersonal conflict and dissatisfaction.

Wanting, needing, and striving are all part of one's basic push toward self-maintenance or self-preservation. They stem from the force Freud called the id. Aggressive and sexual forces are likewise part of the self-preservation drive. Much of the motivation underlying behavior that is in the interest of survival may be unknown to the individual. But if one's drives are satisfied in socially acceptable ways, he experiences a sense of release of tension and a renewal of energy or power. On the other hand, frustration of his wishes and strivings will result in an increase of tension or depletion.

An infant may be said to be all "id." Since every society

has its prescriptions and proscriptions, a child is taught very early in life that uncensored gratification of his id drives (fundamental, subconscious urges) cannot be socially tolerated. He must learn to achieve these gratifications in the prescribed or socially acceptable ways. These culturally induced prescriptions and proscriptions become part of the child's psychic make-up, some of them so early in life—and sometimes so fearfully induced—that as an adult one no longer knows how or where he acquired them. They are brought to bear upon his behavior automatically through the function which Freud termed the superego (roughly, unconscious conscience). Thus anger may be expressed but only in certain ways; sexual gratification may be had but only in approved ways. Wishes and urges, then, are constantly being censored.

The function of the ego is to govern and organize, negotiate and balance these various wishes and controls so that the person may achieve adequate gratification in ways that are constructive both for himself and for his environment. Rising tension frequently heralds inner conflict when one's ego functioning is coping inadequately with id urges and superego demands. When prolonged over a period of months or years, constant, unrelieved tension from unconscious conflict may lead to such somatic manifestations as insomnia and anxiety-laden fatigue.

The counselor is chiefly concerned with ego functions. For the counseling process can proceed effectively only if the client's ego is free enough from unconscious conflict to engage in the necessary task of working toward solution of the reality problems for which the client has sought help. When, therefore, a counselor is faced with the task of deciding whether a client will be able to use counseling, the deciding factor, under ordinary circumstances, is the ego strength of the client.

The other side of this coin is the decision to refer for a

different kind of help. If the client is embroiled in intrapsychic conflict of such dimensions and of such nature as to limit ego powers severely, referral for psychiatric evaluation is indicated. The counselor's decision, then, usually rests upon his estimate of ego strength. Referral need not be made merely because a client is emotionally upset. Most people, when faced with difficult reality problems, become emotionally upset to some degree. What is important is the kind and amount of problem-attacking and problem-conquering power that is available for the task at hand.

Careful analysis of the following points is valuable in assessing ego strength.

1. Perceptive powers. How accurate are the client's perceptions? How close to reality or how distorted are his interpretations of what he "sees" (perceives)? Obviously, an occurrence may be somewhat differently perceived by different persons. A quarrel may be viewed by one spouse as having a different meaning from that accorded it by the other spouse. One of the best available gauges of the client's perception is the counseling situation itself. How does he seem to "see" the counselor and his efforts to help? If he can perceive the counselor only as an enemy, as evidenced by sullen, uncooperative, or belligerent attitudes, something is wrong. The counselor is trying to help in a friendly, respectful manner, but the client behaves as if his helper were an enemy! If the client's hostility arises from being coerced into seeking counseling, the counselor can quickly determine this. Lacking some reasonable explanation, this kind of inappropriateness can be attributed to perceptive aberrations resulting from intrapsychic conflict.

2. Ego protective and adaptive measures. Do the client's defenses really help temporarily to maintain personal integrity and balance, or do they operate so constantly and rigidly that perception is distorted and capacity for adaptation and change is severely limited? Defenses are necessary for the

maintenance of equilibrium so that one is not overwhelmed by day to day "threats" or dangers. Ego defenses,[6] such as rationalization, projection, reaction formation, and over-compensation, are constructive if they are used momentarily for integrity protection to regain balance sufficiently to take some sort of adaptive action.

Unfortunately, however, these protective devices can become so constant and so rigid that instead of merely protecting the organism temporarily until adaptive action can be taken, they so constrict the ego that its adaptive powers are lessened. This phenomenon may be observed in some persons who come for counseling but cannot really enter into the task of grappling with the problem and reaching toward its solution because the very rigidity and fixity of their defenses wall them off from any real examination of their role in the interpersonal conflict.

When such rigid ego defenses as this are observed, a counselor should view it as an indication of the severity of the disintegrative threat or as an evidence of lack of ego strength. Usually a client whose defenses are so inappropriately used finds great difficulty in tolerating his own id impulses or in satisfactorily meeting superego demands.

The hallmark of the strong ego is resiliency. Defenses are used, but they are pliable, not rigid. Demands of id and superego can be tolerated and controlled. Realistic choices are made on the basis of available alternatives, rather than on a rigid either-or, non-adaptive basis. Judgments are made and action is taken in an endeavor to resolve the problems one faces.

These executive functions of the ego may be obscured in many persons who seek counseling. At first, they may employ many defenses, appear confused about the issues involved in the difficulty, and seem quite unable to take appropriate ac-

---

[6] Anna Freud, *The Ego and the Mechanisms of Defense* (London: Hogarth Press, 1937).

tion toward resolution of the problems. This is probably due to the tendency of emotional conflict to distort perception. When perception is distorted, accurate judgments become difficult, and the individual either cannot act in his confusion, or takes inappropriate or ineffectual action.

These persons can make good use of counseling. With help, they soon begin to see the problems and themselves more clearly. When the issues and self and spouse involvement in the difficulties become clearer, the original confusion and helplessness begin to fade and plans of action toward problem resolution begin to take form.

The weak ego, in contrast, lacks this kind of resilient strength. It is easily overwhelmed by the tension it can neither tolerate nor ward off. It is defenseless because its defenses are insufficient or so rigid that perceptive functions are constantly awry. At times the ego's perceptive and executive functions appear impoverished because so much energy constantly goes into the struggle for ego protection that little or nothing is left for adaptive functions. The ego then may be likened to a football team that expends so much effort in defense that when the time comes for offensive action, insufficient energy remains.

When a counselor sees these evidences of lack of ego strength, he should recognize also that counseling probably cannot be effective with this person and that referral for psychiatric evaluation may be necessary. A weak ego often means intrapsychic conflict, which precedes and elicits interpersonal discord.

Practical application of the foregoing theoretical considerations may be made by assessing the following factors that are usually revealed by a client in his counseling sessions:

(a) Is the client able to enter into relationships with other persons and participate in the relationships with a reasonable degree of warmth? Can he maintain relationships without difficulty? Can he give of himself in relationships with others?

(b) Does the client see himself as a worthy person? The

manner in which he dresses, his grooming, his attention to recreational activities, and his interest in good working conditions and appropriate living conditions all reflect his estimate of self-worth or self-respect.

(c) Can the client identify himself with and interest himself in something outside himself? His participation in his family, his work, his church and civic groups provides some indication of his ability to focus part of his energy upon something other than his own needs.

(d) Can the client accept frustration of his wishes, ambitions, and desires without much loss of composure? If most of his ambitions are centered upon short-term goals, frustration of them may be less tolerable to him than to a person whose ambitions center around long-term goals. Another important gauge of a client's frustration tolerance is the equanimity with which he copes with sexual deprivation.

(e) Can the client tolerate guilt feelings without resorting to overly defensive measures? Does he use his feeling of guilt as a propulsion to constructive action, or does he tend to immerse himself in his guilt in a self-punishing manner? A corollary of this point is how well the client tolerates anxiety.

(f) Can the client participate pleasurably in a sexual relationship, and does his attitude toward his spouse provide evidence that he considers the sexual relationship as a cooperative one? Or, does he use this relationship in a hostile manner?

(g) Does the client's conscience function in an appropriate and realistic manner? Does he feel guilty when his behavior and attitude should cause him to feel guilty? Can he allow himself legitimate pleasures without experiencing guilt? Does he make unreasonable demands on himself and berate himself when he cannot meet these demands?

(h) Can he deal directly with crises? Or must he withdraw, deny the existence of crisis, become ill, or turn to alcohol to forget the problem? Frequently, a person whose ego strength is inadequate becomes more passive in crisis situations.

(i) Can the client see humor in some of his difficulties? Can he laugh a bit at himself? Can he see ludicrous situations as they are? Or does he view himself and his world in a resigned, cynical, grim manner?

(j) Does the client use defenses appropriately and does he seldom resort to projection (unconsciously attributing one's thoughts or desires to others)? What often sounds like projection in an unhappy client soon diminishes and becomes merely spouse-blame out of anger if the client has good ego strength. Real projection as a chief defense is an ominous sign of a weak ego that cannot tolerate recognition that one's difficulties are related to himself.

4 THE COUNSELOR

A great deal of thought is being given to the education of professional counselors. Recently several universities and counseling clinics have established programs of study and clinical experience for the training of marriage counselors. Most of these training programs follow essentially the standards set forth by the American Association of Marriage Counselors.[1]

Theoretical formulations concerning the didactic and even the clinical training of counselors are relatively simple to evolve. In essence the process is to enable the student counselor to acquire the philosophy, skills, and techniques which have been found to be effective for counseling practice. In practice this usually means that a mature person who has already had considerable experience in the general field of human relations, possessing either the M.D. or Ph.D. degree (or the equivalent), or who is working toward an advanced degree (ordinarily in psychology, sociology, or social casework), is accepted by a university or a clinical training program for advanced study in counseling. Such training programs provide the student counselor with supervised practice as well as with didactic training.

In the evolution of a profession careful evaluation of training programs for the profession in terms of goals is of utmost importance. At the present time several professions are busily engaged in work on the same problem. To mention a few, clinical psychology, social work, and psychiatry are presently being closely scrutinized by workers in these fields with regard

[1] From "Report of the Joint Subcommittee on Standards for Marriage Counselors of the National Council on Family Relations and The American Association of Marriage Counselors," (New York: 1947), pp. 1-3 (unpublished).

to the goals of training and the effectiveness of training in these disciplines.

What characterizes an adequate counselor? Perhaps this is the most important question to be asked concerning the training of counselors. Any real answer to this question will of necessity be concerned with integrity, character, and sensitivity to the suffering and other feelings of people as well as with intelligence and the ability to learn.

The Counselor as a Person

Transcending all other training considerations in counseling is the importance of the counselor as a person. The client is always aware, as the counselor should be, that he is talking to another *person*. Counseling cannot proceed merely on the basis of what the counselor knows: It also proceeds on the basis of what he is as a person and what the client thinks about him as a person.[2]

Like the client, the counselor is a bio-psycho-social organism adapting to a world of people and things. He, too, began his existence with a biological inheritance; his life experiences have been associated with the processes of maturation and socialization through interpersonal relationships. From the time of his first cry as a newborn infant to the time he says, "Good morning," to the client he has been reacting to stimuli from without and within himself and has been finding ways of adapting to his world. All of these experiences have had their effect upon him. Did he feel secure and loved in the early environment of the home? Did he learn out of the experience of being loved to love? In the process of socialization did he learn freely the give and take of social interaction? Was his own early inner security great enough for him to learn to empathize with others? Has he found gratifying solutions to conflicts engendered by his struggles to find expres-

---

[2] Much of the material presented in this section was originally published in *The Bulletin of The Menninger Clinic*, No. 17 (1953), pp. 29-35. It is used here by permission.

sion for his inherent wishes and drives within his social milieu? These and many other experiences and conditions from the past have contributed to what he is today as a person.

A counselor can never be first of all a counselor. He is inevitably first a human being. He has become a counselor as a result of his past experiences and his own wishes and defenses. He is not a counselor merely because he wishes to help other people, but also because counseling brings certain emotional satisfactions, the need for which depends upon the counselor's individual ego and defenses and his basic wishes and drives. This is not to say that he does not truly wish to be of assistance to other persons, but that he probably has other and often unrecognized motives in entering his professional work. A not uncommon discovery in the process of his training is that one of his formerly unrecognized reasons for wanting to become a counselor was to obtain help for himself. Not infrequently such motivation underlies the choice of psychiatry, psychology, social work, or counseling for one's professional vocation.

The counseling situation itself provides many opportunities for the gratification of very deep human desires. The "ease and confidence between the patient and the counselor and . . . identification with one another" described by Cuber (1948)[3] and the permissive atmosphere described by Rogers (1942)[4] as warm, understanding, and objective, allow the client to bring to the counselor his most personal and frustrating problems in the hope that the counselor will help him.[5]

Because this accepting environment places the counselor at the center of the client's appreciation and feeling that "at last I have found someone who really understands me," a

---

[3] John F. Cuber, *Marriage Counseling Practice* (New York: Appleton-Century-Crofts, 1948), p. 69.

[4] Carl R. Rogers, *Counseling and Psychotherapy* (Cambridge, Mass.: Riverside Press, 1942).

[5] *Ibid.*, p. 159.

counselor who does not understand his own motives may in this very situation find himself indulging in narcissistic gratifications. For here he finds some satisfaction for his wish to be liked and approved and the wish to be important or superior. And if he is unable to become aware of his own motivations, his counseling probably will suffer.

Early in the development of psychoanalysis Sigmund Freud recognized the necessity for a training analysis for every person entering the profession. He saw this as the most practical means of giving the analyst not only a knowledge of what constitutes psychoanalysis and the psychoanalytic method, but also an intimate knowledge of the dynamics of his own personality. The training analysis, he believed, would tend to minimize the analyst's emotional blind spots and, by uncovering his unconscious motivations, enable him to better understand the patient and meet the patient's needs therapeutically while controlling his own needs.

This effect is equally desirable for the counselor. To say, however, that every counselor should have the experience of a personal analysis would be to take an extreme position. Psychoanalysis is time consuming and expensive and is therefore beyond the reach of many persons. Other (and for most counselors more practical) methods for increasing self-understanding are readily available.

First, a counselor must see the necessity for—and genuinely desire—a comprehensive knowledge of his own motivations and of the characteristic methods he uses to secure his satisfactions in life. Second, he should envision the acquisition of self-understanding as a lifetime process in which he incessantly examines his reactions and studies his responses to clients and others. Third, he may take advantage of available opportunities for supervised counseling experience. If the supervisor is psychoanalytically oriented, he may be particularly adept in leading the student-counselor toward insightful self-evaluation.

Effective counseling demands that one be objective enough

to keep his value system from interfering with his work as a counselor. No person is value-free, nor would that state be desirable in counseling. What *is* desirable is the ability to accept that other persons may have a different set of values and to be able to refrain from judging their behavior by one's own values. A counselor is a human being, with human emotions, and with life experiences not entirely dissimilar from those of his counselees. Complete objectivity is therefore impossible. The counselor reacts subjectively to emotional stimuli and so cannot maintain complete objectivity. However, the attainment of a high degree of self-understanding, knowledge of the dynamics underlying human behavior, and the acquisition of skill in applying these understandings in counseling can all contribute to one's objectivity.

A fourth practical method for increasing self-understanding is that of securing personal help, perhaps psychotherapy, as one recognizes his need for it. Such help can be of tremendous value to a counselor by helping him to become more objective through clearing up some of his own unfinished (psychic) business that has been finding its way into the counseling situation to the detriment of the counseling process. Psychotherapy can also provide a personal experience that graphically reveals the powerful forces of (unrecognized) ambivalent, paradoxical, and antithetical attitudes in human behavior. Thus, through an experience which reveals and illustrates the existence and operation within one's own personality of nonrational but extremely powerful behavior-motivating forces, one is in a much better position to understand his clients' motivations, attitudes, and behavior.

This is not to say, however, that psychotherapy is an indispensable experience for *every* counselor. In the first place, not all counselors need it, and in the second place, if one does not recognize or feel a need for personal help, little is likely to be accomplished by entering into such an experience. Moreover, the specialized training and supervision indicated above will be adequate for some counselors' needs. What is of utmost importance is that a counselor possess a willingness and ability to utilize constantly the opportunities that are available to him for the deepening of his understanding of his own motivations.

A counselor once remarked that prior to his supervised training in counseling he had firmly believed that his whole purpose in entering the work of counseling was to provide help for other persons because he liked people. In the process of counseling under supervision, he discovered that his underlying (and formerly unrecognized) motive was to obtain the appreciation, respect, and admiration of others. He then began to realize that these attempts were rooted in early childhood experiences which left him feeling basically unloved and rejected. With the assistance of his supervisor, this counselor's self-understanding was deepened to the extent that he no longer needed to use the counseling situation for his formerly unrecognized purposes. He became an excellent counselor and his understanding of other persons who tended to react on a nonreality level was greatly enhanced.

The counselor himself is the most effective counseling tool he can possibly have, provided he can come to understand and accept his own subjectivity. He can never help the client by being so coldly objective that he is completely emotionally detached from the relationship between counselor and counseled. Only as he uses his subjectivity effectively, can the counselor feel, sense, and anticipate the reactions and emotions of the counseled.

The self-understanding of the counselor, then, is of primary importance for effective counseling. One cannot fully utilize his own subjective reactions unless somehow he has come to understand and accept many of these reactions. As long as he has only a minimal understanding of his own subjective reactions to emotional stimuli, most probably he will "get in his own way" in counseling. Only through the understanding and acceptance of his own motivations and the dynamics of his own reactions is he freed enough from his emotional blind spots to understand others and to function adequately as a counselor.

A marriage counselor who has not learned to recognize and handle his own needs may (unknowingly) react to a client as he once reacted to his parents. For example, the counselor may, in effect, hold punitive attitudes toward a client who is expressing hostility toward him, or the counselor may form an identification with one of the marital partners with whom he counsels and, without recognizing what is happening, take the side of the person with whom he has identified.

Annette Garrett (1941), writing for social caseworkers, concludes: "This phenomenon [which she equated with the psychoanalytic concept of countertransference] makes necessary continued supervision even of the most experienced caseworkers, even of supervisors, even of those who have been analyzed." [6]

In Chapter Eight, we will consider those attitudes on the part of the client that are inappropriate to the reality situation in the counseling relationship. Such phenomena are sometimes referred to as *transference*. This is a psychoanalytic term which has been variously defined by writers in the field. Freud found that a patient often reacted to his therapist as if he were some significant person in the patient's past. Freud called this phenomenon *transference* and considered it to be related to the patient's inability or difficulty in recalling a repressed memory to consciousness. Instead of recalling the memory, the patient "relived" it in the present. Freud called this tendency to distort present reality in accordance with past experiences the *repetition compulsion*.[7]

Something akin to transference occurs in counseling as well as in psychotherapy. Karl Menninger, one of America's fore-

---

[6] Annette Garrett, "Transference in Casework," *The Family*, April, 1941, p. 45.

[7] Vide Sigmund Freud, "The Dynamics of the Transference," *Collected Papers*, 4th ed. (London: Hogarth Press, 1946), II, 312.

most interpreters of psychoanalysis, defines transference as "the unrealistic roles or identities unconsciously ascribed to a therapist by a patient in the regression of the psychoanalytic treatment and the patient's reactions to this representation derived from earlier experience." [8]

What Menninger describes under the concept of transference *does not* occur in counseling. The entire psychoanalytic treatment structure not only facilitates regression but also, in a sense, encourages its development.

The counseling structure and process, to the contrary, neither encourages nor facilitates regression. Indeed, the problem-solving work in the counseling situation discourages transference in the strict psychoanalytic sense of the term.

Nonpsychoanalytic workers, such as social workers and psychologists, have long observed unrealistic attitudes and responses by their clients. Strongly influenced by psychoanalytic theories and findings, many of these professional helpers have applied the term, *transference*, to a wide variety of attitudes and responses that seem inappropriate to the reality situation in counseling.

In an attempt to encourage clarity and to differentiate between two sets of phenomena that appear to be similar but are, in operation, quite dissimilar, the author has avoided the application of the psychoanalytic terms *transference* and *countertransference* to counseling phenomena. Mention has been made that something akin to transference occurs in counseling. This refers to the frequently observed phenomenon which is characterized by client attitudes, maneuvers, actions, and verbalizations that are not appropriate to the reality situation in counseling. On close examination, these responses to the counselor seem to be on an "as if" basis. That is, the client responds to the counselor "as if" the counselor's role were different from the role the counselor believes he has, and different also from the role that is *appropriate*

[8] Karl A. Menninger, *Theory of Psychoanalytic Technique* (New York: Basic Books, Inc., 1958), p. 81.

for him. For example, a client supposedly comes to the counselor for help in reaching some solution to his problems; yet, we frequently observe that instead of responding to the counselor in a manner commensurate with this objective, the client reacts *as if* the counselor were a tyrannical and punitive judge who, far from being a helper, is instead a hinderer, a thwarter, a frustrater who deserves the client's hostile attacks.

In short, the roles *ascribed* to the counselor by the client, however far from objective reality they may be, are quite *real* to the client and constitute one basis for his inappropriate responses. But another facet of this phenomenon is to be seen in the client's view of his own roles in relation to the counselor. Not only are his responses as if the counselor's roles were different from the reality roles but also as if the *client's roles* were different from the roles that would be appropriate to the reality situation.

One of the impressive features of the "as if" responses is the immaturity that appears in them; for example, the petulant, seductive, teasing, baiting, nonchalant, hostile, stubborn, daring qualities that are so readily observable in children. In different language, a client's ascription of unrealistic roles to the counselor and the taking of unrealistic roles for himself have a referential quality. While the behavior occurs in the present, the point of reference for the expressed attitudes and the emotion-laden responses lies in the past in one's relationships with other persons who were singularly significant to him in a psycho-social sense. Thus, counselors sometimes observe that they have apparently become a father-figure to a client.

We have applied the term *referent reaction* to this phenomenon. Further consideration of the client's responses and techniques of handling them in counseling will appear in Chapter Eight.

For our present purposes, the idea of referent responses can now be applied to the counselor in relation to his need for self-understanding.

Since referent reaction is irrational (reaction toward the counselor is inappropriate to the actual situation and is as though the counselor were an important person in the client's past), usually unconscious (the client does not realize what the sources of his reactions are nor why he feels toward the counselor as he does), and uncomfortable, the more neurotic persons are likely to form these kinds of relationships. Counselors who see clients only two or three times may observe these phenomena, but they are most likely to flourish and become apparent in the close, continued counseling relationship.

If the counselor is sensitive to this phenomenon, it is readily observable in almost any of the helping relationships. A pregnant unmarried girl, for example, who comes for help to a social caseworker in an agency may carry into that situation the assumption that the worker has the same moralistic attitude toward her that the client has toward herself and may, therefore, react toward the worker on the assumption that the worker considers her wicked and no good. Again, a client may regularly come to his counseling appointment twenty or thirty minutes late, thus reacting toward the counselor in a hostile, aggressive manner which is inappropriate to the reality situation but in accord with his past reactions toward persons of authority. Both of these are examples of ways in which individuals may unconsciously transfer to the counselor attitudes originally held toward other persons.

Obviously, the counselor who understands his own reactions (through analysis or some other method which has uncovered his unconscious motivations and emotional needs) should be better able to understand and accept referent reactions in his clients. In accordance with Freud's discovery that time is the principal factor in the development of transference, he then expects that whenever he is counseling with a client over a fairly long period of time transference-like phenomena may occur. This is not to preclude the possibility that some persons may develop such reactions very quickly, as for example, persons with hysterical reactions (and such persons are frequently encountered in marriage counseling).

The important matter is not whether referent reactions occur, but rather what the counselor does about them, how he reacts when they do appear. And here we are involved with the counselor's own reactions. The danger is that a counselor whose own neurotic traits and unconscious conflicts remain unknown to him may find himself emotionally involved with a client to the extent that he seeks unconscious satisfactions in his practice. If a counselor cannot recognize his unrealistic feelings, obviously he will not be able to control them. Not infrequently a counselor treats a client as if the client were a projected part of himself, and so attempts to reform the client because the counselor feels that a part of himself is bad and needs reformation. Nor is it unusual for a counselor to find that hysterical, seductive women easily "wrap him around their fingers" to the detriment of the counseling situation. Some counselors react to clients with such strong sympathetic feelings that their counseling judgment becomes impaired. In short, a counselor's referent reactions may involve excessive sympathy, overfriendliness, seductiveness, resentment, hostility, or authoritative and demanding attitudes. Counselors generally do not talk very much about such things because first, they are not aware of what is happening, and second, they often are not willing to admit their own reactions.

Counselor referent reaction is not entirely bad, even though the client's progress may be hindered if the counselor remains unaware of his own personal needs and becomes overinvolved with a client whose reactions affect the counselor. To a very considerable degree, effective counseling depends upon the ability of the counselor to permit himself to become a part of the total counseling situation, and this involves one's own reactions. Probably the counselor does best to admit to himself quite honestly that at times he enters into feeling tones similar to those being experienced by the helpless, distressed client. Empathic response to the client's distress does not mean, however, that the counselor identifies with the client. To do so would take away counselor objectivity and thus remove the counselor from his role of helper. The art of counseling lies, to a very considerable degree, in the counselor's ability to sense and understand what is going on in the client's mind and emotions because of what is going on in his own mind and emotions through empathy.

Effective counselors frequently experience a sudden insight into the client's personality and problems and respond accordingly. People are helped no more with indifference and cool detachment than with overfriendliness and excessive affection. The important matter is that the counselor know what he is doing and why. This is impossible unless the counselor understands to some degree his own psychodynamics.

Since each counselor has his own particular personality structure, he will also have his own individual set of motives. The important point is not that he has a particular set of motives but that he becomes aware of the methods by which he seeks his gratifications. For example, if the counselor has a deep desire to be omnipotent, he will probably become enmeshed emotionally in the need to cure or to succeed in bringing all of his clients into a happy and successful marital relationship. When this need is not gratified in a particular case, the counselor may become frustrated with resulting difficulties.

Every counselor wishes to help his clients, but this desire should not obscure the reality of the factors involved in each particular case. For one thing, every counselor will encounter clients who do not really want help and others who are unable to accept it. Moreover, clients very quickly discover whether a response can be produced when they express hostile, aggressive attitudes toward the counselor or when they express doubt concerning the counselor's ability to help them. The obvious danger here is that the counselor who has a strong need to cure may react with a defense of overcompensation and become intent upon demonstrating his ability. Or, he may find himself reacting with hostility and resentment.

But to speak of the counselor's need to understand himself psychologically is not enough. Psychological factors are intertwined with cultural factors in the life and reactions of an individual. The counselor who grew up in a happy, congenial family with parents who were obviously loving and considerate toward each other may endeavor to bring his clients to an acceptance of his ideals and models. It is sometimes difficult to accept the fact that some couples actually prefer to quarrel rather than to live in an atmosphere of constant congeniality.

Too, the counselor who is culturally conditioned to believe that the democratic type of marriage is superior to marriage in which the husband is the distinctly authoritarian person may find that in counseling he is trying to impose his ideals upon couples whose cultural conditioning is different from his own.

Understanding one's own culturally induced convictions, prejudices, class consciousness, and religious and moral principles is a necessity if one is to avoid the temptation of treating as lesser persons those clients whose ideas and behavior are different.

In essence what has been indicated thus far in this chapter is that the counselor's ability to become somewhat objective about his own subjectivity is of the utmost importance. If he can recognize that he, too, has needs and problems with which he must cope, and that his professional adequacy depends in no small measure upon his ability to separate his own needs and problems from those of a client's, the acquisition of counseling skills and techniques becomes largely a matter of learning and experience. But without self-understanding, skills and techniques have little meaning and less effectiveness.

The Counselor as a Professionally Trained Person

A marriage counselor needs to be both scientist and artist: a scientist in the sense that he is ever alert to his responsibility in searching for truth; an artist in the sense that he is able creatively to use himself constructively in his relationships with people. Counseling is not merely an art, nor is it simply a science. It is both.

If counseling could be thought of only as a science, then all one would need to do to become an effective counselor would be to find out through research based on experiment what counseling techniques are most effective in achieving the desired results. But this would be like saying: "Here are tubes of paint, brushes, and canvas. This is art." Real art involves much more than the ability to mix various paints in such a way that one evolves the desired shade of color. Form, color, and perspective are all important to painting, but of equal or more importance is the appreciation of beauty and the possession of a creative desire. The artistry involved in counseling is in a similar manner related to one's feeling about himself, things, and people. It also involves one's personal philosophy, point of view, scale of values, and ability to discipline oneself in order to learn to become more effective as a counselor. This involves learning to control one's own emotions, preconceived ideas, and value system in the interest of understanding others in an empathic manner.

A great deal has been said and written recently in the field of counseling concerning the importance and the dignity of persons. To be effective an attitude predicated on man's worth must be genuine. It cannot be put on in the interview hour and put off in the counselor's home. This involves *a basic philosophy of life*. Does the counselor really believe that every individual is a person of worth and therefore worth helping? Is he quite convinced that human life has meaning and that that meaning is purposeful and good? Does he genuinely perceive the world as a friendly place? Is he diligent in seeking out those positive and constructive elements in the persons with whom he has contact? Does he care about and understand the feelings of loneliness, inadequacy, uncertainty, and hopelessness experienced by many of the persons with whom he works? If he does not and if he cannot acquire these attributes, he will do well to seek some other vocation—for his own sake as well as his client's.

Alongside this philosophy should be placed the counselor's *faith in* the inherent *capacity of most persons to adapt* themselves to their life situation, to change that situation, and to compromise or in some other manner consistent with their own wishes and abilities find solution to their difficulties. For counseling is not a matter of solving problems *for* people. It is, rather, a way of aiding the client toward a *self-determined resolution* of his problems. If a counselor cannot find within himself faith that individuals possess such adaptive capacities, he will be in danger of imposing upon other human beings his own values, judgments, and solutions to problems—solutions which might be adequate for himself but not for his clients.

If these are admitted to be essential prerequisites for counseling, then the counselor as a person is much more important than the counselor as a scientist or technician. What he can learn to *do* in terms of counseling skills and techniques can only be supplementary to *what he is*. The very nature of the close interpersonal relationship between client and counselor demands that the value systems, ideals, standards, and interests of the counselor be ethically above reproach. If he does not have these characteristics before he enters into training for counseling, he probably cannot acquire them through the training process; hence, the need on the part of the training centers for careful selection of candidates for counselor training. Persons responsible for the training of beginning counselors should in every way encourage the acquisition and development of an adequate philosophy and ethical attitudes, and they should emphasize the fact that the counselor's effectiveness depends to a considerable extent upon the stability and breadth of his personality.

The counselor as a professionally trained person needs to be an individual of *wide cultural interests.* He should have some knowledge of the contemporary and past literary and artistic, as well as social and scientific, developments and achievements. A counselor can hardly be considered professionally trained unless he has a broad knowledge (and, more important, understanding) of the age in which he is living and the forces which have influenced the development of the social and cultural milieu of his time. He can gain a great deal from the study of the social sciences, including sociology and cultural anthropology; the study of these subjects should therefore be included in the didactic training of the counselor. He should be as conversant with the forces influencing the reactions of immigrants as he is with those affecting "first families." He should be able to understand the tenant farm family as well as the penthouse apartment family. The feelings of a tenement dweller who longs for the open freedom of the country, a little boy intently watching a firefly, a worshiper kneeling in his pew, a grief-stricken mourner at the graveside, an old man lost in the fantasies of the television screen—all should come within the scope of his empathic understanding. In the field of counseling, one's professional work is directly related to the breadth and degree of empathic response to human experiences such as these.

Textbooks can never provide the counselor with all he needs to know. The poets, the novelists, the dramatists, and the artists of all ages have portrayed the feelings of themselves and their contemporaries as textbooks can never do. The counselor cannot afford to overlook nor neglect them. Perhaps nowhere are the feelings, the struggles, the tragedies, and the joys of human beings more cogently and thoughtfully set down than in the pages of the Bible. Throughout its pages—from the nameless men who struggled with problems of the origins of mankind to David and his conflicts between love and faith, Job and the problem of evil, Paul and his "thorn in the flesh"—human life and emotions stream. Counselors can gain much from a Wordsworth seeking meaning in life from his communion with nature along the "sylvan Wye," or from a Francis Thompson struggling with his feelings of guilt and describing his flight from God in near-hallucinatory terms. These, also, speak to the counselor of the deep feelings and the struggles of human beings.

So, too, modern literature can afford the counselor heightened understandings of the intricacies of human life. Neither textbooks, lectures, nor seminars can ever provide the deep insights into the vicissitudes of family interaction and the effect of parental viewpoints, philosophies, and ways of life upon family members that one can get through the depiction of contemporary families by some of our modern novelists.

5 CREATING AN EFFECTIVE COUNSELING RELATIONSHIP

Counseling can proceed only under conditions which enable the client to talk about his problems. The client's task is to verbalize his thoughts and feelings in such a way that his total situation can be understood by the counselor. In return, the counselor verbalizes certain of his own thoughts and questions in an endeavor to help the client clarify his ideas and view his situation with some degree of objectivity. The client must feel comfortable enough in the counseling session to translate his thoughts and feelings into understandable speech. The counselor-client relationship is therefore an important consideration. The quality of this relationship depends somewhat upon the physical environment utilized in counseling, but it is far more dependent upon the attitudes, verbalizations, and behavior of the counselor.

Utilizing the Counseling Environment

Counseling takes place under a great variety of conditions; no dictum restricts counseling to the confines of the counselor's office. Effective counseling may take place under quite informal circumstances. However, most professional persons engaged in marriage counseling use a formal setting and utilize the time-space conditions imposed by the setting within which they work.

THE USE OF SPACE. A desirable physical setting for counseling is such that medical and particularly psychiatric consultation and referral are readily available. Ideally, this implies a clinic or agency setting, a medical group affiliation, an educational or a public institutional setting. But, wherever counseling takes place, privacy should be provided so that the client may feel at ease. The counselor and client should work alone. At times in marriage counseling it is advisable for the counselor to see husband and wife together, but aside from these joint interviews counseling involves only two persons.

Most counselors-in-training imagine that eventually they are going to have a lovely, spacious, pleasant room with eye-pleasing draperies and pictures and comfortable chairs. Unfortunately, the vast majority of clinics and agencies in which marriage counselors work cannot provide such an ideal setting. Instead the counselor may be relegated to the almost bare, unattractive little cubbyhole with the one and only window overlooking the street and bringing in the distracting noises of taxicab horns and streetcar wheels. If so, he simply does the best he can with what he has. If, for example, thin or uninsulated walls and partitions allow sound to carry to such an extent that other persons (a spouse, perhaps) might hear what is being said, the counselor may speak softly as an indication for the client to lower his voice.

The counseling room should be large enough that the client need not feel confined or cramped. If office furnishings are pleasant and create a blended, comfortable appearance, the client is more likely to feel that it is a good place to come, and the counselor will find his work more satisfying in such surroundings. In any event, the counselor and the client should have comfortable chairs. A counseling office can become a torture chamber for the counselor who sits six or seven hours a day in a chair that seems bent on cementing his bones to the wood. Nothing in the surroundings, including the chair on which he must sit, should be distracting to the client. Not only should the client's chair be comfortable, but it should be of the same height as the counselor's chair. The counselor who sits in a chair which is raised or padded higher than that occupied by the client may seem to tower over the client. A desk is not a necessary piece of equipment, but it can be a helpful one if properly used. A good counselor does not need to have his client seated on the opposite side of the desk from him, thus using the desk to hide behind or to impress his professionalism or his expert (authoritative) status upon the client. If a desk is used, a good arrangement is to have the client seated at one end of the desk giving some distance between counselor and client, yet without an across-the-desk atmosphere. In any case, neither client nor counselor should have to face a bright light, as for example, from a window. Artificial lighting should not be glaring nor should it stream into the eyes of the client.

The environment is not an all-important factor in counseling, but comfortable, pleasing surroundings and arrangement can contribute to the counseling process. A thoughtful and studied consideration of the use of space is therefore indicated.

THE USE OF TIME. In most clinics and counseling services counseling occurs within certain time limitations. Just as counselor and client must make constructive use of the environment within which counseling takes place, so, too, must time limitations in counseling be utilized. Since time is always involved in counseling, the counselor needs seriously to consider the ways in which it can constructively be used and the problems the use of time may present. Ordinarily clinics and agencies adhere to definite time limitations with regard to the length of individual counseling sessions. Forty-five minutes to an hour seems to be adequate for most interviews. If counseling appointments are scheduled for each hour, there cannot be much flexibility in the matter of extending the time beyond the set limit. However, relatively few emergencies require or justify the extension of time beyond the end of the scheduled interview. Most clients are more comfortable in the knowledge that they have a certain length of time in which to discuss their problems, and they readily fit into the time structure.

If a client consistently comes late for his appointment, the counselor may be interested in this fact, but he need not be very concerned about it. If, instead, the client is always so late that his hour is half gone before he arrives, the counselor and the client should examine the reasons for this missue of time. For example, Mrs. A. was 35 minutes late for her first two interviews. She came to the third session 25 minutes late and began by saying: "I'm sorry I am so late. I am always late getting anywhere. My husband is always fussing at me about it." The counselor sensed that Mrs. A. was wondering if the counselor (a man) would treat her as her husband did. He therefore commented, "The hour from 10:00 to 11:00 has been set up each week for your use. You may use it as you wish." The following week Mrs. A. came to her appointment on time. In this instance the client initiated the discussion concerning her tardiness. If, after the first few sessions, a client continues to come late for the appointment, the counselor may approach the subject by saying, "I notice that it seems a bit difficult for you to come at 9:00 (or whatever the hour happens to be). Would another time fit into your schedule better?" If such a question is asked in a friendly, interested manner the client need not feel rebuked. Frequently tardiness and appointment-breaking are indications of the client's doubts concerning the benefits he may receive in counseling. By opening the way for a discussion of the matter of time, the counselor is simultaneously enabling the client to discuss his attitudes toward counseling. If these attitudes are not uncovered, progress is unlikely.

Clients sometimes attempt to prolong the interview by bringing up questions or topics at the close of the hour which would obviously require lengthy discussion. If the counselor says, "Suppose we discuss that next time," the client may learn to use the time available to him in a more constructive manner. In many cases the client is reassured to discover that he cannot manipulate the counseling structure at will.

The Counseling Relationship

Marriage counseling is essentially a matter of interaction between client and counselor. The client experiences an interpersonal relationship which is unlike the social interaction in his everyday life. This relationship is different in that it is permissive—the client is free to discuss matters about which he is concerned without eliciting punitive responses from the counselor. Such a relationship is quite different from those the client experiences in his everyday life. Other persons may punish and reject, indulge and protect, or ignore him. The accepting, permissive environment of the counseling relationship provides an atmosphere in which the client is able to clarify and formulate his ideas and feelings concerning his situation, and to share them through communication with the counselor. Such a relationship must emerge as a product of the client's desire for help and the counselor's understanding and helpful attitudes; it does not automatically occur with the arrival of the client in the counselor's office.

ESTABLISHING CHANNELS OF COMMUNICATION. Almost without exception the client's first attempts to receive help are tentative and exploratory. He is not quite sure how he should approach this new relationship. He does not know what to expect, so he reaches out in a tentative test of the situation. For example, a young man came to the receptionist's office in a marriage clinic and said, "I have heard that you people do some marriage counseling here." The receptionist replied, "That's right." He immediately sat down, folded his arms, and said, "Well?" In effect this was a tentative and exploratory test of the new relationship. What he really meant was: "I understand counseling is done here. I am in difficulty. I need help. I do not know how it works. I do not know how to go about getting help. Please show me." When first seen by the counselor, he went into the office, sat down, and immediately said: "Well, I don't know how this thing goes. What am I supposed to do, or what are you supposed to do?" In another case, the client who had been a psychology major in college began with the exploratory comment, "Well, I know something about nondirective counseling. Do you people here use Rogerian techniques?" Both of these clients were making tentative attempts to get help. Neither of them knew exactly how to approach the matter. The reactions of both were conditioned by their past experiences.

Most clients want to know what to expect from counseling. This is one reason for their tentative exploration of the relationship. If the counselor structures the situation by giving some idea of what the client may expect in counseling and thereby creates an awareness of the responsibilities of both persons in this relationship, the client is freed to proceed in a more comfortable atmosphere. Such structuring removes erroneous ideas one may have concerning counseling. Many clients approach counseling with the same ideas they have in going to a physician. They expect that something will be done to them and for them in a very direct way. Similarly, they may expect that when they have told their story, the counselor will tell them what to do about it. Such erroneous ideas may be corrected directly or indirectly. The counselor may respond directly to the client who has such an impression by saying: "You would like me to tell you what I think you should do. I can understand that, but our experience has been that most people are not able to carry out decisions that someone else makes for them, so we do not make decisions or give advice to anyone. We try, rather, to help a person arrive at adequate decisions for himself." The client then realizes that in this relationship he is expected to take certain responsibilities. He sees, also, that the counselor is willing to take certain responsibilities. In one sense, creating an effective counseling relationship is like a game. The client makes his move; he casts about in an attempt to discover whether his impression of the relationship is correct, and the counselor, in turn, makes his move to correct or confirm the client's impression.

Since counseling occurs in a situation involving social

interaction, much of the structuring may be indirect. The client discovers what the relationship can be and how the counseling situation is structured through his experience in that situation:

Mr. and Mrs. Y. arrived in the counseling clinic, were greeted by the receptionist, and then seated in the waiting room. The counselor came to the waiting room, greeted Mr. and Mrs. Y., and invited them to his office. As they came into the office the counselor noticed that the office was warmer than the waiting room, and he said, "It may be a little warm in here for you." (An expression of concern about the welfare of the clients.) Mrs. Y. replied, "Well, it feels good to me right now."

When they were seated, the counselor commented, "Dr. M. wrote us that you would like to have an appointment. He didn't give us any details about the situation. I wonder if you would like to tell me first how you decided to come to us at this time." (The counselor is indicating that there are certain rules of the game and that certain responsibilities rest with the clients. At the same time, he is attempting to discover what concepts the clients have about counseling, what their motivations are in coming, and how they expect him to be of help to them.) Mrs. Y. replied, "The doctor recommended it to us." (She seems to be testing the relationship. She may wonder whether they have come to the right place for help. She may not be certain that she wants to enter into this relationship, and, more important, she does not know just how to go about it.)

The counselor responded, "Have both of you been going to the doctor, or just you, Mrs. Y.?" (This opens the way for the couple to discuss the reasons for consulting the physician and the reasons for their seeking counseling.) Mrs. Y. explained, "Well, he didn't go. I didn't have anybody to turn to and I went to the doctor for advice. He didn't feel like he was qualified to give it to me. He said I needed help from somebody that knew more about it—especially me. He said I needed someone who knew more about it than he did." Mr. Y. interrupted, "In other words, I think maybe we both need help, and we don't know just where to start. We've got to find the trouble and see what the trouble was and what it is." (In this conversation Mr. and Mrs. Y. are moving rapidly from uncertainty and confusion about counseling toward acceptance—"perhaps you do seem to be interested and concerned about us.")

Effective counseling can proceed only if the relationship established between counselor and client is one in which the client can feel free to express himself. This relationship is fostered through the growing understanding on the part of the client that the counselor consistently accepts him and is permissive in this context. Acceptance refers to the total attitude of the counselor in treating the client as a worthwhile person. Other persons may have rejected him, scolded him, or condemned him for his actions. The counselor does none of these, but instead, reacts to the client in an understanding manner. The counselor is not interested in telling the client he is right or wrong, good or bad. Instead, he shows that he is interested in understanding the client's situation, his ideas, his feelings about himself and his problems, and what the client has thus far considered as a possible solution to his dilemma. Since this is quite dissimilar from the reaction the client has experienced from other persons, he is free to express himself more readily. The counselor's nonverbal communication expresses to the client this feeling: "I consider you an individual of worth. I believe in your ability to cope with your problems, and I stand ready to aid you in clarifying your own thinking and planning." Within this kind of relationship the client experiences a permissiveness which allows him freedom to express himself without fear of recrimination, judgment, or admonition. Since he does not have to guard against allowing himself to express ideas or wishes which in ordinary social communication are censured, he can be more comfortable in verbalizing his thoughts and feelings; as such verbalizations occur, his wishes, expectations, goals, and desires may become more clear to him. He is then in a position to choose a course of action from the various available alternatives. The acceptance and permissiveness of the counselor, therefore, aid the client in arriving at a self-determined resolution of his problems.

Behavior in the Counseling Relationship. The permissiveness already described is essential for the development of a counseling relationship. But such permissiveness refers to the client's freedom to say anything he wants to say. It does not mean that the client should feel free to behave in any way he wishes. Time and space limits, for example, are not permissively but rather authoritatively set by the counselor. The general behavior and the attitude of the counselor must convey his expectations to the client. The client learns that he has a certain amount of time in which to talk about his problem, and the counselor's attitude conveys to him the expectation that he will assume responsibility for use of that time. He also learns that the counselor, by expressing certain of his own thoughts, attempts to understand and to aid the client in seeing himself and his situation as clearly as possible.

The interpersonal interchange during an interview is not wholly a verbal one. Many attitudes, thoughts, and feelings are exchanged through nonverbal communication. *How* either one of the two persons says what he says may be more revealing than *what* he says. The counselor should, therefore, be observant of the total behavior of the client, but he need not be permissive of all kinds of behavior. A client may attempt, for example, to involve the counselor in an argument, and this may be his way of approaching the counseling relationship. By refraining from arguing, the counselor may convey to the client that he understands and accepts even the client's negative approach.

Some types of behavior show the client's reluctance to deal with his real problem (sometimes termed resistance). For example, Mrs. C. came into the office, greeted the counselor with an amiable smile, sat down and said: "Oh, you've changed things around in here, haven't you? What kind of plant is that over there?" Then she exclaimed: "Oh, it's beautiful! Who painted that picture? Did you do that?" She rushed on into talking about form and shade of color in the painting. The counselor then drew her into the accepted structure by asking a general question, "Where would you like to begin today?" In this example, the counselor maintained consistent attitudes—and consistent behavior—in the counseling relationship. He recognized that the desire of the client to place the relationship on a social rather than professional plane represented resistance to engaging in the painful task of problem-solving. He also recognized that his task as a counselor was to help the client resolve her problems. His responsibility, then, was to encourage her to come to grips with her situation. Had he allowed the relationship to change to a social level, his inconsistent behavior would have been apparent to the client.

Most clients are troubled by a number of inconsistencies within themselves and their families. If the counseling relationship is one upon which the client can rely, it acts as a stabilizing influence in his life. He knows that the relationship has a certain and dependable structure which will not be changed by his own inconsistencies. If the client could modify the relationship according to his momentary whims, his confidence in and respect for the counselor would rapidly be dissipated. The counselor must never forget that his aim is to aid the client to a self-determined resolution of his problems. He must remember, too, that what he says and how he behaves in the counseling situation are important determinants of how well the client can profit from the counseling process.

6 THE BEGINNING INTERVIEW

Counseling begins in the first interview, but the initial interview differs in purpose and function from later interviews and different problems related to interviewing are involved. Consequently, different techniques are utilized.

The Initial Interview

Many agencies and clinics distinguish sharply between the initial interview and those which follow. The intake interviewer may or may not be the counselor who will work with the client. In some agencies one counselor is assigned periodically to do all of the initial interviewing for a designated period of time. Following intake, a different counselor may be assigned to work with the client on a continuing basis.

The initial interview is extremely important for then the client first asks for help, presents his problems and his own view of his situation. The interviewer's task is to attempt to see as clearly as possible the client's situation and the problems with which he is grappling. He attempts to discover why the client is seeking help at this particular time and just what he expects from counseling. Some evaluation is then made as to whether the client's problem is one which the agency or clinic is prepared to handle. It is almost entirely an exploratory interview; the counselor asks questions and, as the client talks, the counselor begins to see the client's total situation.

The initial interview is controlled and directed by the counselor. It is controlled because the interviewer needs to get the essential facts involved in the client's situation as quickly as possible. He also needs to evaluate the client's motivation in seeking help. Further counseling will be effective only if the client is sufficiently motivated to come to grips with his problem and seek a solution to it. Another reason for the counselor's control of the intake interview is that he is trying to help the client to understand what counseling is and what the client may expect and what he should not expect. Unless this is done, a client may anticipate that the agency will solve his problems for him. If by being passive, the counselor allows the client to talk without direction, and thus fails to guide the interview, the client may anticipate that by pouring out his difficulties he will be able to shift the burden of them onto the counselor, who will then arrive at solutions for him.

Beginners in counseling sometimes have difficulty in recognizing that the counselor can be permissive and directive at the same time. Permissiveness is largely an attitude which results from the fundamental acceptance of the other person as he is. In effective counseling acceptance is never a façade. It stems directly from a fundamental respect for persons and from a real desire to be of help to the client. Permissiveness is evidenced through the counselor's behavior in the interview. His courtesy, his willingness to listen to the client's story, his patience, and his uncritical acceptance of whatever the client may talk about are all evidences of his basic attitudes. These attitudes cannot be merely a professional façade. If the counselor himself is relaxed and at ease, and if he is able to create an atmosphere in which the client can feel comfortable, the whole counseling process is facilitated. The initial interview is directed to help the client present his problems without great discomfort and gain the security of knowing what he can expect of the agency and what the counseling process will probably involve.

We can best illustrate the difference between a first interview and a subsequent counseling session by presenting an initial interview with interpolations to indicate the significance of certain client productions and counselor questions and responses. The initial interview with Miss A. is here presented as an illustration of previously enumerated principles. The reader will note that the techniques utilized have a direct relationship to the principles involved. Miss A., a 17-year-old high school senior, planned to be married within the next six months. Her parents objected to the marriage and asked the daughter to consult a marriage counselor.

Counselor: Would you like to tell me what it is that you came to see me about? (Focus of the interview is immediately centered on the desires and expectations of the client in coming for counseling.)

Client: Well, (laugh) I want to get married. (Client is a bit nervous, does not know what to expect.)

Counselor: You want to get married? (Counselor's aim is to keep the client talking concerning what she wants to get from the counseling situation. This question indicates to the client that she should elaborate on her prior statement.)

Client: Yes, sir, and I want to know if you think it would be a good idea. (This is probably a test statement. Will the counselor take the same position in this matter as that taken by her parents?)

Counselor: How did you decide to come to see me just at this particular time? (Counselor has sensed that the client's statement was intended to test him; therefore, his move now is toward finding out just what motivation the client has in coming. This question also serves the purpose of getting parental attitudes out in the open.)

Client: Well, Mother wanted me to come because she doesn't especially want me to get married, but she said she would feel better if I talked to you. (Counselor cannot know, at this point, just what the client's motivation may be. Is she coming simply because her mother wants her to come?)

Counselor: I see. She's not quite ready for you to get married? (Counselor wants to explore the client's prior statement concerning the mother's desires before he explores the client's motivation in terms of what, specifically, Miss A. expects in counseling.)

Client: She thinks I ought to go on to college. She doesn't want me to get married before I have some college.

Counselor: What did you think about coming to talk to somebody about it? (Counselor now knows something of the mother's wishes, and he knows that before progress can be made in counseling he will have to deal with the client's motivation.)

Client: It's all right, I guess. (Laughter) (At this point the client appears to have come only to satisfy the requirement or expectation of her mother. If the counselor does not discuss this, he may expect the client to resist entering into counseling. To leave this matter as it now stands is to allow the client to assume that the counselor is on the side of the parents and will assume attitudes toward her similar to those of the parents.)

Counselor: All right to please your mother about it? (Is this all the client wants? If so, little can be accomplished in counseling, but if by this time the client has sensed that the counselor is an understanding person who wants to be of help to her, she may tentatively feel out the counselor's attitude to further test him. If he passes the test by showing her that he is concerned about her wishes, counseling may proceed.)

Client: Oh, not just for that reason. Well, if it is the wrong thing then I would be better off to be more sure about it. I think it is the right thing, and I want you to help Mother. (Laugh) But if you don't think that it is right, then I will think it over some more. (She is really saying: "I would like to talk the situation over with you, but I am afraid you may be like my parents." "I wish I could ask you to persuade my mother to agree with me, but I doubt that you would be willing to do that. Moreover, I am not quite certain that my wish to be married at this time is wise. Anyway, I'm willing to listen to what you have to say about it.")

Counselor: Well, I'll tell you—I wouldn't want to say to you that I think it is the right thing or the wrong thing. (The client can be free to fully explore her situation only if she knows that the counselor is not going to sit in judgment.)

Client: I thought that was what you would say. (Laugh) (So, she was testing.)

Counselor: Because deciding whether to get married, or even whether to get married just at this time is rather a far-reaching decision, isn't it? (Counselor is capitalizing on the response of the client in order to lead the client to further bring out her own wishes. At the same time he is recognizing with her that the matter is a very important one to her.)

Client: Well, it is about the most important decision I will ever make. (Counselor's response has been effective, but he will need to further explain the structure of the counseling situation.)

Counselor: And you are concerned about making the wisest decision possible. I believe I will be more help to you if I do not say that I think it is the thing to do or that I think it isn't the thing to do. Sometimes it is of help, though, to talk about it and see what some of the situations may be that you are going to be encountering. Perhaps you can make your decision more easily and clearly in talking it over that way. Of course, you see, I don't know the situation at all, do I? (Now that reassurance has been given the client that the counselor is not going to try to make her decision for her, and that it may be important for counselor and client to talk the situation over, counselor leads her into a discussion of just what is involved in her situation.)

Client: No. Do you want to ask me some questions? (Client doesn't know how to begin to tell her story.)

Counselor: Would you like to just tell me what the situation is? (This is a general question which allows the client to start wherever she wishes. In the event she is concerned with a particularly pressing problem, she is free to begin with that problem.)

Client: Where do you want me to start? (Client finds it difficult to begin. Is this because she is still afraid that the counselor will be like her parents? Perhaps the counselor needs to guide Miss A. into a little further discussion of the child-parent conflict.)

Counselor: Well, apparently your feeling is that the problem right now, so far as you are concerned, is that you want to get married and your mother is not so sure this is a good idea.

Client: Uh huh, kinda. (Laugh) And Mamma says that—no, Mother and Daddy—I guess I shouldn't limit it to Mother because they agree on it. They say they probably can see—Oh, maybe you will know something! Isn't the minimum age to get married without the parents' permission in this state 21? (Client agrees that the counselor has stated part of the problem correctly but that more is involved than that. She begins to talk about further implications of the problem, but stops and asks a factual question. It may be difficult for the client to get into the problem. On the other hand, perhaps another aspect of the problem came into her mind and prompted the question.)

Counselor: I believe so. (The counselor responds to the factual question. If the client is having difficulty in talking about the problem, this may allow her a bit more time and make it a bit easier for her. If she is grappling with an aspect of the problem with which the question is concerned, the factual answer will allow her to discuss it.)

Client: And so if we—they said they don't want to give us their permission to get married, and I don't especially want to get married without their permission because that just isn't right. But I'm going to go ahead and do what I think is right whether they think it is or not. (Now the relevance of the factual question is apparent. It is also apparent that Miss A. is now ready to discuss her conflictual feelings concerning her problem.)

Counselor: You would rather not if you can get their permission. (Counselor demonstrates to the client that he understands something of the conflict.)

Client: Definitely. (Laugh) But I do want to get married in the church. (This is another aspect of the conflict.)

Counselor: So, when you think about the church wedding, that involves, usually, your parents. And if your parents were in on it, it would give you a lot nicer feeling. Is that it? (Counselor again demonstrates that he understands something of what the client is feeling.)

Client: Yes, if they are really—and golly! I want to share it with Mamma and Daddy. They are always against it, and it is not much fun to tell anybody when they're so set against it. (Client now feels that the counselor really wants to understand and be of assistance to her.)

Counselor: When did you decide that this is what you wanted to do? (Counselor could have continued responding in an understanding way to Miss A.'s expressions of feeling. However, this is a first interview and the counselor needs to know more about the situation. Now that he has passed the client's initial test he can proceed to gather information that will enable him to see the client's problem more clearly.)

Client: Well, I started going with him—let's see—our two year anniversary was February 21. I had known him before, but I didn't think he was especially interested in girls. (Laugh) But I went to a dance, and he came and danced with me. We remembered each other and talked and then after that we saw each other at church and places and we talked. Then he called me up for a date, and pretty soon we were going steady. It wasn't too long after that that he told me that he loved me, but I wasn't quite so sure then. I wanted to take a little more time before I said anything. Then we moved away from there and that put us a little bit apart, so he had his own car and he came up on weekends. We went to church and places together. I guess we knew we were going to marry each other before then, but we definitely said it on Easter. And then—let me see—we didn't tell Mamma and Daddy right away, because it wasn't anything definite. It was just some time in the future, and so it has been back and forth when we were going to get married next summer, and I felt that I ought to tell Mamma what I wanted to do. I didn't want to go sneaking around about it, so I told them and they got real upset about it.

Counselor: When did you tell them? (Counselor wonders how long Miss A. and her parents have been struggling with this problem and just what is involved in the parent-child interaction.)

Client: Oh, I don't know. I talked—just recently—it has just been a couple of weeks ago since I told them about this, but we considered getting married next summer and then I told Mamma and Daddy. But we talked it over, and we didn't see how we were going to get any money, so then we said we would wait until we could see how we could get some money. So then it has come up again about two weeks ago, and we think we can swing it.

Counselor: What is he doing right now? (This allows the client to talk further about the recent decision of the client and her fiance.)

Client: Well, he is working right now. He plans to start to college next fall.

Counselor: In—(name of college)?

Client: Uh huh. He is pretty sure that when he gets out he can make about five thousand a year.

Counselor: If he goes to school what about the financial picture then? (Counselor is drawing the client into a factual discussion of a problem the client has already intimated.)

Client: Well, we talked about—we both want to go to college. We both feel that we need to, and we both want to. So we felt that it would be more important for him to get his education first, so I will work. And I'm going to a business school this summer and take courses in secretarial work so I can get a job. When we get married I will go down where he lives and where he will be going to school, and I'm hoping that I will be able to get a job there. (Laugh) (Apparently this is the way Miss A. and her fiance have discussed solving the financial problem. The counselor cannot know whether Miss A. is quite convinced that this will solve the problem. She indicates some doubt by saying that she is hoping to be able to get a job and by laughing as she says it.)

Counselor: You are hoping that by doing this you can work and bring in some money? (This response enables the client to think further about it.)

Client: I should be able to. There are a lot of people who know me down there. He is well known, too. (She seems to recognize that there is some question about this plan working out.)

Counselor: So it is just a little difficult to know just what the financial picture would be at this time? (Counselor has recognized the tinge of doubt in the client's mind, and leads her to discuss it further.)

Client: Yes. We plan to have some money saved up by then. I've got a little bit of savings, not much, but we are going to try to get at least five or six hundred dollars by the time we get married, and then if I have a job maybe we can make it. I don't know. Do you think it would be possible? (Laugh)

Counselor: You wonder just a little whether you can make it on this? (The counselor cannot possibly know whether the couple could survive in this manner. Even if he had a definite opinion on the matter, it is unlikely that he would be of much assistance to the client by stating it at this time.)

Client: I think we can make it if we have to. I mean, I know some people who got married, and they borrowed ten dollars to get married on, and they are doing all right. (The counselor's question has probably been accurate in terms of the client's doubts, but it is somewhat threatening to her, and she returns to her wish to be married in spite of the difficulties involved.)

Counselor: Will he be working while he is in school? (Again the counselor is eliciting factual information which he hopes will be weighed by the client as she talks about it.)

Client: I don't think so—well, just a little bit.

Counselor: So about the only income would be what you would be able to make?

Client: Uh huh. He may work. We haven't discussed him working. I don't especially want him to because I want him to concentrate on his college work and get that over with. (Some important facets of the problem have not yet been thoroughly discussed by Miss A. and her fiance. The counselor needs now to be concerned with some details of these facets.)

Counselor: Will he have to spend some time in the service?

Client: Well, if he keeps his grades up and scores on that selective service exam and stays all right on ROTC, he probably wouldn't be drafted for the first two years. But if it does happen, and I hope it won't, but I imagine I will go to college while he is in the service. (It is more and more apparent that further detailed consideration needs to be given to aspects of the situation which have been passed over lightly in the couple's planning.)

Counselor: Then from a financial standpoint a lot hinges on your working and your being able to keep on working?

Client: Well, I guess so. It would. But, if worse comes to worse, there wouldn't be anything we could do. (Laugh)

Counselor: I suppose that means, too, that you don't plan to have children soon? (Has she carefully considered this aspect?)

Client: I hope we can wait until he gets out of college.

Counselor: That's something you hope will put itself off, huh?

Client: Uh huh. Really a lot of chance things come into this, but I think that no matter what happens, we will be able to work it out. (More evidence that much of the client's plan is based on hope, rather than on a realistic consideration of the problem involved.)

Counselor: You have probably discussed that possibility of a baby coming along before you planned for it?

Client: Uh huh. (Laugh)

Counselor: And what would you plan to do then?

Client: I really don't know. It depends. There are a number of different things we could do, and I don't think we have to decide right now. (Laugh) (She recognizes now that she has been depending on the chance element in the situation working out to her satisfaction. The laughter may be an expression of this recognition with the counselor.)

Counselor: That is just a little hard to think through, isn't it? I can see how that is something you would hope very strongly about, though much seems to depend on it in terms of your planning. (Counselor gives reassurance that he understands something of what the client is feeling, and he also encourages her to consider the matter more carefully.)

Client: Well, I don't know. I was just thinking over some possibilities right now. Well, we could leave the baby with his folks. His mother brought up five children, only I don't especially like that. Or, he could just go on to the Army and get some of that over with, and then when he got out he could go to school on the G.I. Bill. Or, well—I don't think that he would just stop and go to work without going to college or something like that.

Counselor: I get the impression that you feel that this is something that is pretty urgent. You really want to do it, but there are some problems in the way. (Counselor senses that the discussion of the financial aspect has served his immediate purpose of encouraging the client to think more carefully about the problem, and he guides the interview now into a discussion of the immediacy of the client's wish to be married.)

Client: I want to get married. (Laugh)

Counselor: What's the plan—what alternative is suggested by your parents on this? (Again focusing on the immediate from the standpoint of the conflict between the client and her parents.)

Client: Well—wait.

Counselor: Wait until?

Client: They are really vague about wait until when. (Laugh)

Counselor: Just wait, huh? What about his parents? (Another element is introduced here. Are both sets of parents in agreement about waiting? Is the couple faced with a conflict on both sides?)

Client: They say it is all right.

Counselor: Do your folks give you reasons for waiting?

Client: They want me to go to college. That's about the main thing. They say they will feel better about it if I have a little more experience, and they say that college gives you a better rounded view. They would like for me to have a little more behind me than just high school. I have studied marriage in high school, and I've taken courses in Home Economics. That's what I want to major in—Homemaking and Family Living. I'm hoping that if I work that I can take a few hours of college work in the evenings, but I don't know if I can. It all depends.

Counselor: You would really like to continue your education?

Client: Oh, yes. I intend to go on if everything works out all right, and if I can take it during that time and in the summers, I will not have but one year after he gets out of school and a summer. Then we will both be through with our college education and be ready to start our family.

Counselor: You have been going with him for quite a while. Had you dated quite a bit before that? (Counselor thinks that he should have more information before leading the client into more detailed discussion of these points. Moreover, enough discussion has taken place to set the client thinking concerning some of the aspects she has lightly passed over thus far.)

Client: Oh, I was pretty popular. I had dates for any occasion that I especially wanted to go.

Counselor: Have you been in love before? (Is Miss A's intense love feeling at this time something completely new?)

Client: Uh huh, when I was—let's see—I guess I was just a freshman in high school. I don't know if I was really in love. I guess I thought I was at that time. Anyway, this was a boy who was in the Army, and—well, he said that he loved me. I never told him I loved him, but he said that he wanted to marry me. But—well, we—I write to him about once a year.

Counselor: But you feel more strongly about this time?

Client: About now? Yeah, this time. Uh huh. (Counselor now recognizes that the client's present feelings are being measured over against probably only one previous experience. This may be further considered at a later time, but the counseling hour is drawing to a close at this point.)

Counselor: I wonder if there are some things in your situation that you are wondering about. I don't mean now just what your folks have talked to you about, but is there some particular thing you would like to talk about? (Again reassurance that the counselor is interested in the client's own problems and welfare.)

Client: Well, I don't think that there is anything. Mother asked me if I had a problem and I said no. I think we've got what it takes to go through with it no matter what, and well, we—I don't—there won't be any question of a divorce. We both have family backgrounds of no divorce, and neither one of us believe in it. And so we—there just won't be any of that. We don't want any way to get out of it. So, when we get married it's going to be permanent. We've talked it over—well, not—we know a couple of married couples and they say that lots of times—I guess even with Mammas and Daddys that questions come up in a family. And we know there are going to be arguments and disagreements and a lot of hard times, but we feel that our marriage will be more important than either one of us, personally. So I think that we can sit down and work it out. Whenever we have fusses now, we really pour it on to each other, but we sit down and talk about it and work it out.

Counselor: You think you have reached some pattern of solving your problems now and that would probably continue into your marriage?

Client: I think so, and we both feel very much at ease with each other. We aren't afraid to tell each other if there are other things that we would like, especially. And we don't get to see each other except on weekends, although we try to remember the things that we think the other person will like to tell each other.

Then whenever either one of us has any problems or—well, since I have come here I don't have any real close friends that I see a lot. I have some good friends, but it is such a big school here and I don't have any classes with them so I hardly ever see them. So I always feel better because I can tell him just about everything. I tell him all about my school work and different things—things that I am worried about—and that makes me feel better about it. And whenever he gets worried he tells me about it.

Counselor: You can talk frankly and easily to each other.

Client: Uh huh, and when we are mad at each other we talk frankly, too. (Laugh) He doesn't get mad very much—maybe every three or four months, something like that, and then we have our little fuss and make up again.

Counselor: Does he know your friends here, or—

Client: No, he comes on weekends and maybe we go to church in the morning, and he comes home and eats dinner with us. Then if I wash dishes, maybe he will go out and play with my brother. And sometimes we—oh, in the summer we go swimming and on picnics and all. We have taken other couples swimming. Sometimes we double date that way. Usually we go riding in the afternoon and to a show at night. (The client is talking freely and easily now and apparently a good rapport has been established. The interview is about to draw to a close and the counselor will need to aid the client in reaching a decision as to whether she wishes to continue counseling. He will also need to explain further what will likely be involved in the counseling situation.)

As yet, the information is too meagre for the counselor to know all of the problems involved in the client's situation. At this point the counselor has been able, however, to make a tentative evaluation of the client's suitability for counseling, and he has gathered enough information to enable him to decide that the case may properly be handled by the counseling agency. He has observed no manifestation of serious emotional disorder. He has recognized that the client is intelligent, able to verbalize her problem easily, and interested in achieving an intelligent solution to her difficulties. Moreover, the counselor has been able to aid the client in overcoming some of her initial doubts and fears concerning the counseling process.

The Joint Initial Interview

If a couple seek counseling together, the counselor may believe that the clients' problems may be clarified more readily if he interviews the couple jointly, than if he sees them separately. The joint interview often helps the counselor to gain a reasonably clear picture of the manner in which the two persons communicate with each other. It also has the advantage of providing the counselor with both sides of the problem simultaneously. Since each person knows that the other is aware of certain important facts, he is not as likely to color these facts to his own advantage as he may be if the counselor sees them separately. On the other hand, the counselor must not allow the interview to degenerate into an argument between the two persons. In the event he cannot adequately control the interview, he will do well to terminate the joint interview and see each person individually.

The following example is presented as an illustration of the advantages and disadvantages of the joint initial interview. Mr. R., thirty-one years of age, and Mrs. R., twenty-eight, sought counseling together. The couple had three sons, aged four and one-half, three, and sixteen months. They had been married eleven years.

Counselor: Won't you sit here, Mrs. R., and you here, Mr. R.? Now I, of course, know nothing about the difficulty or just how you decided to come to us. I wonder if you would like to tell me about it. (Since the counselor knows nothing whatever about the couple, he attempts to focus the interview on what they want to achieve through counseling.)

Mrs. R.: Well, my mother—this marriage has been pretty bad for about three and a half years, and—we were overseas at the time, and I had been writing to my mother this and that and different things. She was very upset because she has always thought he was wonderful, and she was always trying to smooth things over for us. Finally, it got as bad as it could get recently, and she was getting bad headaches over it and she heard about this counseling center so she was going to go up where she lives for them to talk to her in order to try to understand our situation so she wouldn't be so upset about it. And they told her that there was also a place here that we might go to, so she cancelled that other deal and told us to come here.

Mr. R.: She was actually, in a way, blaming herself for the way Ann (the wife) was acting, you know, and it bothered her so she was trying to get help in that respect, I guess. She must have felt something was wrong to have you act the way you do.

Counselor: You were saying that it has been pretty bad for about three and a half years? (The counselor is avoiding the possibility of an argument developing. He is also attempting to discover what the marriage has been like during the time that the couple have been experiencing difficulty.)

Mrs. R.: Well, there is a reason for that. I mean, being overseas is very bad on marriages for many reasons. We had to be over there because of his job. It was rugged work most of the time, and he was not home hardly at all, and I began to feel sorry for myself. I was doing everything that I could to keep myself interesting to him. I kept my appearance up, but I never seemed to get him to notice, and the first thing I did write home to my mother was that he was not paying any attention to the little boy, which to me is the most important thing. I mean, I seem to demand a lot of—I want him to be around as much as possible, but the fact that he ignored the child hurt me very much because we had tried for five years to have children. Then this miracle finally happened and continued to happen for three children (laugh). So, that was the beginning of it, and then he began to be very good friends with a fellow who worked with him. He was with this one person who I didn't think was a very nice character at all. They went hunting constantly, so he was never home, and in the meantime, I became pregnant, and—well, I admit I might have been a neurotic, pregnant woman which is very common, but I became more discontent and began to feel more and more neglected. I mean I was very, very hurt, and then finally it didn't hurt any more. And I haven't cared for him since then, and that was over three years ago. At this point we are just staying together because of the children, and I can't see spending the next fifty years that way.

Mr. R.: Well, since that time you have been back in love with me a couple of times.

Mrs. R.: No, I haven't.

Mr. R.: Well, I think you thought you—at the time you said it you probably did believe it, but when any little thing comes up—

Mrs. R.: Well, that's it. It is not actually a love; it is just that he is a nice person, and he is very nice now. If he had been this way before, I don't think anything would have happened, but I don't care any more. It just is—it isn't there. (This interchange between the clients is a serious, friendly one. They do not seem to be trying to hurt each other. Since it seems not to be threatening to either of them, the counselor allows the interchange to take place, because it is providing an opportunity for him to see what their communication is like.)

Mr. R.: Well, your values change, and I think you are growing up now. You must admit that you weren't a real prize housewife for many years, either.

Mrs. R.: No. We never seemed to get synchronized in our feelings. When he was—when I was madly in love with him, he was off running around, and when he was madly in love with me, I didn't care anything about him.

Counselor: You just haven't been able to get together.

Mrs. R.: We have been married eleven years, and the first four years of our married life—he went overseas two days after we were married, and he was gone fifteen months—but I was not true to him for the first four years of our marriage. And then when I finally was true to him, he was not around so we never seemed to get together.

Counselor: And you say that it has been pretty bad for quite a while, but that recently it has become about as bad as it could be? (Counselor is beginning to see something of what the situation has been like but he needs to know what has recently happened that caused the couple to decide they must do something about the marriage.)

Mrs. R.: Well, I want to leave him, and I have just been going on now for all these years, and I finally—I just want to do that.

Mr. R.: Well, last October she wanted a divorce, and after we had the trouble overseas she had an affair with a fellow, so she wanted to get a divorce and marry him. I told her I would just forgive her everything, and she could just remember it as a nice memory, you know, but we would just keep the family together. We have the children. Then, in the middle of the trouble, I was transferred (to another country), and when we got over there she continued to go out with other fellows. She was very bitter toward me at the time, and then she got pregnant, which made her more bitter. She blamed me entirely for it, although I didn't plan it that way. It was just one of those things that happen. Then we got back here, and we were living in first one place and then another. Then, last November—or October—she wanted to get a divorce again. So I argued again, and we discussed it and everything else, and I asked her not to leave and to forget about it, you know. She wanted to take the children and go back to this fellow she had the affair with. Well, three or four months later, for some reason, we got very close then. So she said she was so glad that I talked her into it, that she was in love with me again. So then we were very close for about two months, and then she went home to see her folks and about three weeks later I went up there and she was very cool again. She said it was all a story she had been telling me. Well, that was sort of a shock. We were there for a few weeks, and on the way back she said she wanted to go back to this man and get it all cleared up. She wanted to take the children, and they had been dragged back and forth so much, and she admitted it was not the best thing for them. So I said, "Well, you go ahead." First I asked her not to go, and she said she had to get it off her mind, so then she can come back and we can start all over again. But she said that until she talked to this fellow she can't get it all straightened out. At the time I said, "What are the chances of not getting it straightened out?" She said, "They are so remote that you don't even have to worry about it." Then she said, "For the first time I am afraid to lose you." Well, anyhow, she had not heard from him for a couple of years, but I said: "Even if the chances are one out of a hundred that things will get fouled up again I would rather you wouldn't go. You stay here and I feel that as time passes by we can smooth things over and get as happy as you would if you went up there and ended everything right away." So she said she was going to go even if I wouldn't help her, which she possibly could do. I would just come home some night and she would be gone. So she went a few months ago and was gone for about five or six weeks, and I took care of the children. Then after she had been there a couple of weeks she called up and said, "Well, I have decided, but you aren't going to like what I have decided to do." So now she wants to get a divorce and marry this fellow. So, as far as my actions overseas, I can't exactly define them myself, although you know the first four and a half years she always said she loved me, but still I know she was constantly running around. (None of this seems to be threatening to Mrs. R. She nods in agreement from time to time.)

Mrs. R.: Well, I was only 16 when I got married. I didn't know I loved him. I didn't know what love was until I actually fell in love.

Counselor: When you made your decision to come here, how did you think of our helping you? What did you really wish? (Counselor tries to focus attention on what the couple wants to achieve through counseling.)

Mrs. R.: Do you want to know frankly my reason for coming here?

Counselor: Yes.

Mrs. R.: Every time that I do something or I am going to do something that my husband doesn't think I should or he doesn't want me to do, he runs and tells my mother, and I get pretty tired of that. She can be pretty wonderful, but if I don't mind her, she can be very vicious and she suggested we come here. If I don't come here, she will make it very difficult for me. That's the reason.

Counselor: You felt that you had to do this in order to meet her requirements? (The question enables the client to express her own wishes concerning counseling.)

Mrs. R.: Well, I mean I wanted to come if you can help either of us. You won't help us stay together because that is definitely finished, but I thought if you could help us accept it as it is, or—I don't know really what it could be, but I knew if I didn't come here my mother would give me a lot of trouble, which she is very capable of doing. I mean, she can think of things that nobody else can think of (laugh), even to the point where—Well, she doesn't want our marriage to break up because she has a nice son-in-law. (Laugh)

Mr. R.: Of course, other people don't have to live with me.

Mrs. R.: You—no one is—I mean—well, if it came right down to it she would help me, but she will struggle to the last breath, and then she will go over to me, but in the meantime she will—she even offered to—if he could get the children, she said she would come and live with them and take care of the children. I know she actually would not do that if it came down to it, but she does all these things to make me unhappy and confuse me and force me to stay with him, because it may—I want my children definitely and he has been a very good father for the past year, but he has not been so good before that.

Mr. R.: Well, that sort of varies with the way she happens to feel. She said I didn't pay any attention to the first child, but then when the next one was born she said I didn't pay any attention to him and that I paid too much attention to the other one.

Mrs. R.: The time when he first started picking up the second boy and playing with him, it was just when he knew he was leaving and the boy was fourteen months old by that time. He never paid any attention to him before, living in the same house, and when he finally did try to play with the boy and offer to do things for him, the boy was so surprised he didn't want to go to his father. It was such a shock to me because I feel like it is a big fraud. We planned—I went through a lot of discomfort. I went to many, many doctors through all these years to get children, and I thought, Boy! I'm going to have the best father for the children in the world. Well, I don't know. Maybe I expect too much. I don't know.

Mr. R.: Well, I used to feed him, and he would sit on my lap and eat. Most of the time he would eat sitting on my lap. What a chow hound that guy was! (Laugh)

Mrs. R.: We have three fine children.

Mr. R.: Yes, we have three fine children. I guess maybe I feel a little closer to the one that I supposedly neglected. He was always wanting to sit on my lap and stuff like that.

Counselor: Mrs. R., apparently you feel that things might have been different if it had been like that all the time?

Mrs. R.: This past year? Yes.

Counselor: But you find it difficult to accept what is now?

Mrs. R.: Yes. There is just no feeling at all. If we stayed together it would be maybe six months or a year, and it would fall flat on its face again.

Mr. R.: Not if we both made a genuine effort, honey. I know I don't want you unless you decide in your own mind that you want to stay, and that you are going to really try to make a go of it and make something permanent.

Mrs. R.: We just go along every two months, and then four months—it has just been going like that for two years now, and it doesn't get any better. It is just an existence.

Mr. R.: Well, it could if you made up your mind. That's how I feel about it. Of course if you really don't want to, there is not much you or anyone can do about it.

Counselor: Suppose we talk separately now for a little while, and then we can get together again.

Mr. R.: Okay. Why don't I step out for a while?

Counselor: All right. You will find reading material out there, and we will get together again after a little.

Mr. R.: All right.

The counselor has chosen a good point to terminate the joint initial interview. The couple seem to have moved closer together in their communication during this session, and the counselor is now in a better position to see the husband and wife separately. Note that the counselor has had opportunity to explore briefly with the couple their reasons for seeking help, what kind of help they expect to receive through counseling, and some of the problems with which they are struggling. The joint interview has also provided opportunity for the counselor to observe the way in which the husband and wife relate to each other and the manner in which they communicate their feelings to each other.

In the interview just cited, the counselor said very little, but the interview—not the clients—was under proper control throughout. The initial interview should establish an atmosphere of mutual confidence and a working relationship. The first task of the intake interviewer, then, is to listen. The counselor needs to glean facts about the client's situation, but he should not focus attention so thoroughly upon fact finding that the client feels thwarted in telling his story.

Although a counselor should not approach the intake interview with the conviction that he must find definite answers to a group of specific questions, he will be wise to remember that he should come to the interview with certain goals. The counselor's ability to listen to the client's story has been emphasized, but such listening should be purposeful beyond the catharsis afforded the client. If one is a good listener, many of the facts necessary for adequate understanding of the client's situation will be answered without questioning on the part of the counselor.

The assumption should not be made that one need not ask questions, but rather that the counselor's questions should serve to clarify (both for counselor and client) the problems presented and the hopes and expectations of the client as he seeks help.

The following considerations are presented, not as a list of questions the counselor may ask, but rather as a summary of the kind of information that will be helpful to him as he begins to make a tentative evaluation of the client and his problems:

1. Observe the kind of person the client seems to be. How does he relate to the counselor? How does he begin the interview? What are his beginning words in the interview? What seems to be his affect at this point?
2. What is the source of referral and what is the client's reaction to referral? Does the client himself have some motivation for coming for counseling? Will he probably have enough motivation to make use of counseling?
3. What precipitated the client's seeking an appointment here at this time? Usually some event has brought the client to seek help.
4. Has the client made previous efforts to obtain help for his problems? If so, what were the circumstances and what was the outcome?
5. How has the client hoped or expected marriage counseling would benefit him?
6. What does the client see as his problems in marriage? How does he describe them? Are these problems of recent origin? When did he recognize that he had the problems?
7. If the client is currently under medical treatment, has the doctor referred him, or does the doctor know about his coming for marriage counseling? If not, is the client willing for the counselor to confer with his physician? Note any significant health, economic, social, or cultural factors.
8. If the client is married, did he discuss his desire to obtain marriage counseling with his spouse? Does the spouse wish to see a counselor also? If the client wishes the counselor

to see the spouse, what is the client's expectation or hope? Are parents or families of either of the marriage partners (or premarital couple) involved in the problem? What is the attitude of these persons toward the marriage or proposed marriage?

9. At the close of the initial interview the counselor should carefully evaluate his impression of the client and of the marital or premarital situation. In particular, he should note:

    a. Whether the client has been able to delineate his problem so that he has defined that with which he wishes to have help.
    b. What factors seem to have contributed to the emergence of the problem in this particular relationship?
    c. Is the client more concerned with the relationship or with his own personal problems?
    d. How has the client reacted and how is he now reacting to his situation? Do these reactions appear to be appropriate to the reality situation?
    e. What is the counselor's evaluation of the client's strengths? Is the client probably going to be able to make good use of counseling?
    f. What is the counselor's conclusion at this point concerning whether this problem should be handled by marriage counseling?

The above suggestions include making tentative evaluations. These may be reformulated as further counseling proceeds. Impressions at this point must in many cases be merely tentative subject to revision after further exploration. The counselor may at this time consider further factors which probably should be explored in future interviews. For example, if there have been previous marriages, what were circumstances of the marriage and divorce. If this is a premarital case, perhaps there have been former engagements. If so, what were the circumstances? In a marital case there may have been other times and/or areas of dissatisfaction or times of particularly happy relationships. Have any crisis events occurred, such as operations, separations, miscarriages, deaths, and so forth? A general rule of thumb for beginning interviews is for the counselor to obtain a rather general idea concerning the client's situation rather than to seek details.

7 EARLY PHASES OF COUNSELING

A person who has problems that are serious enough to cause him to seek the help of a counselor usually needs more than one interview to alleviate his difficulties. Very few clients are able to do more in the first interview than to present in broad outline their problems and life situation. Frequently, after a first interview, a counselor feels that the problems have not yet been delineated; therefore, he wishes to continue talking with the client for two or three more sessions in order to be able to evaluate properly the client's difficulties. A counselor cannot make an accurate appraisal of the client's suitability for marriage counseling until he can evaluate the kinds of difficulties being experienced by the client, the effects of these experiences, the kind of person the client is, and his ability to work toward resolution of his difficulties. In addition, the counselor must arrive at a decision concerning whether counseling will be of adequate help for this individual, and whether this particular kind of problem—and person—should be accepted for continued counseling or referred for other help.

Accepting the Client for Continued Counseling

The counselor has an obligation to himself, the client, and the clinic or agency involved to evaluate as accurately as possible the advisability of accepting a client for counseling on a continuing basis. After such an evaluation has been made, the counselor may decide that psychiatric assistance for the client would be more helpful than counseling. A counselor should never attempt to help a client with problems or situations beyond the counselor's competence or outside the scope of his agency's function. This means that a conscientious counselor often refers clients for different kinds of help.

This kind of assessment demands considerable skill. The counselor listens, observes, questions, and comments in an endeavor to understand the client and his problems. At the same time, he is keenly aware of his obligation to become reasonably certain that the agency has an appropriate service to offer and that the client wants and can utilize the available help.

The counselor enters into this period of initial evaluation, therefore, with certain aims. His goals during this period may be described as follows:

1. *To understand the client's current situation:* Most persons who seek counseling quite readily describe their life situation; some persons, however, are hesitant concerning talking about their marital difficulties and can be aided by the counselor's factual questions and understanding comments.
2. *To understand the manner in which the client has previously endeavored to handle his problems:* The client may have tried to use help at some former time. Perhaps he feels that other persons have not helped him. If so, he may assume that this effort, too, will fail. He may find certain satisfactions in having (and keeping) his problems.
3. *To understand the client's view of the problem:* In the intake interview the client usually states his problem as he sees it. The opening remarks frequently contain the *presenting complaint.* As counseling proceeds, the meaning of the problem to the client becomes clarified.
4. *To understand the client's motivation for seeking help:* Does he come because he recognizes his need for assistance with his marriage? Or does he come because someone else (spouse, parents, physician, or the like) thinks he ought to have help? Does he come for counseling because the

agency has a name to which he relates his problem? (Some clients who seek marriage counseling in a psychiatric setting may be indicating that they wonder if they really need the help of a psychiatrist and are approaching psychiatric help in this manner.)

5. *To understand the client's emotional reactions:* Disturbing life experiences always involve emotional reactions. A counselor's ability to recognize and estimate the seriousness of such reactions depends upon the competencies he has acquired through training and experience. A counselor whose training has been largely in social casework cannot be expected to make the same kind of evaluation a psychiatrist might make (nor should he attempt to do so). Some decision must be made, however, concerning the client's suitability for counseling and the counselor's (or agency's) ability to offer the kind of help most needed by the client. Therefore, some evaluation of the client's emotional reactions needs to be made. Certainly a counselor should be able to recognize evidences of gross pathological reactions. Also helpful is the ability to identify various ego defenses, such as those that are usually predominant in persons with hysterical or compulsive reactions. The emphasis here is upon understanding the client's emotional reactions rather than upon placing the client in some specific category. However, certain elements of an individual's reactions he has in common with other persons of similar personality make-up. The significance of the emotional reactions and behavior of a specific individual may, therefore, be more quickly understood if the counselor recognizes that this person's reactions are similar to those of other persons he has already come to understand.
6. *To endeavor to understand the client's current situation in the light of this total context:* What the client is experiencing at this time has some relation to his total life experiences. We are able to observe a continuity in the behavior of an individual if we are aware of many of his

past experiences. Moreover, desirable changes in attitude are much more likely to occur when counselor and client recognize and understand the reaction and behavior patterns that have led to the current behavior under consideration at this time.

7. *To arrive at a tentative estimate of the client's strengths:* If the counselor is to reach a valid conclusion concerning the kind of help the client can best utilize, he will need to make a tentative estimate of the client's ego strength. The counselor needs, therefore, to consider carefully how well the client tolerates anxiety and how flexible or rigid he seems to be. How does he view himself? Does he have a healthy self-respect? Can he give himself to social causes, such as civic organizations and the church? Can he relax when he has opportunity to do so? Has he a healthy conscience? Is his guilt feeling appropriate, or is he neurotically guilt-ridden or relatively conscienceless? Are his defensive reactions appropriate? Does he project all his difficulties upon someone else? If so, counseling may be inadequate for his needs. Moreover, excessive use of projection can be an indication of serious emotional illness. Does he have meaningful relationships with other people? If so, he probably will be able to gain something from the relationship involved in the counseling situation.
8. *To make an evaluation of the total problem:* Here we are concerned not only with what the client states as his problem but also with what the total problem seems to be in view of all the factors we have enumerated. A meaningful appraisal will include the counselor's estimate of how much of the stress being endured by the client is the result of external factors and how much of it is due to internal conflict. This is seldom clear-cut, but a skillful counselor will be able to make an intelligent appraisal of the degree to which a client is immobilized by pressures from within. In this sense, the decision to accept the client for continuing counseling rests upon the counselor's evalua-

tion of the problem. If the internal stresses are extreme, the counselor will be wise to refer the client for help more appropriate for his needs. Chapters Eleven and Twelve provide detailed consideration of psychiatric referral and consultation.

9. *To clarify the problem with the client:* As the problem becomes clearer to the counselor, he may aid the client in examining the problem and in focusing attention upon what the client really wants to accomplish through counseling.

Rapport

The objectives outlined above can be attained only if a cooperative, confident relationship between counselor and client has been established. As here used, the term "rapport" implies that the qualities of respect, trust, and confidence are present in the relationship. There is nothing mystical about this. Rapport is a prerequisite to adequate and satisfying interpersonal communication in everyday life. Since counseling involves an interpersonal relationship in which two (or more) persons are communicating with each other, rapport must necessarily be established early in the counseling process.

The chief key to the establishment of rapport is the counselor's attitudes. The warmth, respect, acceptance, and permissiveness (see Chapter Four) brought to the counseling situation by the counselor serve to dispel many of the initial fears of the client and thus eliminate or minimize his reluctance to share his thoughts with another person.

If the reader will again study the case of Miss A. (see Chapter Six), he may gain a clearer conception of the manner in which rapport may be increased. When Miss A's initial interview began, she was obviously dominated by her emotional reactions to the counseling situation. These reactions involved fears associated with seeking help. For example, she was afraid the counselor would react as her parents had reacted. The counselor's attitude dispelled this fear and thus emotionally disarmed the client.

Miss A. also exhibited fears that the counselor would treat her as a lesser person and judge her. This fear was alleviated by the counselor's direct and implied assurance that he would not want to tell her that what she planned to do was right or wrong, but that he was interested in helping her to arrive at a decision with which she could be satisfied. As a result, rapport was greatly increased.

Unfortunately, many inexperienced counselors, through reading literature in the field of counseling, acquire the impression that by learning the proper responses to make to the client they can thereby succeed in establishing rapport. But we are here concerned with attitudes far more than with words. Interpersonal relationships in everyday life amply illustrate the importance of attitudes in establishing rapport. In the first meeting we may gain the impression that here is a person who is genuinely interested in us, who respects us, and who is to be trusted. On the other hand, we may be impressed with the absence of these qualities in a person we are meeting for the first time. Why are our impressions so different? Certainly words have not made all the difference. Probably closer to the truth is that we have obtained a general impression of the person's attitudes.

Similarly, a client gains his impression of the counselor's attitudes toward him not only through what is said but also through how it is said. Perhaps even more impressive is the counselor's total behavior, including how he looks at the client, how he reacts facially as the client talks, and the tone of voice he uses. All of these matters are related to the counselor as a person and are reflections of attitudes which cannot be assumed in the counseling room and discarded after hours.

When we speak of rapport, then, we are designating a counseling atmosphere in which the client feels secure. Such security is engendered through the client's perception of the counselor as a warm, friendly, accepting, objective, and sincere person.

The Client Talks: The Counselor Learns

In the early stages of counseling, one of the counselor's major tasks is to learn as much as possible about the client and his problems. The process by which this goal is reached is not unlike the process involved in painting a picture. First, a small segment of a broad outline is observed. Other portions of the outline then gradually emerge until a bare sketch of the picture appears. Later, the details are filled in, and very gradually the subtle shading tones become apparent.

In painting his picture, the client's major implement is speech and a concomitant use of his body in communicating his thoughts to the counselor. As the client talks, the counselor learns. Counseling is a cooperative endeavor with each person contributing. The client's major task in the early stages is to convey as accurately as possible a picture of himself, his total life situation, and the problems with which he is concerned. The counselor's task is to facilitate this process in every possible manner and to understand the client (including, of course, the client's problem). This is accomplished through the use of three major techniques: (1) listening, (2) questioning, and (3) commenting.

Adequate counseling always demands purposeful listening, but nowhere is the demand more insistent than in the early phases of counseling. Many counselors believe that the way to secure needed information is to ask questions. Certainly some questions should be asked, but they should be used sparingly and judiciously. If the counselor constantly asks questions in the beginning phases, the client may assume that what is expected of him is merely to reply to the questions. Or, what is worse, he may assume that when the counselor finds answers to all his questions, the counselor will then tell him what to do, advise him, or prescribe the remedy for his problems.

If the counselor can listen with interest and a sincere understanding attitude, many clients will provide a large proportion of the desired information without questions being asked.

The following excerpt from a counseling session is presented as an illustration of the use of the *purposeful listening* technique. At the close of the initial interview with Counselor A, plans were made with Mrs. M. for continuing counseling with Counselor B. The interview with Counselor B began as follows:

Counselor: Just have a chair there, Mrs. M.

Mrs. M.: You don't look a bit like I pictured you.

Counselor: Is that right?

Mrs. M.: Uh huh (laugh). I thought you'd have long white whiskers and be quite old and quite a fellow. (Laughter, client and counselor.)

Counselor: I understand you live in . . . (town) . . . How did you decide to come to see us?

Mrs. M.: Well, I didn't want to talk to anyone I knew, so I knew about this and just decided to come here.

Counselor: Uh huh.

Mrs. M.: Until I talked to . . . (Counselor A), I had never talked over my problems with anyone before. I did see my doctor briefly about it, but he's been my doctor all my life, and I couldn't say a word. I've thought (laugh) he probably thought it was something terrible when he didn't know anything, but I just couldn't tell him.

Counselor: It isn't very easy to talk to people you've known so well.

Mrs. M.: It certainly isn't. It's really difficult to talk at all. There are things you would like to leave unsaid, and I'm not sure of myself at all. But I would like a divorce. That's what I want. But naturally I'm under obligation to my three children, and I want to get the thing settled, too. Yet I don't want to have a duty to marriage and be living with someone I don't love for the rest of my life for my children's sake, because we don't get along. It's my fault now. At first it was his fault, but now it's my fault because I don't want to be interested in marriage other than for my children and I don't try. I don't have any incentive there to try. I mean . . . I could if I would (laugh). I mean . . . that's what I've used in my thoughts. There's a lot of factors there, but I did try until after the children were born, and it's been very provoking. However, we didn't get along from the first. I kept saying to myself I wouldn't go back and live with my folks and have them support me, no matter how badly he treated me, so I stayed until my children were up out of the baby stage and I went to work, My folks—they're keeping strictly out of it, but naturally they're hoping we'll stay together. Maybe I'm just not seeing it right. Maybe you can help me with that. But about my folks, they've never had a good marriage in anybody's language. They've been married thirty years and have four children, and we're all three years apart. And we fought all through school, except when somebody else said something to one of us. Of course, you're always willing to fight, you know. But we never had anything in common, so now we're all through school and married. But my folks never had a good marriage. Of course, other people don't know that. And my mother stayed with my dad because of the children. Of course, when she was coming along it was the thing to do. There was no choice. It has been an impossible situation to be brought up in, and I don't think it has influenced my marriage. But, I mean it looks like I am going to do what my mother did before me, but I just refuse to stay married for a duty marriage because of the children. There's enough of that. That's just the way I feel about it. Of course, that much has influenced me, knowing that if I can't live and be fairly satisfied and fairly companionable I'd rather not live with a person at all. I've made up my mind I don't love him. Or, I don't think I do. I believe he's a good person basically, and he's just as good to me as he can be, but . . .

Counselor: How long have you felt this way about it?

Mrs. M.: Well, for quite some time now. One thing—I guess I feel cheated. I mean, when I met him, I was only fifteen, and I'd never gone out with anyone except on my own age level. He was older and, well, I guess I was just infatuated or crazy about him. He was very jealous, and as a kid I thought that was just fine. No one ever felt that way about me before. Well, I guess I really took it as a big compliment. At that time I had just no confidence in myself at all. One thing my mother always said, "Don't do this and don't do that. People will talk." That was her theme song. She always wanted me to get in with the best crowd, but I couldn't because I just didn't see things their way. I couldn't snub other people the way they did. Now I wish I had gone with other high school boys and girls—I mean with the better crowd, as my mother said. You see I didn't have much confidence in myself when I met him. And he cared a lot for me, he really did. But the trouble came because I was young and pretty and among some people, popular. And he was so jealous. He had a fit if anyone even looked at me.

In this illustration, the technique used by the counselor was that of listening with an understanding attitude. Because this client verbalized quite easily, a wealth of information was provided without the necessity for questions. At this point, the counselor had acquired an impressionistic picture of an unhappy wife who was actually uncertain as to whether she wanted to remain with her husband or secure a divorce, who felt obligated to remain because of the children but also felt she had missed the normal good times of teenage dating. In her high school years, she had been constantly reminded by her mother that she should belong to the "best" crowd, but she did not feel comfortable with this group, lacked confidence in herself, and turned to the one person who seemed to want and need her. She married an older person who provided some satisfaction for her need to be loved and wanted, but she now doubted that she loved her husband.

Persons who cannot verbalize easily may need far more help from the counselor than this client required. Questions may be asked and comments may be made to facilitate verbalization.

Mr. D's initial interview was with Counselor A. Agreement was reached that he would work with Counselor C in subsequent sessions. At the beginning of the first interview with Counselor C, the client appeared ill at ease and uncertain of how to begin.

Mr. D.: Well, I guess Dr. N. explained some of the trouble we are having. (He is trying to find a way to begin and wonders how much the counselor knows about the problem.)

Counselor: Yes, we talked some about it. But perhaps you'd like to tell me just how you see the situation. (Counselor encourages him to continue talking.)

Mr. D.: Well—you see, we are both in college, but I'm graduating in two months and she's just a freshman. And, I don't know . . . when I got pinned . . . at the time it didn't bother me too much and maybe it shouldn't now . . . but we're in love and we're planning to get married some day, and I just don't know exactly what she and I . . . I'm probably going to be drafted and we'll be apart. I mean . . . It makes you think, especially when you're fixing to get . . . you know, not be around any more. (Client has difficulty in putting his fears into words.)

Counselor: You are wondering whether, under these conditions, it will work out all right? (This question indicates that the counselor is trying to understand. If the client feels he is being understood, he will continue expressing himself.)

Mr. D.: Yeah, I mean it's a problem and I never realized it was such a . . . you know. But this won't happen . . . I mean, I don't think it will. (Verbalization is quite difficult for this client. He now assumes that the counselor understands an unspoken fear. The counselor will need to make certain that this fear becomes clarified for it appears to be part of the problem.)

Counselor: You're wondering whether the relationship would remain the same? (Counselor senses the client's insecurity in the relationship with the girl and he endeavors to aid the client in talking about the changes that may occur in the relationship.)

Mr. D.: Yes, I was wondering about that. That worries me . . . Well, I'm not worried, exactly, but . . . well, yeah, about separation. (Counselor's understanding has enabled the client to state his concern.)

Counselor: What particularly concerns you about that? (Now the counselor endeavors to help the client specify his doubts and fears.)

Mr. D.: Well, I'm just . . . well, I don't know whether . . . well, what gets me is this, that so many other people . . . you know, a lot of my friends go away or get drafted or something and they . . . I mean they just . . . I don't know, something happens and they forget it, you know. And I'm sure that . . . well, I know I don't want it to happen and yet it just happens, you know. (Now the problem begins to take shape, but further clarification is needed.)

Counselor: You're a bit afraid that being separated so long it might happen to you? (The question conveys understanding and encourages amplification of the problem.)

Mr. D.: Yes, and I'm . . . well, if I don't have to go into the service everything would be fine because I've got a good job and everything. It's just that that's kinda worrying me . . . of course, she doesn't know I'm thinking this way.

Counselor: You haven't talked it over then?

Mr. D.: No, I haven't talked it out with her and I . . . I'm sure that . . . as a matter of fact, probably if I wanted to get married she'd probably get married, you know. But I just don't want to jump into anything like that.

Counselor: So you are wondering whether it's a good idea to continue as you are?

Mr. D.: Yes . . . I mean, as far as we're concerned we're definitely going to get married. We just haven't decided when yet. The logical time for me would be to wait until I get out of service, which would be two years. I mean, that's the way I want it and I'm sure . . . I don't know whether that's the way she wants it or not, but I . . . you know, that's kinda the way we agreed on it. We didn't exactly agree, we haven't exactly decided. And that's the part . . . two years, you know, that's a long time. And especially when you're going to be apart two years. A lot of things change. It's not that I'm afraid . . . well, maybe I am. You've just gotta face it, I guess.

With this client the counselor has utilized the technique of asking questions in order to encourage verbalization. The client has been helped to express some of the fears that were difficult for him to talk about. The kinds of questions asked also served to increase rapport by conveying to the client the real interest and desire of the counselor to be understanding and helpful.

At times reflective comments may be used by the counselor to help the client express what he is feeling and thinking. Moreover, reflective comments enable the client to examine and evaluate what he is saying. Frequently, a client will express thoughts and feelings without recognizing exactly what they mean to him. When these verbalizations are reflected to him, he may be rather surprised that these thoughts and feelings really are his own.

Client: I guess the reason I feel the way I do is that I am really almost afraid to be as happy as I could be.

Counselor: You are afraid something might come up to take away the happy feelings.

Client: Yes. I mean, when we were first married, I just saw the best side of things, but I had never had anything go wrong in my life before. But now, I just don't give any more. I guess I feel the less you give the less you get hurt. Sometimes I think that's just part of why I refuse to believe in him as much as I could.

Counselor: Afraid you might be hurt again.

Client: I really am. But that isn't very fair to him. After all, he is trying so hard, I ought at least to be fair to him. I do want to believe in him and trust him.

The illustrations cited are illuminative with regard to some of the techniques that help the client talk about his problems and clarify his thinking and feeling concerning them. Apparent, also, is that the use of these techniques is in accordance with the aim of marriage counseling, namely, to aid the client to a self-determined resolution of his problems.

Deterrents in Counseling

The term *resistance* is frequently used by counselors and other professional persons to denote a defense or force within the individual which opposes the efforts of the helping person. Resistance is usually thought of as an unconscious phenomenon that serves the purpose of warding off any threatened change in the "neurotic" equilibrium previously established through the use of characteristic defenses.

If the goal in counseling were one of effecting fundamental changes in personality, the counselor would be faced with the task of lessening or nullifying resistances by interpreting them in an endeavor to alter the balance of the person's wish-defense system. Personality alteration is not, however, the marriage counselor's goal. If a client can be helped only through personality change, referral should be made to a competent psychiatrist. The counselor needs, therefore, to become aware of client resistances and to observe their characteristic patterns.

Unfortunately, the term *resistance* can become a catchall appellation for any undesired reaction to what the counselor believes would be helpful. Responsibility for what is frequently called resistance may rest squarely upon the counselor's shoulders. For example, if the counselor too early attempts to lead a client to consider his own involvement in his marriage difficulties, the client may react with denial. On the other hand, if the counselor is more patient and understanding, allowing the client gradually to experience a relationship in which he need not feel threatened, then in his newly found freedom, the client may begin to explore his involvement in the marital relationship.

In considering the counseling process, the author prefers to think of the client's negative reactions chiefly as the results of threats to his self-esteem or *deterrents* rather than as resistances.

Assuming, then, that the marriage counselor is working with persons whose intrapsychic functioning is not seriously impaired but whose major difficulties lie in the interpersonal relationships in marriage and family living, examination of the sources of deterrents in counseling is practical and profitable. In a great many instances, simply to say that the sources lie in the client's personality structure is not enough. True, the client reacts in a manner that is idiomatic for his personality, but so do we all. What is important for the counseling process is that the counselor take cognizance of what, in the process, has threatened the self-esteem of the client and resulted in the observed deterrent.

Some deterrents are practically inherent in the counseling situation. For example, most clients are reluctant to talk about their most intimate problems in beginning interviews. This is not necessarily a resistance, in the sense of an intrapsychic defense against attempted disturbance of the psychic equilibrium. Rather, it is a phenomenon common to most beginning interpersonal relationships. The client is a person, and like all other persons who begin new relationships, he cannot know what the other person is like, whether he will understand, what he will think, or how he will react. He must, therefore, wait a bit before divulging to the counselor his most bothersome and intimate problems.

Similar consideration may well be accorded the frequently observed tendency of clients to present their problems in a manner which tends to exonerate them from any possible responsibility for their troubles. This "best-foot-forward" attitude is common in all newly-formed relationships and may be defensive only in the sense that the client is unwilling to let down his guard until he is reasonably certain that no serious blow to his self-esteem will be forthcoming.

To say to ourselves that a client who reacts in this manner evolved his characteristic pattern of defenses (including this one) in his early relationship with his parents will not solve the counselor's problem in dealing with the client. The practical problem for the counselor is how to provide the kind of climate in the counseling situation that will be conducive to the development of confident, trustful feelings on the part of the client.

One of the greatest virtues a counselor can possess is patience. Far too many persons who seek help terminate after only a few interviews and go away resentful because the counselor was unable to be patient and to accept the fact that some time must elapse before the client can become confident enough in the relationship to proceed to deal with his more serious problems.

If a counselor becomes impatient, the danger is not only that the client may sense the counselor's lack of understanding but also that the counselor may prematurely confront the client with what he is doing to produce conflict in the marriage. Such confrontation may arouse anxiety related to a threatened loss of self-regard, and if the anxiety is too discomforting, the client may fail to keep the next appointment or terminate. In counseling, as elsewhere in human relations, exceedingly few substitutes exist for kind, interested friendliness. This does not mean that one does not need, at times, to be firm, but when firmness is necessary, it can be blended with kindness.

The people who come to us for help are, like ourselves, more or less grown-up children. When a child feels unloved, unwanted, uncared for, and rejected, he acts to defend himself. He may find a defense in becoming outwardly compliant and inwardly hostile, or he may angrily lash out at his world of people and things or find some other way to protect his self-esteem. Grown-up children do the same things and for the same reasons.

If, then, a client initiates counseling with resentful, hostile attitudes, we may be assured that such defensiveness has the aim of protecting him from some kind of hurt, or feared hurt. Frequently, such uncooperative attitudes are evoked by the fear that the counselor may attempt to manipulate his life as other persons have done.

While this kind of reaction doubtless is rooted in the individual's early relationships with important persons in his life and could be thought of as transference phenomena, the counselor's task is in the present. If his own reactions do not get in the way, he can provide an accepting, permissive climate in which the client can become freer to release some of the hostility he feels, without recrimination and without manipulation of his life by the counselor.

Not only does the patient, accepting, understanding attitude of the counselor provide an atmosphere in which the client can experience a relationship that lessens the necessity for hostile reactions; it also tends to strengthen the client's motivations for seeking solutions to his problems.

8 COUNSELING ON A CONTINUING BASIS

Most counselors have a genuine desire to be of help to the individuals with whom they counsel. Therefore, they are sometimes perturbed that many clients begin a counseling relationship only to terminate it a few sessions later.

In this chapter we shall consider the various aspects of this problem and its important correlate, the delineation of dynamic factors involved in a sustaining relationship which are usually present when counseling is continued beyond beginning phases.

The Initial Period of Testing

We have noted that most persons who seek counseling do so in a rather tentative manner. It is as if they must first test the counseling situation and the counselor to make certain that the experience into which they are entering is one they really want. Like the skater who cautiously tests the strength of the ice before he is willing to entrust himself to it, a client may need to explore his new relationship. This is a new experience. He cannot yet know whether he wants to enter into it fully. He, therefore, feels his way along, testing the counseling situation and exploring the counselor-client relationship from time to time.

During this initial period of testing many clients terminate. That a person whose marital relationship is seriously enough disturbed to seek outside assistance can gain adequate help in one or two hours is highly improbable. In a great many instances this is not even enough time for a clear delineation of the client's problems.

Why, then, do so many terminations occur after only a few

interviews? Certainly there can be no one answer, but no counselor should be content to ignore the question or merely to assume that these clients received that for which they came. A counselor's professional growth depends far more upon the discomforting questions he raises about his counseling than upon the comforting answers he is able to muster.

One of the easy but not very illuminating answers is that a client expected too much of counseling and when he recognized that his expectations were not to be fulfilled, he stopped coming. Many clients do begin with unrealistic expectations; for example, the client who wants to know whether he should secure a divorce. If the counselor assumes that this is all the client is asking, he may tell the client that he cannot give him an answer. Now the client's apparent expectations have been thwarted, and he may stop coming.

A skillful counselor, however, would not be content to tell the client he could not be of help. He would explore with the client the meaning of such a request. Let us suppose that this client has come to his clergyman to ask whether he should obtain a divorce. Is this what he really is asking? Doubtless he knows his church's views on divorce. Why does he come with such a question? The real answer may be that his marital situation has become unbearable, yet he does not believe in divorce. He feels helplessly caught in this dilemma and comes to his pastor hoping that somehow this authority (father-figure) will decide for him and perhaps help him to see some solution other than divorce.

Whatever the meaning of a client's beginning request may be, glib answers are not likely to solve his problems. Probably more than anything else, a client wants to find someone who will understand him and how he feels about his dilemma. In a sense, then, beginning requests may be "feelers" to aid the client in arriving at a decision as to whether the counselor can understand him and therefore help him.

Probably, then, many of the persons who discontinue their

counseling sessions after only a few hours do so because they feel that the counselor does not understand them and is coldly objective and detached from the client's feelings. Perhaps he participated too little in the interviews, with the result that the client felt that the whole burden of the counseling sessions fell upon him and that the counselor was not really interested in him. Or, the counselor may have talked too much, thereby giving the client the impression that the counselor was lecturing to him. Again, the client may have felt thwarted in telling his story if the counselor participated too actively.

Obviously, each person reacts in accordance with his own personality needs. A skillful, understanding counselor will soon detect evidences of the client's needs and will constantly be aware of them in the counseling sessions. This is one of the reasons for our conclusion that a counselor needs to be flexible. If, instead, he has to work with all persons in the same way, his rigid personality patterns will seriously limit his effectiveness as a counselor.

Up to this point, we have considered testing of the client-counselor relationship as phenomena occurring in the early phases of counseling. Now we must add that such explorations of the relationship continue in some manner and to some degree throughout the course of counseling.

The Continuing Relationship: The Client's Viewpoint

When people are helped by counseling, exactly *what* has helped them? If we knew fully the answer to this question, doubtless we could greatly reduce the number of persons who seek counseling but do not receive much help from it. Evidently, the answer does not wholly lie in the techniques used by the counselor. Two counselors, both very successful in their work, may be poles apart in the techniques used. Why are both successful? Again, how do we help people who come to us with their troubles?

Whatever else is involved in the helping process, one primary factor is the client's perception of the counseling situation. By this, we do not mean the preconceived ideas with which many persons seek counseling, but rather, the way in which the client experiences the counseling sessions. Although preconceived ideas and expectations of counseling strongly influence the manner in which the sessions are initially perceived, in most instances skillful counseling can greatly diminish that influence.

Increasingly impressive evidence is accumulating to indicate that improvement in counseling depends largely upon how the client perceives and experiences the counseling sessions. But what determines the client's perception of the interviews? Certainly the counselor's attitudes, mannerisms, sex, and age have some influence, but much more than this is involved. That a client will experience counseling in much the same way he has experienced other interpersonal relationships is doubtless true, but this answer, too, is insufficient.

Perhaps, at the present stage of our knowledge, all we can do is recognize that the helping process, at its best, involves the client's perception of the counselor as a trustworthy, warm, understanding person who is genuinely interested in, and desirous of helping, the client. Indeed, this perception probably supersedes all others as an important factor propelling the client toward effective resolution of his problems. In other words, a counselor's skills, techniques, and personality have little effect in the interview unless their combined totality somehow is experienced by the client as a relationship with an understanding, interested person. Expressions of clients who regard their counseling sessions as beneficial emphasize this:

> I was afraid at first that he (the counselor) wouldn't really understand. Maybe that was because I didn't quite know how to explain what was bothering me, I don't know. Anyway, he seemed to be interested and listened to me. Another thing, he didn't push

me or try to get me to talk about things I didn't want to discuss. I got the impression that he somehow knew how hard it was for me to speak of some things. But after a while, I did find myself able to talk with him about anything and everything.

He made me think. It wasn't pleasant but it was helpful. At times I think I resented having to think things out, especially when I faced some of the things I was doing to wreck our marriage. I guess the thing that kept me going back for more was that I knew he would understand and not look down on me.

To be really honest about it, I do not think I ever really liked my counselor. He was so reserved and not the kind of person I like. After the first appointment I thought I wouldn't go back, but I did and I kept going. At first I had the idea that he was just doing his job and that he wasn't really interested in me and my problems. I was so wrong. No one ever did so much for me.

The thing was that someone could understand the way I felt. I was so mixed up I did not know how to explain. But he seemed to know how I felt. I can't explain what it was exactly, but I felt he was a real friend, not just a counselor. Not like other friends, though. He sure didn't dish out sympathy like so many do, and he didn't blame me, either. He just knew me better than I knew myself and helped me to see myself and my husband better.

Statements of this kind provide some insight into how these clients experienced their counseling interviews. Their tendency to evaluate counseling in terms of the client-counselor relationship is typical. While, admittedly, sufficient data are not available to justify definite conclusions, the following impressions are offered for consideration and further study: (1) Persons who view their counseling experience as having been helpful tend, in retrospect, to see it as a learning experience. (2) These people usually look upon the counselor as one who has been a friendly guide in the learning process. (3) Progress in counseling is accelerated when the client perceives the counselor as one who understands him and accepts him as a worthy person.

We should remember that the counseling situation is a dynamic one and that the client's perception of it may change somewhat as he moves from one stage or phase to another. We may say that he faces certain tasks in each phase and that the counselor needs to recognize this fact and help the client to fulfill his tasks. To clarify this point, a chart of the various phases and tasks frequently noted is here presented (see Figure 8–1). Experienced counselors will recognize that not all clients move from one counseling phase to another in the order indicated, nor do all clients experience all phases. We believe, however, that the chart provides a conceptualization of the client-counselor relationship in terms of the counseling process as it emerges dynamically in continued counseling.

Figure 8–1

STAGES IN COUNSELING

I. THE BEGINNING

Client's Needs	*Counselor's Tasks*
To begin to surmount initial fears and doubts related to seeking help.	To establish rapport through warm, accepting, uncritical, understanding attitudes.
Important but unverbalized attitudes may be:	Important but unverbalized attitudes may be:
I wonder if this process will really help? I am not certain I want to talk about my difficulties. What will counselor think of me? Will he think I am bad? Will he think I am losing my mind? Will he really be able to understand me? What am I expected to do? How does counseling work?	I know it is difficult to ask for help: you feel inadequate because you can't handle your problem. I know you have fears about entering into this counseling process. You wonder how I will react and what I will think.
	My chief concern at this point is to help you overcome these fears. I am trying to understand you and your problems. I will never treat you as a lesser person, nor make judgments concerning your behavior. I will only try to understand and help you.

II. INCREASE OF MUTUAL UNDERSTANDING

Client's Needs

To continue the reduction of fears and doubts related to seeking help and to accept the structure of the counseling process.

To provide counselor with clearer details of the difficulties and to clarify thoughts and feelings related to the problems.

Important but unverbalized attitudes may be:

> You seem to be interested in what I tell you, but sometimes I wonder if you are really sincere in your interest. I wish I could be certain. Can I really trust you? I am beginning to tell you things I never thought I would reveal to anyone, but I am not sure I want to go on with counseling. Some things—the really important matters—are so painful that I sometimes think I should never have begun talking about them. Yet I feel I ought to discuss everything related to my problems. If only I could be certain this painful process will help. But what if I go through all this and get nowhere?

Counselor's Tasks

To establish a practical structure in which counseling may proceed and to aid client in becoming more secure in the counseling situation through increasing rapport and through adequate meeting of test situations, questions, and comments.

Important but unverbalized attitudes may be:

> I understand your feelings of doubt concerning me, my sincerity, and my ability to understand you. You need not feel badly about having such feelings. I want you to know that I am here to be of assistance to you. I cannot supply you with direct and exact solutions to your problems, but I am raising questions and making comments as you talk so that together we examine your thoughts and feelings about your troubles.

III. EMERGENCE OF BASIC PROBLEMS

Client's Needs

To gain an increasing feeling of security in the counseling relationship so that the more basic problems may be discussed and clarified.

Counselor's Tasks

To provide in the counseling hours an atmosphere of acceptance which promotes client's feelings of security and self-acceptance.

Important but unverbalized attitudes may be:

I know that I have not been able to talk about some of the things that are bothering me. I was afraid to do so—afraid of what you would think and afraid of what I would see about myself. But you have understood me even when I have not been able to respect myself. Sometimes I find myself thinking that you seem so calm and assured I wish I could be like you. I wonder what you really think of me and the trouble I am in. You make me angry at times, especially when you press me for details or amplification of something I mention. But then I begin to see that I am passing lightly over something that is very important to me, and I know you must have understood that I was really avoiding dealing with these matters. I wonder if you know how angry I was. Sometimes I think you are stupid, and I tell myself I'll never go back for another appointment, but I always go.

Important but unverbalized attitudes may be:

I know that you are still fearful concerning me, but you need not feel badly that you have these fears and doubts. I accept them because they are part of you and I accept you as a worthwhile person. I believe in you and I want to help you. You have mixed feelings about counseling. You want to solve your problems, but it is a painful task, and you wish the pain could be avoided. Sometimes you are angry with me because, as you face the problems, you also experience unpleasant feelings. Yet this is all necessary if you are to find ways of dealing adequately with your difficulties. If you are angry with me, you will find that I remain calm and accept your anger just as I accept other feelings you may have. The important matter is that together we continue working on your problems so that you may eventually be able to cope with them satisfactorily.

IV. STRUGGLE WITH BASIC PROBLEMS

Client's Needs

To attain a level of self-acceptance and self-esteem enabling client to face basic problems with a view toward their solutions.

Important but unverbalized attitudes may be:

Counselor's Tasks

To maintain rapport through a consistent attitude of interest, understanding, respect, and belief in the client's ability to come to grips with basic problems and to eventually reach adequate solutions.

I know now that, to a very great degree, solutions to my problems depend upon me. You have helped me to recognize this by not offering me ready-made solutions or prescriptions. Somehow, you have helped me to believe in myself and to see that I have some strengths I had not recognized. You never helped me when I could help myself. This angered me at times, but I am really glad you have kept to that policy. Still, there are times when I ask you for advice and I want to depend upon you. So I really have mixed feelings. I want to be able to arrive at the best possible decisions, but I cannot trust my own thinking, and I want you to approve whatever I do. At times I respect and admire you. You seem to know me better than I know myself, but that angers me, too. What do you know about me that I do not know? As this counseling process has gone on over the past weeks, I have talked about many things, but now I find myself thinking of how I have contributed to the difficulties, what my attitudes and feelings have been, and how I have hurt myself and those I love. I have gone this far; I must go ahead and tell you all that has bothered me. You have helped me to face other problems; I believe you will help me face and deal with these difficulties, also. Yet, I am reluctant; you will have to help me talk. I tell you what I have never told anyone before. I feel

Important but unverbalized attitudes may be:

You would like to be able to depend upon me and have me tell you what to do. Yet you long to be able to depend upon your own judgment and your own strength. I will help you to come to grips with your problems. I believe in your ability to find adequate solutions. Your task is not easy, but you may be stronger than you think. You like me, but you sometimes dislike me too. I understand how you feel. You have moments in which you would like to stop coming here. Yet, you want to continue until you are sure you can cope with your problems. I know that it is painful to recognize that you have made many problems for yourself. But I also know that such recognition can help you to solve the problems.

The things you are revealing are very difficult to relate, but you feel that you must talk about them. I accept these revelations as I accept all else you say. Together we can recognize how much they mean to you and how you feel about them.

ashamed, hurt, angry. Can you really understand? Can you still respect me? Since I have told you these things I feel relieved, yet I wish you did not know such things about me.

V. ARRIVAL AT AND TRIAL OF TENTATIVE SOLUTIONS

Client's Needs

To move toward solutions to difficulties with sufficient flexibility to accept and learn from some defeats, and to try out tentative solutions and plans.

Important but unverbalized attitudes may be:

Now that we have discussed those things I most disliked talking about, I feel I can face almost anything. It seems strange to me now that I placed so much importance upon a few matters. They seem much less important now. Yet, I must deal with them. You listen as I tell you how I have thought of coping with these matters and you help me to clarify my thinking. I still wish you would tell me whether my plans are right, but I know you will not. Even after I have begun to put some of these decisions into practice, you do not tell me I have done the right thing, but you do help me to evaluate my own thinking and feeling about it.

Counselor's Tasks

To maintain attitudes consistent with the counseling structure previously established so that the client may remain secure as he begins to put tentative solutions into practice.

Important but unverbalized attitudes may be:

You feel better about the counseling situation now that you feel that you can talk about anything you think about. You also resent my knowing some things about you. I know that you have mixed feelings, but we can continue to work together as we have done except that now you need not feel guilty about withholding some topics from our discussions. As you begin now to see some possible solutions you feel stronger as a person. I believe in your strength too. These are your decisions. I will help you to examine your thoughts and feelings about the possible solutions, but you will be stronger for having made the decisions. As you try out the possible solutions, you want me to approve your actions. Yet the important matter is still that you arrive at solutions that you, yourself, can approve and find satisfying.

VI. TERMINATION

Client's Needs	*Counselor's Tasks*
To arrive at the decision to terminate and to carry out the decision despite doubts and fears as to client's ability to go on his own strength. Important but unverbalized attitudes may be: I know that I have made many gains while in counseling, but I am not at all certain that I can get along well on my own. Still, I am doing quite well. I feel much better about my situation. The problems are not all solved, but I have considerable confidence in my ability to cope with them. Sometimes I feel that you almost want me to stop coming here. You seem to believe that I can get along without help now. I am glad you believe this, but at times I am angry with you because I feel you may abandon me. Yet, you surely would let me return if I need your help again sometime. Perhaps I ought to try to get along without help anyway. I don't really want to have to depend upon someone else all my life.	To share in client's decision to terminate counseling and to recognize client's feelings about the decision. Important but unverbalized attitudes may be: You want to be able to get along on your own strength, but you have some doubts and fears concerning your ability to do so. You will dislike discontinuing counseling in some ways, but you will go out on your own because you know that you are much more able to cope with your situation now. It is good to feel that you are strong and that you no longer need help.

Referent Reactions

In any kind of human relationship, the perception that one is being understood and accepted by another person tends to create an interpersonal bond with that person. In a counseling situation, this bond tends to be sustained by the client's positive feelings toward the counselor. This is not to say that one's feelings are always positive or negative. The client, like the rest of us, may often have mixed feelings, sometimes liking, sometimes disliking the counselor. Mature persons who are not emotionally disturbed usually view the counselor rather objectively and react to the situation as it is and to the counselor as he is. The counselor is liked largely because he has shown himself to be a likable person. He is admired on the basis of skill and ability to help.

Some clients are less mature and less free from emotional disturbance, and they may experience the relationship in a different way. To these clients, the counselor may not be seen clearly as a counselor. He may, instead, be perceived in a distorted manner, as is the case, for example, when the client reacts with attitudes which were once held toward his father or mother (or other influential persons in his past) but which are hardly appropriate in the present situation. This phenomenon is sometimes called *transference* and is thought to indicate unconscious motivation. Since the term "transference" has been used in so many different ways and with various meanings, we have attempted to distinguish between transference in the psychoanalytic sense and transference in the sense in which it is considered here by applying the term "referent response" to the transference-like phenomena in counseling. When we speak of referent response, we are speaking of reactions which are inappropriate to the reality situation. If, for example, a counselor should deride, belittle or frankly insult a client, the client's anger would then be an appropriate response and certainly not a referent response. However, if the client should become angry because the counselor wears tweed suits, then the inappropriateness of the response indicates the possible presence of referent phenomena.

Through the observation of the client's actions, behavior, and verbal productions we may recognize the presence of referent reactions. The client does not ordinarily tell you that he feels toward you as he felt toward one of his parents, for he is not usually aware that these feelings are repetitions of the feelings he had toward some important person in the past. He is, however, conscious of his feelings toward you. In thinking of what referent reaction is and what it is not, we need to bear in mind that in reality a counselor may be in some respects like a parent, particularly if he gives reassurance, makes suggestions, and becomes something of a guide for the client.

Some of the client attitudes which may be indicative of referent response are as follows:

(1) *The "I want you to give me affection" attitude.* The *realistic* role for the counselor is one in which the counselor shows interest and understanding for the client. However, if a client is repeating and reliving feelings that he has had toward other important persons in his life, his attitude in the counseling relationship may express his wish for affection and be revealed in his attempts to secure praise or sympathy or other evidences from the counselor which suggest to the client that he is liked. He may do this by asking for suggestions or by exaggerating the difficulty he is experiencing in his life situation, or he may try to do favors for the counselor.

A corollary of the "I want you to give me affection" attitude is an over-reaction to a very slight rejection when the counselor does not fulfill the role in which the client has cast him. This may sometimes be observed when a client wants to change his appointment to a different time and the counselor explains that that time is not available. The client may reveal by his "hurt" attitude that he senses this as rejection, or he may actually feel jealous of other clients or of the counselor's own family.

(2) A second type of referent reaction may sometimes be observed in the client's *"I want to be like you" attitude.* Probably the reason that the individual casts the counselor in this role is that he wishes to achieve some of the calmness, intelligence, balance, and other qualities he believes he observes in the counselor. Thus we can think of the client as having a wish to become adequate to cope with his problems through

the achievement of some of the qualities he sees in the counselor. In this sense an identification process may become evident in the client's intense interest in the counselor's books, pictures of his family, the way he is dressed, and similar evidences of the counselor's tastes and interests.

(3) Along with this "I want to be like you" attitude may be a concomitant *attitude of "I want to please you."* The counselor should be aware that unfortunately when a client becomes overly concerned with being sure that he pleases his counselor, he is certain to have some punishment and reward ideas, such as he once held toward important persons in his life. One needs, also, always to remember that the other side of this coin is a dislike or anger, which may eventually be directed toward this "powerful" figure. The counselor therefore needs to be cognizant of this fact when he observes his client being overly polite, overly solicitous, and overly agreeable.

(4) A fourth kind of referent reaction is the *"I must outmaneuver you" attitude*. The counseling situation may become like a game in which the client tries to out-guess the counselor, as if the two were locked in a tournament-like competitive struggle. Such phenomena may at times be recognized in such statements by the client as "I knew you were going to say that" or "You probably think so and so but that's not the way it is at all' or "This is the way I'm going to run my household and nobody can change me" or "You seemed to think thusly, but I tried it and it didn't work."

In some types of psychotherapy, transference is extremely important for the reason that treatment of intrapsychic conflict seems to depend largely upon the reactivation of infantile attitudes, fears, and hostilities so that they may be recognized for what they are in the present. In this manner, one gradually becomes free from the necessity of reacting inappropriately.

Character alteration is not the goal of counseling, and transference-like phenomena do not have the same significance they have in psychotherapy. Referent reactions are apparent in counseling, but much of the client-counselor relationship is based upon current realities. Ordinarily referent reactions are not interpreted, but they should be recognized by the counselor.

Several factors in counseling serve to keep these phenomena peripheral to the main focus of the relationship. Counseling is a method of helping a person clarify his problem and rationally sort out the various factors involved. The client is also helped to examine alternative choices and courses of action which may be open to him. Counseling, therefore, is focused upon reality factors. The goal for the relationship is to enlist the client's conscious ego in the task of finding adequate solutions to the reality problems.

The Use of Structure

Every relationship exists within the framework of some kind of structure. Moreover, the structure has an important bearing upon the kind of relationship that develops. A father-son relationship is quite different when the son is living with his father and mother than it is when the father and mother are divorced and the father periodically visits the son. In the latter case, there is still a relationship, but the structure is different. The relationship is not the same. The structure has made a difference.

One facet of the structure in which counseling takes place is represented by the *place* where counseling is done. To talk over one's problems with another person while walking in the garden or on the golf course is to experience the relationship in a different manner than one would experience it while consulting a person professionally in a clinic or agency. The helping person in a clinic is identified with his agency and—to the client—becomes the agency's representative. Therefore, the helping person is presumed to stand for what the agency stands for. A person who seeks help from his minister may assume that he should talk about his behavior in terms of its moral implications, whereas if he visits a psychiatrist he may think he should relate painful past experiences or his disturbing impulses or conflicts.

This is not merely a matter of preconceived ideas. As a matter of actual fact, the helping person does work within the limitations imposed by his agency. The agency has certain regulations, certain traditions, and, usually, a set of accepted procedures. The counselor and client work within this structure.

Another facet of structure involves *time*. Modern life is, itself, time-oriented. We earn a livelihood by working a stated number of hours daily. In order to get to work on time, we set the alarm clock, we eat at a certain time, we stop work at a certain time, and who knows how many times we look at our watches or clocks in a day? All relationships involve the time element, but in counseling, time is ordinarily a very definite part of the structure. Unlimited time is not available. If fees are charged, usually time is the basis for the fee. Appointments may regularly be one hour in duration, and the time interval between interviews may be set at one week.

Whatever the time stipulations may be, they become part of the structure in counseling. Time limitations can profoundly affect the course of counseling. If a client realizes that he has only fifty or sixty minutes per week in which his difficulties may be discussed with the counselor, the time factor may stimulate motivation sufficiently to overcome defensive avoidance of significant material. Some counselors are so convinced of the motivational value of time limits that they begin a series of counseling interviews with the stipulation that counseling will be limited to a certain, definite number of sessions. While this procedure may have desirable effects with some clients, it is of doubtful value with others. Indeed, such rigid use of time structure can evoke undesirable anxiety in some persons. One may feel so burdened with his problems that he doubts that there is any help for him. If so, to say to him, in essence, that if he is to receive help, he will have to do so in six, eight, ten sessions or whatever is stipulated, may overwhelm him so that he feels he is expected to do the impossible.

A different, and quite valid, use of time is that of setting a definite time limit for evaluating the problems and deciding upon the next steps in securing help. Rather than being disturbed, the client is reassured if the counselor says at the beginning, "Suppose we use the next five or six interviews to try to see just what the problems are, and at the end of that time, we can talk about what kind of help will most likely be of value to you." This type of structure places responsibility upon the client to explore his problems, sort them out, and come to grips with his feelings about them. He does not, however, have to labor under the pressure of trying to reach a solution to his difficulties within a certain period of time.

Every experienced counselor knows that structure frequently reveals very clearly some of the basic difficulties with which a client may be struggling. Moreover, if a counselor is unaware of what is happening, he may fall into the error of fitting into the problem rather than aiding in its solution. The following illustration reveals many ramifications of structure:

> Mr. T. called for an appointment, saying that he could come any time except Friday or Saturday. His work did not permit his absence on those days. His wife was to come with him. A Wednesday appointment was agreed upon. However, the wife telephoned to tell the counselor that she would be unable to accompany her husband, but that she would like a Monday or Tuesday appointment for herself.

In this instance, the counselor was faced with a dilemma. A structure had been agreed upon by the counselor and the husband. Now the wife was endeavoring to change the structure. While the telephone conversation with the wife was in progress, the counselor might well have wondered just what this action meant to Mrs. T. Was she avoiding a joint interview? If so, why? Was she trying to arrange matters so that she would be able to state her side of the situation first? Was she a controlling person and was this telephone call an attempt to control the counselor as she controlled others?

All this may have gone through the counselor's mind, and his judgment concerning the possible answers must have influenced his immediate decision. Upon inquiry, Mrs. T. explained that she and her husband had agreed that they should not both be away from their business at the same time and that Mrs. T. should try to secure the first appointment. Later, they would be able to come to appointments together. The counselor suggested that perhaps Mr. and Mrs. T. might want to talk over the possibility of finding a time when they could both be away from the business. Mrs. T. replied that such an arrangement would not be possible for about three weeks and that she and her husband wanted to begin working on their problems as soon as possible.

Several alternatives were available to the counselor. He could have insisted that he could see Mrs. T. only if she came with her husband. He could have stated that if the marital problems were pressing, perhaps both husband and wife could afford to leave the business in other hands for the time necessary to keep appointments. The counselor chose, however, to accede to the client's request as stated. The first interview with Mrs. T. revealed that her request was quite valid and that the counselor's decision was justified. In this case, the structure and the client's problem did not become mingled.

Considerable similarity may be observed in the case of Mr. and Mrs. V.; yet, the outcome was quite different. Mrs. V. telephoned on Thursday for an appointment for her husband and herself. The hour agreed upon was the following Monday at four o'clock. Friday Mr. V. telephoned to say that owing to prior arrangements he could not come to the Monday appointment with his wife. However, he could accept a Saturday appointment. He also said that his wife would keep the Monday hour since she could not be away from her work on Saturday. The counselor agreed to this arrangement.

Very early in the hour with Mr. V. the counselor became aware that the client's real motive in changing the time structure was to attempt to persuade the counselor that Mrs. V. intended to make untrue statements. Mr. V. wanted to put a different story before the counselor. The result of this change in time structure was that the counselor allowed himself to become caught in the middle of a husband-wife conflict. His task was now doubly difficult. Mrs. V. could easily feel resentment toward the counselor for allowing the husband to manipulate the situation. Moreover, she might feel that husband and counselor were teamed against her.

No less important is that the counselor, in one sense, gave his support to what, apparently, was one of Mr. V's personality problems, that of attempting to exonerate himself, cast blame on someone else, and control the persons around him.

This is not to imply that, once decided upon, structure should never be changed. One ought to be flexible enough to allow change when it is warranted by circumstances. Common sense can be a very good guide here. One ought, however, to weigh carefully the possibility that a certain asked-for change in structure may really add to the problem by fitting into the defensive and controlling maneuvers of a client.

Part of the problem of persons seeking counseling is that there is so little in their environment upon which they can depend. Counseling can be helpful in this respect by the establishment of a dependable relationship, and part of the setting of the relationship is a dependable structure.

The Metaphor in Counseling

A frequently overlooked phenomenon in counseling—yet an extremely important one—occurs when what is said has an altogether different meaning than the words may seem to imply. The metaphorical language used by a client is often more revelatory of actual feeling than are his other utterances. Although the words and phrases used metaphorically by an individual are common terms, they have a particular meaning for the speaker.[1] For example, a client who had difficulty in telling a straight story frequently prefaced what he said with the word, "Honestly." "*Honestly,* I don't know why she walked out on me." "*Honestly,* I wasn't drinking." "I'm no angel, and I'm not trying to impress you with any goodness, but *honestly,* I've never stepped out on her."

> A client came in the office for her seventh interview, sat down and sighed, "It's such a nice day out: I'd like to be outside all day." The counselor commented, "Yes, outside it is nice." She replied, "I guess I really dreaded coming in today to talk about problems again."
>
> In his fifth interview, a client who had previously sought help from three other counselors and each time had terminated after a few hours said: "Well, I try to make my wife happy. Sometimes it's better to make people think you care. If I have a man working for me on the job, I'll make him think I like him, but if he can't deliver, out he goes." The counselor commented, "You'd like to find some solution to your problems, but perhaps you wonder sometimes if this sort of thing can help."

The counselor could have responded metaphorically—and less threateningly—by saying, "You'd chuck him out quickly if he didn't meet your expectations. Is that it?" This kind of comment could enable the client to gradually approach the matter of his expectations of other people and perhaps eventually his expectations of the counselor.

Action is frequently metaphorically meaningful. An observant counselor can learn a great deal from gestures and other types of bodily behavior of the persons he interviews.

> A client came into the office and was invited to be seated. The counselor did not indicate a particular chair, but silently awaited the client's choice of the three available chairs. She looked briefly at the chair opposite the counselor's desk, then went quickly to the chair closest to the counselor's chair. The ensuing interview

---

[1] For a psychoanalytic interpretation of metaphor, see Ella Sharpe, "Psycho-Physical Problems Revealed in Language," *International Journal of Psychoanalysis,* XXI (1940), 201.

disclosed the fact that the client had a strong wish for an emotional closeness with others. Her action in choosing the chair nearest the counselor seemed to be a metaphorical expression of this wish.

A man who, in his counseling sessions, constantly constructed first in his mind what he was about to say, would then carefully—and in an obviously withholding manner—speak the words he had so carefully chosen. He had the habit of toying with his pipe, and would carefully light it before replying to a question or comment. The habit seemed to serve the purpose of gaining time for the construction of a "harmless" reply. Metaphorically it appeared to express his withholding tendency.

What is of importance to the counselor's work, then, is that he be cognizant of the fact that the client is constantly communicating something of his attitudes, fears, hopes, and patterns of reaction. Some of this communication is verbal, and some of it is nonverbal. In any event, part of it is metaphorical, and this part is easiest for the counselor to miss. Yet, this part of the communication may be most meaningful. Like many other aspects of counseling, learning to recognize and understand metaphorical language is not a quick process, nor a simple one. Such learning usually begins with the recognition that much everyday social communication abounds in metaphors. Once recognized, these phenomena begin to be observed in increasing frequency in counseling sessions, and they add a further dimension to the impression the counselor is obtaining of the client and his situation.

Withheld Information

Most clients do not tell the counselor all the facts about their problems in the first few interviews. This is quite understandable since the relationship between client and counselor is new. Confidence is an important element in counseling, but for it to appear full-blown in the beginning hours is highly unusual. This is one reason for the maxim, "Try to acquire a general impression of the problem in the first interview: wait until later for specifics." As the client's confidence in the counselor grows, the more specific and hard-to-talk-about factors are more easily discussed.

Experienced counselors have become aware, however, that the matter of confidence frequently is not the entire explanation for the tendency of some clients to withhold certain information. If one is understanding and patient, usually clients eventually speak of matters that have not previously been discussed with other persons. To the client, such material frequently seems to have the quality of a secret. It is as if the knowledge of a certain happening, event, or experience has long been concealed, thought about, or even, in imagination, relived by the client, but not imparted to any other person.

When this kind of material is disclosed, one is impressed by a seeming contradiction. While, on the one hand the client seems to be somewhat ashamed or guilty about the secret, he often seems also to have cherished the memory of the experience. When the experience is revealed, the client may talk about it with a great deal of emotion. If the counselor discusses this kind of material as he has discussed other material, ordinarily the client feels relieved and after a time, less guilty. Sometimes the telling of such an experience is followed by the client's assertion that he now wonders why he had attached so much importance to it.

If, instead, the counselor has probed for material, he may discover that this type of client later reacts hostilely toward him for having been encouraged to divulge the secret to which he had clung so tenaciously. Experience indicates that the better course to follow is that of patient understanding without asking questions that would bring the client prematurely to the point of discussing the withheld material.

Quiet Stages in Counseling

Certain clients who continue in counseling over a period of several weeks or months eventually reach a point at which they feel that they do not know anything else to say about their problems. Sometimes this is due to the counselor's failure to provide a structure consistent with the aims of counseling. If, in the beginning stages, the client gained the impression that his task was to verbalize his problems and that the counselor's task was to provide solutions, the quiet stage may simply indicate that the client is really waiting for the solution.

In other instances, clients seem to reach a stage in which they recognize that they are not yet ready to terminate counseling but do not quite know what to talk about next. Analysis of interviews that take place during these periods often reveal the presence of more than the usual number of silences. If the counselor is not made uncomfortable by the silence, frequently the client uses these moments to think through some point of discussion and then begin again to verbalize his thoughts.

Sometimes clients say that they do not know what to talk about next and then after a brief thoughtful silence, go ahead talking as usual. On the other hand, if a client makes such a statement with a look of appeal to the counselor, some comment may be made to help the client find a starting point.

> In his tenth interview, Mr. P. said, "Well, I just don't know where to start today." After a brief silence, he continued, "I guess I've talked about everything that's bothering me." The counselor replied, "I believe you had planned to go on a little trip over the weekend. Did that . . ." Mr. P. interrupted, "Oh, yes, I took my wife with me, and we left the children with her folks. You know, I thought it would be a good idea if we got away for a couple of days, just off by ourselves. You know how it is when you have to be watching out for the kids all the time. And I thought I'd get a chance to—well, sort of talk to her and try to show her how I felt about her. But it didn't work out. She acted so distant and just like she'd rather have stayed home, so I . . . I just got tongue-tied, I guess. I couldn't . . . I didn't even feel like trying to talk to her when she acted like that."

Mr. P's counselor recognized the validity of helping him to get started in the interview, and although the counselor indicated a definite topic, he did so with the prior knowledge that this was a matter with which the client was presently concerned. Moreover, the counselor's question indicated his interest in the client's attempts to work out a more satisfactory relationship in the marriage. This very fact can bolster a client's desire to continue working on his problems.

Counseling with Both Spouses

The focus of marriage counseling is upon the interpersonal relationships in the marriage or in the premarriage state. While these relationships may be improved when only one of the partners obtains help, the desirability of counseling with both spouses seems obvious. Usually both persons in a marriage have some involvement in the problems and dissatisfactions that appear in the relationship. The first major step is taken toward improvement of the marriage when the two partners decide to seek help together. The decision in itself implies a mutual concern and a mutual task.

However, certain problems may arise out of a structure in which both partners are interviewed by the same counselor. Those most frequently encountered are considered here.

Situation (a): Only one spouse comes for counseling.

Counselor: What does your wife think about the matter of getting help on these difficulties?

Client: I don't know. I didn't tell her I was coming here today.

Counselor: You haven't talked it over, then?

Client: No, we haven't . . . I . . . it's not very easy for me to talk to her about it. She . . . I don't think she is aware of anything being wrong, really. (Silence) Still, she must know something's not right with us. (Silence) Maybe I could talk with her and at least tell her I came to see you and ask her if she would like to work on it with me. Would you . . . would you be able to see her Monday if she wants to come?

Counselor: I think so. If she wants to talk with me, I'll be glad to see her. She can just call the office here, and we'll set up an appointment.

Situation (b): Client asks the counselor to secure participation of the spouse in counseling.

Client: I really feel a little guilty about saying all these things about my husband.

Counselor: Guilty?

Client: Well, yes . . . I mean, he would have a fit if he knew I had talked to anyone about our trouble. He thinks anything like that is just private and we ought to work it out ourselves.

Counselor: You've talked about working it out by yourselves?

Client: Oh, we've talked about it, but we just don't ever get anywhere.

Counselor: You've tried, but it doesn't seem to work, huh?

Client: Yes, I just don't think we'll ever work it out by ourselves. It's gone on too long and too far. But I don't think he would ever try to get any help on it.

Counselor: You think he is not interested in working on it with you?

Client: Well, I don't know. I . . . maybe he would be if . . . if he knew I was trying to get help.

Counselor: You're wondering if he'd want to come in, too, if he knew you wanted to try to work it out.

Client: Well, I was just wondering if . . . if you would call him and say you want to see him, maybe he would.

Counselor: I'd be very glad to see him. But I think I could be of more help if he comes here because he wants to do that. You know, from what you have said it seems that he doesn't really know what you want to do about your marriage and you don't really know what he wants to do. Is that about it?

Client: I guess it is, really. I think I see what you mean. After all, I didn't even tell him I was coming here or ask him if he would go with me.

Situation (c): The client seeks information from the counselor concerning what the spouse has said in separate interviews.

Client: Well, I suppose she told you all the things she thinks I've done to her. (Silence) I may not be the most perfect guy in the world, but she's no great prize, either. I suppose she told you all about that Christmas blow-up. Did she tell you about that?

Counselor: You seem to have some concerns about it. Do you want to talk about it?

Client: Well, I know about what she would say, and I know I'm not as bad as she makes out I am.

Counselor: It seems you're pretty concerned about how your wife might see it.

Client: Yeah, I am. She's got a completely wrong notion about me. Since that Christmas thing, she won't have anything to do with me. Acts like I'm nothin' but dirt under her feet. That makes me mad.

In each of these three situations the counselor helped the clients to come to grips with some difficulty in interpersonal interaction. In each case, the counselor recognized that counseling could be effective only if communication between the spouses could be improved. The immediate focus was, therefore, upon this problem.

Situation (c) illustrates not only lack of communication between spouses but also fears and doubts relative to the counseling situation itself. The counselor picked up the immediate concerns of the client. He recognized that these fears were blocking the way to any real attempt to work with the marital problems. If the counselor had merely replied to questions, the client's real concerns would have been disregarded.

Except in unusual circumstances a counselor will not need to reassure a client directly concerning the confidential nature of the interviews. Although a spouse may speak of matters that he does not want imparted to the partner, he will ordinarily assume that such matters will be treated confidentially. Reassurance on this point is most effective when it is conveyed by the counselor's whole attitude, manner, and method of handling such information. Situation (c) provides an illustration of one technique a counselor may utilize to convey to the client the fact that the counselor does not pass information from one spouse to another. The counselor is interested in the client's concerns, and it is this interest and focus that enables the client to move on to a discussion of the problem. To be sure, occasionally one may feel that direct reassurance is necessary, but that is the exception rather than the rule.

Counseling with both spouses demands skills not otherwise necessary. One can easily become the "middle man" for the playing off of each spouse's grievances against the other. No counselor needs to be put in the position of having to referee a bout, however, and if one is skilled in counseling with both spouses, he will not allow the sessions to degenerate to such an ineffectual level.

Presumably, a husband and wife seek the aid of a counselor with some wish to work out adequate solutions to their problems. If a counselor allows the focus to shift from the problem to the counselor as a judge, referee, or decider-of-which-one-is-wrong, he loses his chance to be of help. Most people are not really helped if another person makes decisions for them. If, instead, a counselor helps his clients to apply their reasoning powers to the problems with which they are concerned, he may, indeed, be of genuine help to them.

Ending the Counseling

When should the client terminate the series of counseling interviews? This is an extremely difficult question to answer. Ideally, we would hope that the decision to terminate would be reached only after the client has achieved an understanding of himself, his marital partner, and their relationship sufficient to enable him to function in the marriage and elsewhere with a degree of adequacy that is satisfactory to him and (hopefully) to those near him. But this is, admittedly, an ideal. Not all clients will achieve the ideal. The counselor will have to be content with limited goals, and he must remember that the client's goals and wishes will be the important factors in any consideration of termination.

If the disrupting or unpleasant factors in the client's marriage have been ameliorated to a comfortable level, he may decide to terminate counseling. The decision may be quite realistic and valid. The client may feel quite confident that he can get on now without further help. This confidence may be rooted in the fact that he has made certain decisions designed to better the marriage relationship and has been able to carry the decisions through satisfactorily. If so, his decision to terminate counseling may be the outgrowth of increased confidence and feelings of self-worth. In short, he may no longer need the help of the counselor.

At times, however, evidences that the client really is ready for termination are lacking. Yet, he wishes to stop coming. The desire to stop may be an expression of resistance to going farther in working on the problems. Perhaps this process is too painful, and he is reacting defensively. The counselor should treat this decision as he would treat any other decision. It should be discussed in terms of the client's wishes and thoughts about the matter. After discussion, the client may revise the decision. If he does not, the counselor need not attempt to dissuade him.

If, however, a client states that he has decided to stop coming for counseling and then expresses some doubt that he will be able to get along on his own strength, these doubts should be recognized. Nothing else needs to be done with the doubts. The counselor can recognize with the client that the client has some doubts about it. But the doubts do not have to be resolved, and the counselor need not attempt to resolve them. After all, the client may not actually be able to carry through on his own and may again seek help.

Occasionally, a client may express some anger upon terminating. He may be finding difficulty in detaching himself from the counselor, particularly if the counselor has, in effect, become a parent substitute. Or, he may feel abandoned by the counselor if the counselor does not attempt to dissuade him from terminating. Some clients react as if the only way they can terminate the relationship with the counselor is by becoming angry. The counselor should recognize and identify the anger, but he need not try to deal with it except to say, "I understand your feelings," or some similar statement which conveys understanding.

Some clients ask if they may feel free to return for additional sessions if needed. The real concern is frequently related to the client's doubts about whether he should stop coming. In addition, he may fear that the counselor will be displeased. The counselor should not over-assure the client about coming back. A better course is to recognize the doubts and simply say that if he feels the need for further help, he may call for an appointment.

9 COUNSELING SKILLS AND TECHNIQUES

Far from being a bag of tricks, counseling techniques are the ways in which a counselor treats the persons with whom he works. What he does and says in attempting to provide help for people who come to him is a direct reflection of how he feels about people and about himself. If, for example, a counselor really feels that people are to be used for his own purposes, the techniques he uses will reveal his motivation. Few counselors acknowledge or recognize any tendency to use clients for the purpose of finding satisfaction for their own personality needs. Nevertheless, this is a matter that deserves close scrutiny by every person who chooses this kind of work.

The following examples illustrate some of the dangers in counseling when the counselor uses the counseling situation to seek satisfactions for his own needs:

> Counselor R. constantly reported to his supervisor an unusual number of crying episodes in his sessions with women clients. Careful examination of his records revealed excessive and unwise use of confrontation as a technique. When the matter was brought to his attention, the counselor began to recognize that he felt a sense of power in the presence of a crying woman. Without realizing what was actually happening, he had used confronting statements and questions that resulted in the crying episodes.
>
> Counselor V.'s clients regularly talked more about sexual matters than about other topics. The supervisor pointed out this fact to Counselor V. who began to wonder what it meant. He arrived at the conclusion that he was unknowingly leading his clients into discussions of sex because he was curious about the sexual behavior of other persons.

How one thinks and feels about people and about himself is revealed in the way he treats the persons who come to him for help. Few enterprises can be more fruitful for a counselor than to give careful thought to the principles upon which must rest the techniques he utilizes.

Relation of Principles and Techniques of Counseling

Since techniques are the implementation of the counselor's accepted principles of counseling, certain principles should be particularly germane to the field of marriage counseling. Indeed, we have become convinced both by experience and by observation of other counselors' experiences that a few principles provide a basic foundation for counseling. These principles form a core philosophy out of which adequate techniques may emerge.

1. THE PRINCIPLE OF THE WORTH OF HUMAN PERSONALITY. The highest and best development we know about in the universe is human personality. Nothing in the world is as important as human beings. Nothing else bears within itself the tremendous potential for the development of loving and creative action. If counseling is to be effective, the counselor must believe in and work with this potential. Moreover, his techniques will reflect whether he possesses this conviction. For if his counseling is based on this principle, he will feel a kinship with all other humans and will attempt to help those who seek his aid by being a helper, not a dictator.

2. THE PRINCIPLE OF THE FREEDOM OF THE INDIVIDUAL FOR SELF-DETERMINATION. In part, this principle rests upon convictions stated in the first principle. Freedom to choose one way of life over another way of life seems to be inherent in human personality. We would scarcely be human without such freedom. Automatons cannot be men. Therefore, a counselor who seeks to choose for his client some specific solution to a problem or to impose upon a client a model which may be adequate for the counselor but not for the client, in effect, seeks to limit the client's freedom of choice. This is one of the

serious defects in advice-giving or telling people what they should do. Another defect is, of course, that advice-giving seems so seldom to be effective. Perhaps one reason for this may lie in the individual's reluctance to relinquish freedom of choice. If a solution to a problem is not attained by the client, albeit with the counselor's assistance, it simply is not his solution.

A counselor who is committed by his convictions to this principle will utilize techniques of counseling that help the client sort out and clarify his feelings and thoughts about his situation and examine possible alternative courses for an adequate and workable solution. In this kind of counseling, the client never is treated as a less important person than the counselor. The counselor is a helper whose training and experience should enable him to better understand and accept the individuals who seek his aid. Most troubled persons need to encounter precisely these qualities if they are to find help.

If a counselor believes that relatively mature and healthy persons possess the capacity for applying sufficient intelligence and will to their disturbing life situations to reach satisfactory solutions, and if a counselor is convinced that individuals should be free to make their own choices concerning these solutions, such convictions will be reflected in counseling. Clients will not be pushed into solutions that were in reality made by the counselor rather than by the client. A counselor can easily—without recognizing what is happening—lead his clients to a seeming acceptance of the counselor's values, ideals, ideas, and ways of acting. Certainly a counselor should have his own set of ideals, morals, and values. But people in trouble are seldom helped by the counselor who imposes his own model upon them. If, instead, they are helped to think through the various facets of their problem situation, their reactions to it, their involvement in it, and if they are encouraged, in a permissive, accepting counseling environment, to work out a self-determined resolution of the difficulty, they may then arrive at a course of action which is theirs and for which they can accept responsibility.

3. THE PRINCIPLE OF LIMITATIONS. No one person can be adequately trained to provide all kinds of help for people who are in trouble. Counselors must recognize their limitations and adhere strictly to an attempt to provide only the kind of help for which they are trained and competent.

If one's competence is in marriage counseling, he needs constantly to consider whether this is the kind of help which is most likely to be of real assistance to the client. Sometimes a counselor helps most by exploring the problem with a client and by examining with him the kind of help he wants and needs. Frequently the most appropriate help is to be gained through counseling. At other times the counselor will be of more assistance if he refers the client for some other kind of help.

This means, of course, that every counselor should be well aware of his competencies and limitations. It also means that he will need to develop skills and techniques that will help clients to reach adequate decisions concerning the nature of their difficulties and the kind of professional assistance they want, need, and are ready to accept.

The principle of limitations implies also that one should not expect more of himself as a counselor than is reasonable. Inexperienced counselors frequently feel that they must provide help for every person who comes to them. Even when referral to another source of assistance is not indicated, some clients simply are not ready to accept help. In this context, readiness implies a sufficiently strong desire for help that this wish will override any concurrent wish to avoid the pain involved in examining one's problem situation.

Unless a counselor recognizes that he cannot be of assistance to everyone he sees, he may unwittingly try to keep clients coming for counseling when they have not reached a sufficient readiness for continuing. Moreover, the counselor may begin to doubt his counseling effectiveness if he has such high expectations of himself that he feels he should be able to continue counseling with all who begin. Some clients are unready to proceed steadfastly toward resolving their problems, and some seem unable to make use of any kind of talking-out process. With these persons, a counselor can reasonably expect of himself only that he will provide time and his best knowledge and skill. If a client comes in without adequate motivation, and if the understanding and accepting attitudes of the counselor fail to bolster the insufficient strength of the desire for help, the counselor can do little else.

The principle of limitations applies also to what may and may not reasonably be expected of clients. A counselor who expects too much of himself is also in danger of expecting too much of clients. Patience is a great virtue for counselors to cultivate. Clients must progress at their pace, rather than at the counselor's pace. If too much or too rapid progress is expected, clients may feel that it is futile to try. They may become discouraged and resistant if they think the counselor is pushing them with his own expectations.

These three basic principles are not exhaustive. They merely serve to focus attention upon some of the most important bases upon which skills and techniques may be built. Competency always indicates skill; but skill in the field of counseling should encompass far more than merely the ability to use certain techniques. Involved in the art of counseling are the counselor's set of basic beliefs and feelings about himself and others. Whether the counselor wills it so or not, the techniques he employs and the way he employs them will reveal their origins.

Counseling techniques consist mainly of listening, asking questions, and making comments. This sounds quite simple, whereas in actual practice it may be quite complex. Everything a counselor does should be done for a purpose. A counselor should at all times know what he is doing and why he is doing it. Otherwise, his counseling will be in danger of becoming a hit-and-miss variety of doubtful worth.

Listening

In counseling, purposeful listening is of great value. Some clients come with a tremendous need to talk freely with an interested and understanding person. Perhaps they have never before been accorded the opportunity to express freely their thoughts and feelings without any fear of judgment or recrimination. The counselor who recognizes his client's needs and listens with interest and an obvious desire to understand and help provides an atmosphere in which, through verbalization, clients may experience a deep sense of release.

This experience may be quite necessary for some clients as a prelude to focusing upon the problems for which they are seeking solutions. If the counselor interposes too many questions or makes too many comments at this stage, he may arouse antipathy and resistive attitudes that will block progress.

Mere listening, however, is never enough. Most clients come for help, and they know that simply telling their story will not solve their problems. True, there may be a sense of release in merely being able to talk to someone who will listen interestedly. But more than this usually is wanted and needed.

The counselor's task is to help the client delineate the problem or problems and to clarify his thinking about his difficulty so that he may become more objective and begin to apply his rational reasoning powers toward achieving an adequate solution. Mere listening cannot accomplish these aims.

Listening also raises other problems. For one thing, unless the counselor comments or asks some questions, the client knows that his story cannot be accurately understood. He may wonder if the counselor really is interested in helping him. Another danger is that the client will assume that when he has related the facts concerning his difficulty, the counselor will provide a solution. Still another danger is that the client may later blame the counselor for allowing him to expose so much of his feeling of inadequacy or inability to deal with his life situation. Or, he may become quite dependent upon the counselor, thus blocking progress in future counseling sessions.

The counselor needs to be well aware of all these possibilities as he listens. If he does not understand what the client is telling him, he can ask for clarification or say that he is not quite clear about the point being discussed.

All of this demands that the counselor be an intelligent listener. Not only what the client says is important. What he is not saying should also be noted. As he listens, the counselor should be aware of any important omissions. He may notice that a client who has children never mentions his relationship with them. Or a client who complains about his wife's behavior while he was overseas may completely omit any reference to his own behavior during that period of time.

Asking Questions

Like everything else a counselor does in the process of counseling, asking questions of a client should be purposeful. Counseling is not mere social conversation. To be sure, conversation in counseling as elsewhere serves the purpose of communication between the persons involved. But in counseling, the client is the focus of conversation. All the questions and comments and even the listening employed by the counselor are directed toward accomplishing a definite purpose. He wants to be of assistance to the client, and he knows that he can do so only if he constantly tries to understand what the client is thinking and feeling concerning himself, his spouse, and their relationship. The counselor also becomes aware of the strengths of the client and helps him to make better use of the positive factors in himself and in his environment.

With these purposes in mind, the counselor may ask questions of various kinds. Some of the most effective types of questions are:

1. THE CLARIFYING QUESTION. This kind of question that asks for clarification of the information given may be used effectively to help the client become more aware of his own thoughts about what he is telling the counselor. Many clients are confused as to just where the problem lies. Until this is clarified, they are unlikely to be able to work toward adequate solutions to their difficulties.

Counselor: Well, where shall we begin?
Client: I don't know exactly. I suppose what worries me most is whether I ought to go back to my husband or not. You see he's begging me to come back to him and that keeps me all upset. I left him two weeks ago and now I'm living in my own apartment.
Counselor: How did that come about?
Client: Well, he told me to get out. He said he never wanted to see me again. He was mad, and I guess he didn't really mean it, but at the time he certainly acted like he meant it.
Counselor: Why was he so angry?
Client: Oh, I guess he had reason to be. I had gone out with some friends of mine and he doesn't like them and won't have anything to do with them and so he was just real mad about it.

2. THE REFLECTIVE QUESTION. This kind of question helps a client to decide whether what he has just said is really what he means. By reflecting the part of the client's comments that seems improbable, the counselor encourages his client to become somewhat more objective about his situation.

Client: I know that part of the trouble is my mother. My wife doesn't like her. Never has. Of course, we lived with her when we were first married and I guess that was the wrong thing to do. But my mother has always been good to us. Oh, she's not the easiest person in the world to get along with. I know that. But she's old and she won't be here always. I just can't neglect my mother. But my wife hates me for it.
Counselor: Hates you?
Client: I believe she does. Oh, I guess she doesn't, really. But there are times when I feel like she absolutely despises me. Like

the other night. I got off work and I thought, well, I haven't been by Mom's for a couple of days, so I went over there. She was so glad to see me and all, I hated to leave right off, but I looked at my watch and I knew my wife would be mad if she had to wait supper on me. So finally I just called my wife and told her I wouldn't be home for supper.

Counselor: You felt you had to choose between disappointing your mother and making your wife angry?

Client: Well, yes . . . only, I guess really I couldn't stand to feel in myself that I had hurt my mother's feelings by leaving so soon. And if I didn't leave and get home, then my wife would look at me like I was a worm. And then I'd feel bad about that, too.

3. CONNECTING QUESTIONS. Frequently a client can be helped in seeing his difficulty more clearly if interrelated facts or occurrences are connected by a question that makes this relatedness quite apparent.

Client: I don't know what's the matter with us. We used to be happy together but now we just don't seem to have anything in common. It's all just faded out.

Counselor: How do you think the fading out came about?

Client: I don't know, really. It just seems like we had everything in our marriage and then we didn't.

Counselor: You had everything . . . until?

Client: Until . . . well, right up to the time our first baby came.

Counselor: You think there is some connection between the coming of the baby and this difference in your relationship?

Client: There must be. Yes, because we were just real happy up to that time. Then . . . but, of course, we loved having the baby. Only, I think it sort of shocked us when I got pregnant right off again.

4. INFORMATION-GATHERING QUESTIONS. If a counselor is to succeed in gaining enough understanding of a client's personality, his life situation, and his difficulties, certain facts must be held clearly in mind. Most counselors probably keep some kind of record about the persons they interview so they can review pertinent facts prior to each counseling session. But however valuable these records may be, at times in coun-

seling one forgets facts and has to ask about them again in order to fully understand what the client is concerned about at the moment.

In addition, the client may talk about persons, things, or occurrences as if the counselor were quite familiar with the concomitant facts whereas, in reality, the counselor may be completely unaware of them. Under these circumstances, the counselor should ask for the needed and lacking information. If he does not ask, he cannot fully understand. Moreover, failure to ask such questions may later be recognized by the client, who may then assume that the counselor was not really interested in trying to understand what was being said.

Client: My brother once told me that I'd never be able to get along with this girl, but I was so sure.

Counselor: Let's see now . . . which brother was this?

Client: (Name). He's the one, you know, who always tried to tell me what to do. We never got along at all.

Counselor: Mmhm. And you and he talked about (wife) before you were married?

Client: Yeah. He didn't want me to get married. He said she would always keep me broke and we'd never have a dime because she would spend every cent I made. Well, I guess he was right on that. But I don't like people telling me what to do. Especially him. It wasn't any of his business and I wanted to tell him so, but I couldn't. That's another thing . . . when somebody says something like that I just take it. Oh, I think things, but I don't say 'em. I just act like it's all right . . . That's one thing about my wife. She will say something I don't like and I may feel real hurt about it, but I just let it go and say nothing.

Counselor: What do you do?

Client: Oh, I just walk off and leave her. Sometimes I just go get in the car and drive around. You know, something like that.

5. CONFRONTING QUESTIONS. Confrontation (helping a person to examine the meaning of his actions) may validly be used in counseling when a client is unable to recognize that his behavior is leading him into further confusions, conflicts, or dilemmas. But this technique should be used sparingly and

preferably when other—and usually, less threatening—techniques prove ineffective.

Client: Well, I've just about decided to get a divorce. He says he'll fight me on it unless I give him the children, but I guess that's what I'll do, just let him take them.

Counselor: Is that what you want?

Client: No. I don't want that. I love my children and that's the last thing I'd do, but what else can I do? If I don't, he won't give me the divorce. Oh, I don't know what to think. He said last night that he still loves me, and he says he can overlook what I've done and pick up and go on. But I just laughed at him.

Counselor: You laughed at him? Why was that?

Client: Why, the poor guy. Doesn't he know that if he did what I've done, I'd leave him in a minute?

Counselor: How do you think he felt when you laughed at him?

Client: Hurt, I guess. He just looked at me and then left.

Counselor: Do you think you wanted to hurt him?

Client: No, of course not . . . well, maybe I do. Anyway, I guess I did hurt him.

Making Comments

Just as a counselor purposefully listens and asks questions in his endeavors to understand and help clients, he also makes comments or statements in response to what is being said. As a general principle, one should avoid making statements with an air of finality, either in tone of voice or in the content of the statements.

In the following several pages the various types of commonly used comments will be discussed and illustrated.

1. Reflective Comments. When a client is attempting to sort out his thoughts and feelings about his problems, the counselor may give some assistance by restating what the client has said. This reflective technique can be very effective in helping clients who are psychologically minded to clarify their problems and decide upon an appropriate course of action.

In his fourth interview, Mr. L. stated that the relationship with his wife was somewhat better. The improvement was difficult to define or illustrate, but it was something he could feel. He reflected that he was enjoying the children more. He felt that the children were now acting more like children again, and he thought perhaps this change had come about because he was treating them like children. He said that it meant a great deal to him to have the children like him. He wanted them to be able to say that he was a swell guy.

The counselor commented that to have people like him was very important to Mr. L. The client agreed, saying that it was so important to him that he supposed that was part of his difficulty.

After a bit of silence, Mr. L. said, "You know, I have never really trusted anybody. I have always had to do things by myself and so when the important decisions came, I never felt I could trust anybody with them." The counselor commented that this must have made Mr. L. feel very lonely. He said that he had been very lonely without anyone really to depend on or lean on. At this point, however, he said he had found out he could trust his wife and gave illustrations of her helpfulness and understanding.

2. Empathic Comments. The client's perception of the counselor as an understanding person is one of the most potent forces in the counseling process. While sympathy is seldom helpful and, in reality, rarely desired, empathy is indispensable for effective counseling. Unlike sympathy, which tends to be more emotional and often an identification with the client, empathy is largely an intellectual process in which the counselor, with minimal emotional involvement, attempts to put himself momentarily in the client's frame of reference.

Client: (Sobbing) Then he told me . . . he said, I've just lost all the love I ever had for you.

Counselor: (Pause while client continues weeping) . . . That's pretty rough for you.

Client: (Nodding) It . . . I just feel like I can't bear it.

3. Puzzling Comments. Clients who would become threatened by direct confrontation can frequently be helped to move toward more adequate and satisfying courses of action when the counselor exhibits a puzzled or quizzical attitude. In effect,

puzzling comments tend to evoke "soul-searching" on the part of the client without the defensiveness that often results from direct confrontation.

Client: My wife thinks I'm having some kind of affair with another girl, but I'm not. Oh, I'll date one now and then, but that's all. It doesn't mean a thing to me, but she gets upset over it. But that's no problem. I don't think we really have any problem.

Counselor: You know, it seems a bit strange that you feel there's no problem when your wife is so upset over it.

Client: Well, yes . . . yes, I guess from her viewpoint it's a problem all right.

Counselor: I wonder how you see that.

Client: Well . . . She . . . I mean, I guess maybe she's afraid I'll leave her for one of these other girls, but that's silly. I'd rather have her than any girl I ever saw and I've told her so. But she gets all upset about it.

Counselor: Since it upsets her so, it looks as if it would be a problem for you, too. I wonder . . .

Client: Well . . . It is, in a way. I know the answer is to stop doing it. I don't see much wrong in it, but still, if she did the same thing, I sure wouldn't like it, either. I . . . I don't know why I get involved that way with other girls. I've got a good wife. She's a wonderful mother and wife and all that. I . . . I don't know. (Pause) It just bolsters my male ego, I suppose.

4. ENABLING COMMENTS. When a client is attempting to verbalize thoughts and feelings and cannot quite succeed in putting them into words, the counselor can help by making a comment that enables the client to continue his verbalizations. This kind of comment is helpful in two ways: it facilitates client production, and it increases rapport through reassurance that the counselor understands what is being said and meant.

Client: I don't know what's the matter. I love my wife and I'm so fond of the children, but still, I . . . I don't know, I don't know why it is that I . . . Well, I just don't respond to her as I should . . . in little things, I know what I should . . . I don't know . . .

Counselor: You seem to feel that somehow something keeps you from responding.

Client: Yeah, like I know what I want to do or say, and still, I don't do it. Like the other day . . .

5. CONNECTING COMMENTS. Although counseling is not designed to reveal to clients underlying (unconscious) reasons for their behavior and reactions, it must be concerned with specific attitudes and actions. Many persons, far from understanding why they behave as they do, are not even aware of the behavior itself. Doubtless, this is one of the reasons for much of the marital conflict we observe. If, for example, a husband engages in a kind of behavior that constantly provokes his wife to respond with anger, he probably will not attempt to alter his actions unless he can clearly recognize what he is doing to disturb the marital relationship.

Counselors can frequently assist the people with whom they work by helping them to see some connection between one situation and another or between one set of actions and another. Sometimes this involves connecting the past with the present in order to help the client see the continuity of his behavior. This technique should be used with caution, however, and the counselor should be certain that a similarity actually exists between one situation and another before any connection is made. Moreover, a connecting comment should be a tentative comment so that the client can, without embarrassment or excessive defensiveness, reject the connection if it does not seem accurate to him.

Client: One thing we don't agree on is the children. My wife thinks I'm too strict with them, and I think she's too easy-going with them. But I don't want them to be like the little delinquents on our street. She says I expect too much of them. Maybe I do. But I was brought up to toe the line, and I expect my children to do the same. Of course, I didn't like it too well when I was growing up . . . I don't know.

Counselor: Apparently you see a similarity between what was expected of you and what you expect of your children.

Client: Yes . . . Yes, I do. And I feel like it's right, but then I don't want my children to feel toward me the way I felt about my father. I never could please my dad, no matter what I did.

Never. I always had to feel that no matter how I tried, he was always disappointed in me.

Counselor: You felt you just couldn't meet his expectations.

Client: That's right, I just couldn't measure up. And I don't want my kids to have to feel that way.

Counselor: I guess you wonder if perhaps you expect more than they can comfortably produce. Is that it?

Client: Yeah. Well, it's funny. Looks like I'm doing to them just about what my dad did. And Lord knows I don't want them to feel as I did. (Pause) You know, I wonder if I do the same way with my wife . . .

6. CONFRONTING COMMENTS. A confronting comment is one that tends to bring a client face to face with some aspect of his problem or behavior that he has not recognized, or at least not verbalized. This technique should be used with caution. A good rule of thumb for beginning counselors is to use other—and less threatening—techniques before attempting to confront a client. Here, again, patience is a virtue. Techniques previously discussed will be sufficient for many clients to begin to move toward solution to their problems.

Confrontation may be effectively used with some clients who seem stubbornly to avoid any recognition of their own involvement in their difficulties.

A woman client, throughout her first three interviews, blamed her husband for all of their marital difficulties. She exonerated herself completely and assumed a demanding attitude toward the counselor, at times asserting that the counselor should tell her husband to treat her differently. She seemed to believe that he was completely in the wrong.

Client: Well, I'll tell you this, I've just put up with him about as long as I can. You know what he does. I think someone ought to tell him what he does. I think someone ought to tell him what's right and what isn't. (A)

Counselor: You think he doesn't know? (1)

Client: Oh, of course he knows. Anybody knows, but he goes right on just as if he didn't know. That's what I told our minister. I said, you lay the law down to him. (B)

Counselor: And how did that turn out? (2)

Client: Oh, the minister told him, I guess. But it didn't do a bit of good. (C)

Counselor: Looks as if having someone tell him doesn't work out so well. (3)

Client: Well . . . no, I guess not. (D) But what else is there to do? You tell me. I've done everything I know to do. (E)

Counselor: How do you see that? (4)

Client: Oh, I've pleaded with him, I've begged him, I've threatened to leave him, everything. (F)

Counselor: How does he take all this? (5)

Client: It doesn't mean a thing to him. He just says, oh, stop nagging me. (G)

Counselor: He feels you're nagging him. (6)

Client: Oh, definitely. Just stop nagging me, he says. Like yesterday, he started to leave and I said, now, J., promise me you won't do anything like you have done, just promise me. And he got mad and swore and said if I didn't talk about it all the time, he probably wouldn't do it. (H) So there it was again. You can't depend on him any more than a four-year-old. (I)

Counselor: You think maybe he feels you treat him like a four-year-old? (7)

Client: What? Oh, I see what you mean. (J) Why, no, no, I don't think so. Well, how else can you treat a grown man that acts the way he does? (K) (Silence) Maybe he does feel that way. I don't know, sometimes I feel like I've got three children instead of two and a husband. (L)

In this illustration, the basic confrontation is that the client's demands upon her husband and others are unrealistic and ineffectual. The counselor's comments tend to follow this theme. The counselor has recognized that the client cannot move toward grappling realistically with her marital difficulties until she is able to see that her demands are not realistic and that her own behavior has something to do with her marital problems. The immediate counseling goal, therefore, is to separate this sector of the problem and work with it. All comments lead toward this objective, and all comments have in them elements of the basic confrontation. Thus, each successive comment tends to reinforce its predecessors.

Our conviction is that the cumulative kind of confrontation

illustrated above is far less threatening and more effective in the long run than an abrupt, head-on confronting comment. Figure 9–1 illustrates the relation of this technique to the immediate counseling goal.

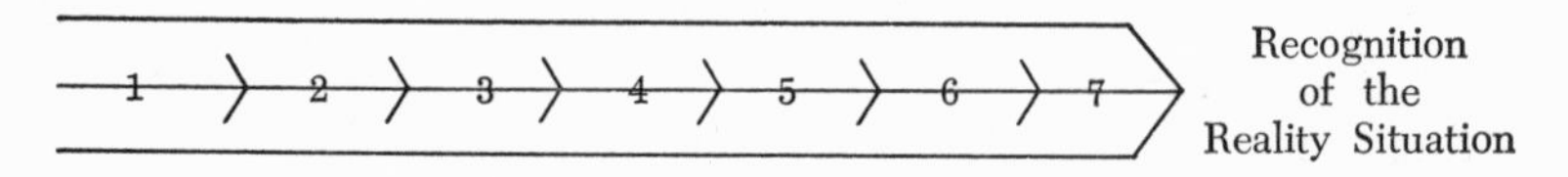

Figure 9–1. Cumulative Confrontation Related to the Immediate Counseling Goal.

Each confronting comment, thus, serves to reinforce its predecessor and to lend weight to its successor. Since all comments lead in a direct line toward the immediate counseling goal, the one basic confrontation is achieved with the cumulative effect of the comments. Moreover, all counselor comments are directly related to, and hinge upon, what the client is saying.

Figure 9–2 represents an analysis of the foregoing case illustration in terms of the effect of the counselor's confrontations as revealed by the client's responses. Note especially how movement toward recognition of self-involvement in the marital problems proceeds in a peak-and-valley fashion rather than in a straight line mode.

What, precisely, has happened in the interview to help the client to move from A to L? The counselor, recognizing that he will be unable to assist the client in reaching a solution to her problem unless she can begin to see her situation and her way of dealing with it more realistically, selects this facet or sector of the problem as the immediate counseling focus. Essentially, what the counselor does is to take the side of reality in a series of confronting comments that challenge the client's distortions of reality. He asks over and over for the real situation. This is an appeal to the client's strength.

Confronting comments may also be used with some clients who almost completely impede progress in counseling by not

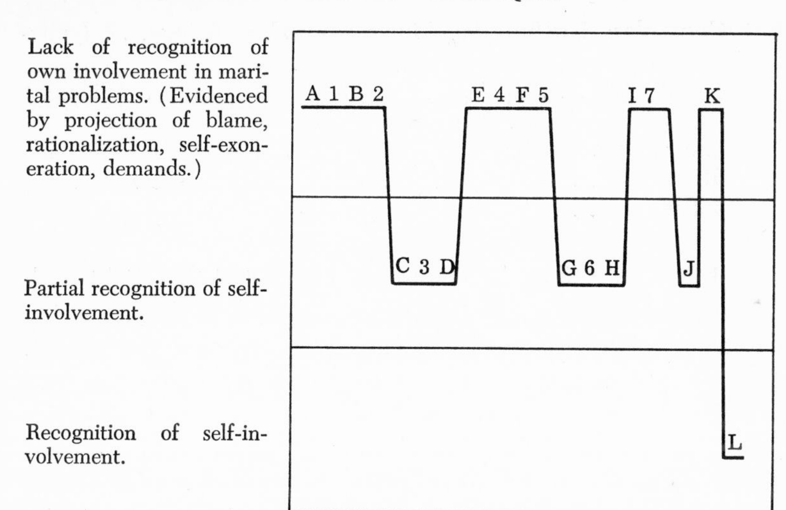

Figure 9–2. Schematic Representation of Cumulative Confrontation in the Case Illustration.

expressing what they are really thinking and feeling. Before using confrontation in this kind of situation, the counselor should be certain that he is working with a person who is not seriously emotionally disturbed. If one is grossly disturbed, his real thoughts and feelings may be very frightening to him, and he may avoid them for this reason.

If, however, the counselor is convinced that the client is relatively healthy and has good ego strength, confrontation may be helpful.

A male client constantly stated that he did not know what his marital trouble was all about. He spoke of his wife only in complimentary terms. She was a good homemaker, mother, wife, and companion. He thought that he had some faults but that he was, in general, a pretty good husband. He wanted to know what the counselor thought the difficulty might be.

Counselor: You seem to be saying that something is wrong, but you can't quite say what. Is that about it?

Client: Yes, yes, I guess so. What do you see in this picture?

Counselor: Well, it seems like an incomplete picture somehow.

Client: Incomplete? That sounds like you think I haven't told the truth.

Counselor: No, but something seems to be missing . . . (quizzical) How does it seem to you?

Client: Oh . . . well . . . I don't know, exactly. (Silence) Well, one thing is . . . This has bothered me, I mean my conscience, for a long time, but I just try not to think about it. Back in 19__, there was this girl, see? My wife never knew anything about it, but . . .

In this illustration, the counselor confronted the client with the improbability of the story as presented. The confrontation was somewhat threatening as is evidenced by the client's defensive accusation that the counselor seemed to think the story was untrue. However, by refusing to react to the client's anger and by being puzzled about the incomplete story, the counselor helped this man to move toward a consideration of the real problem. Obviously, much of the problem was rooted in the client's feelings of guilt. This important factor had been missing, and without it the marital difficulty could not be worked out.

7. Interpreting Comments. Interpretation, in the sense of offering labels or explanations for a client's behavior or verbalizations, is ordinarily unnecessary and usually unwise in counseling. It is unnecessary because the goal of marriage counseling—to aid the client to a self-determined resolution of his problems—is more effectively achieved through the use of methods which encourage the client to pull upon his own strengths. If explanations are to be made, preferably the client should make them.

Interpretation is also usually unwise as a counseling technique because it tends to foster in the client undue dependency upon the counselor. Another danger is that evaluative explanations of client productions and actions may shift the counseling focus to an introspective concern about self. This is not the counselor's task. If the client's chief needs or concerns are centered around his own reactions and his discomfort over them, the appropriate help may be psychotherapy rather than counseling.

8. Informative Comments. Marriage counseling has a place for providing needed information. Although more young people are provided with opportunities for marriage education today than was true of the youth of fifty years ago, many persons still enter marriage without much realization of what it takes to get on well in the marriage relationship.

Some of these couples come to marriage counselors in an endeavor to secure information and to gain a better knowledge of marriage and of marital roles and responsibilities. Many doubts and fears can be alleviated through correction of misconceptions and lack of information. Certainly the counselor can answer questions of fact if they are in his field. Medical questions should, of course, be taken up by the client with a doctor. Similarly, legal questions should be discussed with an attorney.

This does not relieve the counselor, however, of the responsibility for acquiring for himself through his consultative relationships with various professional persons, such information as may properly be utilized in counseling.

The precise information from the various professions that may properly be provided by a counselor is a matter for counselors to discuss and clarify with their professional consultants. Certainly there are questions about economics that the well-informed counselor can handle without the necessity of referral to a family economist. Similarly, an informed counselor may deal with many questions related to sex without needing to refer to the physician. But counselors need to be very clear as to the distinction between providing information that is fairly common knowledge and attempting to provide information which is in the distinct province of a particular profession, such as medicine or law. The following is an example of one type of information the counselor can handle without referral:

> A male client was concerned because his wife objected to the way their finances were handled. He stated that he did not understand his wife's objection and that she had only to ask for the money she needed and if the request seemed reasonable to him,

he would give her the money. When the counselor asked how he and his wife had arrived at this method of handling family finances, he replied that he had told her shortly after they were married that this was the way it was to be done. He had supposed she agreed since she said nothing at the time. This was the way his father had handled the matter, and he could not understand why his wife was unhappy with this kind of arrangement.

As the counselor listened and explored the client's thoughts about the problem, he became convinced that the client was employing the only method he knew and that this method of handling finances did not represent an attempt to control the wife. The counselor asked the client just how the wife reacted to the arrangement. He said she had told him that having to ask for money made her feel like a small child. The counselor decided to provide information at this point and said that many wives would probably feel the same way. Perhaps the client could consider other methods of determining how the family money might be used. Emphasis was placed upon marriage as a sharing, cooperative experience which included handling the money, which is, in reality, family money. The client said he had never thought of it that way, but he guessed that was right. The counselor pointed out that the wife's role as homemaker involves spending some money just as the husband's role involves earning money.

The counselor then asked how the client felt about the way his wife spent the money he allotted to her. He replied that he felt she used good judgment and spent wisely. He wondered how other couples handled the matter. The counselor explored with him the various methods that are commonly utilized and that involve the sharing and mutuality his wife seemed to want. As a result, the client decided he would talk with his wife about these possibilities so they could come to a joint decision. "I just thought I was supposed to do it the other way, but I can see how she might feel about it. This sharing business, I see what you mean about that and that's what I want. Actually, it will be better for me that way, too."

Today, more and more young people are seeking premarital counseling. Some of them want to discuss anticipated problems, or at least adjustments in the coming marriage. Others want to secure certain information relative to marriage. Still others suspect that they are entering marriage with misconceptions, and they want these corrected. In these instances, the marriage counselor has unique opportunities to provide information and discuss concerns of couples prior to marriage, thus helping them to get off to a better beginning in marriage than would be possible if they continued to assume that their misconceptions were facts.

Silence

Silence, when properly timed and astutely used, is extremely valuable in counseling. More than most other techniques, however, effective utilization of silence demands keen clinical perceptiveness on the part of a counselor. In practice, this means that from the way a client is looking, responding verbally and behaving bodily, a counselor needs to estimate carefully the probable effect of any technique he considers using. He needs always to keep in mind the question of how the move he is about to make probably will be perceived by his client.

While this sounds rather complicated and cumbersome, in actual practice, a perceptive counselor gains, through experience, the ability to quickly assess the needs of his client from moment to moment.

Too many counselors are threatened by silences in the interview hour. They feel that they ought to be doing something. The beginner can easily feel that unless he is talking, nothing is really happening. Often the reverse is nearer the truth. Some persons learn to use their counseling hour as thinking-out periods. For these clients, silences are not threatening but moments used in sorting out their thoughts in the problem-solving task.

This is not to say that silence is never threatening to a client: it can be. For example, if, in a first interview, a client is having difficulty in verbalizing his thoughts about his problems, this is not a time to allow much silence to develop. The client needs, rather, to be given some help in the form of questions or comments which will enable him to feel more comfortable and to acquire confidence in the counselor. If, instead, the counselor allows too many long silences to develop, the client may feel anxious because he interprets the counselor's silence as disinterest or as a punitive measure. In other words, at this point, silence may be more harmful than helpful because it is ill-timed and the client perceives it as a threatening, anxiety-provoking matter.

Counselors need constantly to remind themselves that before progress can be made in counseling, a client must see the counselor as a genuinely interested, understanding person who wants to help. After this perception becomes consistent—and it can become so only if the counselor's total attitude and behavior is consistent—the use of techniques which, in the beginning might have blocked progress, may actually promote movement toward resolution of the problems.

If the use of silence is ill-timed, clients ordinarily react in one of two ways. Either they will simply terminate the interviews, with the feeling that they are not being helped, or they will become irritated and express their discomfort directly.

> A woman client had considerable difficulty in verbalizing her problem in the first interview. Long silences developed, and the counselor merely waited while the client struggled for words. Finally she blurted out: "Why do you sit and stare at me like that? Can't you say something? Is that what you're supposed to do?"

Unfortunately, unless a counselor has achieved a reasonably good understanding of himself and his own motivations, he may, without knowing why, actually be punitive in allowing long silences to develop. When, for example, one becomes impatient because a client seems to be withholding and trying to impress the counselor with his own goodness, the danger is that the counselor may punish the client by being silent.

As in the use of all other techniques, the counselor needs to formulate some estimate of when silence is likely to be helpful to the client and when it is not. After a few interviews, if the client lapses into silence and the counselor is fairly certain that good rapport has already been established and he is perceived as an understanding, helpful person, he may sense that the silence is being used by the client as a thinking-out period. In that case, silence can be very helpful and need not be interrupted.

> At the conclusion of his series of ten interviews, a client stated to his counselor: "You know, you helped me lots of times by just being here. It helped me to be calm and to think it out because you were never upset when I was, and lots of times you just sat there and didn't say anything, but I knew you were there and you really believed in me and wanted to help me. I guess it made me believe more in myself, too."

In this chapter, various techniques have been discussed and illustrated. The reader should note, however, that skill in the use of techniques cannot possibly be acquired through reading about them. Skill in counseling is best acquired through actual supervised experience in employing appropriate techniques in counseling sessions. Supervision is important in the acquisition of counseling skill because the experienced supervisor can help the counselor to evaluate carefully the appropriateness of the techniques that are being used and can point out those instances in which a different approach might be more effective.

10 CASE RECORDING

Various agencies—and for that matter different professions—tend to develop particular methods of record-keeping. The aim of this chapter is to evaluate some of the methods in common use and to suggest some ways in which counselors may utilize them to advantage.

Taking Notes in the Interview Hour

A common question asked by beginning counselors is whether they should take notes in the counseling session. The answer cannot be merely "yes" or "no" because the counselor's memory, comfort or discomfort in taking notes, and his ability or inability to write and listen at the same time all must be taken into consideration.

Most counselors feel that they can concentrate more thoroughly upon what is happening in the interview if they do not take notes in the hour but write down pertinent facts immediately after the session. The validity of this procedure depends to a great extent upon how well the counselor's memory functions. Can he retain with exactness the important statements made by the client? Can he recapture the nuances of the interview, such as the points at which the client became tearful or anxious, cheerful, or demanding?

Some counselors become very adept in accurately recording the interview following the counseling hour. For those who can use it well, this is a very good procedure. Its chief advantage is that one's concentration upon what is being said, how it is verbalized, and the accompanying emotional tone need not be interrupted by the process of taking notes. Too, the client's communication may be facilitated by the counselor's undivided attention to the face-to-face interaction.

On the other hand, some counselors discover that their attention becomes more divided when they attempt to use this procedure than when they take notes. The reason for this is that they find themselves thinking of something the client has said that ought to be remembered for the record. Concentration upon this item then serves to interrupt attention upon what is being said at the moment.

If a counselor finds that he cannot rely upon memory for the facts he needs to dictate a proper record following the interview, he should take notes during the hour instead. Perhaps key words or phrases jotted down as the client speaks will sufficiently refresh his memory so that an accurate account of the hour may be dictated later. However he decides to compile the needed information, the sooner he dictates his notes following the interview, the more likely he is to be comprehensive and accurate.

In counseling as in other activities, there are, fortunately, more ways than one to arrive at one's goal. Each person should find, through experience, the procedure that seems to bring him to his goal effectively with maximum benefit to his clients and with minimal discomfort to himself.

The Interview Summary

Most agencies and clinics in which counseling is done maintain some approved form for case recording. Certain facts are considered essential for the record. In some agencies these may be stated in narrative form and may not be accumulated under specific headings. In other agencies, headings are used so that necessary information is integrated under specifically designated topics, such as identifying information, statement of the problem, and so on.

Counselors whose work is carried on in settings in which the kind of case recording is not specified may find some value in developing forms and methods suited to their particular needs. The busy minister, for example, cannot possibly remember essential points in each case if he does much counseling unless he keeps adequate records.

For a first interview record the following essentials may quickly be dictated:

A. Identifying information, including sex, age, color, marital status, occupation, religion, referral source, and physical appearance.
B. Statement of the problem as the client sees it, including a direct quotation as expressed by the client.
C. The counselor's observations of the client, including the manner in which he speaks, how he presents the problem, how anxious he seems to be and how anxiety is manifested, any evidences of depression, aggression, demandingness, bizarre ideas, lack of adequate reality testing, type of relationship established with the counselor, and any other observations which may help the counselor (and, if possible, his consultant) to gain a clear picture of what the client is like.
D. The counselor's impression of the problem, including some estimate as to whether counseling may be the appropriate method of helping the client.
E. Disposition of the case, plans for future approintments, or if the client is being referred for a different kind of help, how and to whom referral is being made.[1]

The following material will illustrate the use of the suggested form for compiling valuable facts following an initial interview:

A. The clients, Mr. and Mrs. X, referred for counseling by Dr. N, came to the office together for the first interview and were seen jointly for one hour on this date.

Mr. X is a twenty-three-year-old, white businessman who works with his father in their grocery store in (city) (state). He is a thin, rather short, wiry, rather athletic-looking man with short-

[1] Forms suggested in this chapter evolved through collaboration with Robert G. Foster, Ph.D., for use in The Marriage Counseling Service, The Menninger Foundation, Topeka, Kansas.

cropped blond hair and pale blue eyes. He presented a well-groomed appearance in his tastefully matched sports clothes.

Mrs. X is an attractive brunette of twenty years who, although somewhat overweight, wears her expensive-appearing clothing and her carefully applied make-up extremely well. Her dark eyes and very white, although not sallow, complexion convey a rather startling impression, as if one might be viewing a painting of fragile femininity.

B. The clients agreed that they desired help in learning to avoid their periodic conflicts which typically result in separation. Mr. X expressed the belief that much of the problem was that his wife was immature, as evidenced by her proclivity for going home to her mother when the couple quarrel. He thought his temper had something to do with it also.

Mrs. X said, "The whole thing is a ridiculous, childish rowing and going home to mother, and sometime this has to stop. I don't relish these separations. He has a bad temper. I knew it all the time before we were married. But I am stubborn. Then, too, my feelings are tender and easily hurt. When he blows up, it scares me and I cry."

The couple agreed that in-laws were a complicating factor in the problem. Mr. X's parents had wanted him to become a lawyer, whereas his interest was in music. He resented his parents' objection to the marriage but agreed that neither he nor his wife realized the extent of the responsibilities they were assuming. Both Mr. and Mrs. X thought her mother "babied" her too much and was too willing for her to return home when the couple were in conflict. Neither considered divorce as a solution, and both clients expressed the feeling that since they loved each other a great deal, they should be able to work out their difficulties.

C. Although Mr. X was very affable and seemed to be attempting to present an appearance of a very sophisticated young man who could be at ease in almost any situation, I noticed that at times his hands trembled. His blasé attitude seemed somewhat exaggerated. He spoke rapidly and rather emphatically as if he needed to reassure himself that he was well in command of himself. He slumped down in his chair, stretched his legs out and folded his hands as if he were completely relaxed, but when I asked a question or made a comment his face became tense and he strained forward as if to be certain he understood every word.

Mrs. X spoke quietly but freely and seemed quite poised

throughout the hour. Now and then she smiled reassuringly at her husband. Occasionally, however, when Mr. X made such comments as, "You think I am rude sometimes, but I think you are rather a snob," she seemed to react by slightly withdrawing, looking down at the floor, and saying nothing.

D. Both clients seem rather immature. Apparently they entered marriage without much recognition of either their marital roles or responsibilities. For the wife to go home to her mother upon seemingly slight provocation has become an easy but, to both spouses, unsatisfactory solution to their difficulties.

Part of the problem seems to stem from their differences in personality make-up, as is evidenced by her obvious tendency to withdraw in the face of his emphatic and sometimes derogatory speech. One senses that with her rather slow, deliberate thoughtfulness she feels unable to cope with her husband's rather aggressive, quick bluntness. Also, while she tends to be somewhat shy, reserved, and quiet, he presents the appearance (probably façade) of one who is in command of himself and his environment.

Indications that this couple may be able to benefit from counseling are to be seen in their love for each other, their wish to find better ways of dealing with their problems, the absence of manifestations of severe personality aberrations, and their generosity of spirit and support of each other evidenced in much of this interview.

E. At the close of the interview both husband and wife indicated their wish to continue the counseling sessions. They agreed with the suggestion that perhaps they could plan to have several separate interviews in which the difficulties could be further considered with each person. Appointments were made for the next interviews.

The Verbatim Record

Verbatim records are those which include the exact content of an interview. Ordinarily verbatim materials can be obtained only through the use of tape or phonographic recordings. Typescripts are later made by playing back the tape or record and typing the material word for word. This is a long, laborious process and is hardly a practical method of record-keeping.

Moreover, counselors who thus record interviews may discover that the tape recorder can become a crutch. It is altogether too easy for a counselor to assume that he can later refer to the tape for any needed information or impressions. A machine can never be a substitute for the counselor's clinical perceptiveness. No less important than what is said in an interview is how the client looks as he says it, what he does as he speaks, and every other factor that helps to produce an impression of the person and his problems. Too much dependence upon a machine can, therefore, become an impediment both to the counseling process and to the professional development of the counselor.

This is not to say that verbatim records are of no value. Properly used, they can be of tremendous value. If, for example, a counselor occasionally tapes an interview and later listens to it, raising questions within himself concerning possible meanings in what the client has said and noting also his own responses and questions during the hour, he may well begin to seek better counseling methods. Too, he may begin to wonder why he responded as he did, why he did not recognize this nuance or that in the productions of the client, or why he failed to respond appropriately at some point.

Viewed as a device for aiding professional development, then, the verbatim record, or at least the use of a tape recorder, can be extremely valuable. Few methods can equal it as a teaching aid. Counselors-in-training who seriously want to learn frequently find in the recorder an invaluable aid to furthering their skills, not only through listening to the tape but also in playing it and discussing it with a supervisor or consultant.

Client agreement to recording an interview is usually given readily, provided the request is forthright and to the point without elaborate explanation or counselor attitudes that leave the impression that the request is not valid. Most clients want help and are quite willing to accept recording as part of the procedure if the counselor genuinely believes that the recording is in the interest of helping the client. If a counselor does not so believe and if he must feel apologetic about requesting the client's permission, he should not record.

Beginning counselors frequently fear that clients will hesitate to express themselves freely if a recorder is used. This fear is very seldom borne out in actual practice. Indeed, many clients feel that recording is an evidence of the counselor's sincere desire to exert every possible effort to be of assistance.

Marriage Assessment Summary

Considering that a counselor is able to observe and participate in discussions with clients for perhaps only one hour (out of one hundred and sixty-eight) per week and that the conditions under which clients are seen are far from ideal circumstances under which to become aware of clients' typical behavior, clearly adequate counseling demands that counselors develop qualities of keen perceptiveness. If counseling were a matter merely of advice-giving concerning a problem, then one could simply take as objective a view of the situation as possible and offer some common-sense solutions. But seldom can one expect to encounter a counseling case that is so simple and uninvolved as to warrant such an approach, even if one believes in the validity of it.

A person who has a problem is a *person.* An adequate solution for one individual may be wholly inadequate for another. Since this is the case, good practice demands as thorough a study as possible not only of the problem but also of the persons who are experiencing the problem. This is not to advocate that counselors should become junior psychiatrists, but rather that counselors make every possible effort to understand their clients in order to be of maximum help as well as to be able to determine when referral for a different kind of help should be made.

A method for making a beginning study of the client and his problems has already been suggested. Let us emphasize, however, that the first interview summary ought to be considered as a first impression which is subject to constant revision as counseling proceeds. Indeed, obtaining a satisfactorily complete and accurate impression of the difficulties and persons in a first interview is most exceptional. Experience indicates that a far more adequate summary may be made after four or five interviews. If this is to be done, however, one needs to formulate some systematized schema for assembling the necessary data.

The following outline is designed to help counselors assemble data from several interviews in a logical, orderly manner in order to estimate with reasonable accuracy the kinds of problems and personalities with which one is working. A further aim is to make an evaluation of clients' assets and liabilities for utilizing counseling. This kind of study enables counselors to organize their material and their thinking in order to clarify what the difficulties are and how clients are reacting and interacting in their major relationships.

Outline for Marriage Assessment

A. Identifying information:
   1. Basic facts (name, sex, age, schooling, marital status, date and place of marriage, employment, residence, referral source, dates of counseling interviews).
   2. Physical appearance (approximate size, weight, skin features, color of hair and eyes, grooming, posture, and voice).

B. General statement of the problem:
   1. The presenting problem (as viewed by the client when he first seeks help).
   2. Quotations from client's presentation of the problem.
   3. Precipitating events that stimulated the client to seek help.

C. The marriage:
   1. Brief factual history of the marriage.
   2. Dynamics of the marriage:
      a. Development of anticipated marital role concepts:
         (1) Childhood models of husband-wife roles and how perceived by clients.
         (2) Early identification figures and idealized persons.

(3) Adolescent identification figures and idealized persons.
(4) Adolescent self-concept: how developed; values, goals, aspirations.
(5) Adolescent interaction pattern with parents, siblings, peers.
(6) Role concepts in dating, courtship, and mate selection processes. (Include extent and quality of relations with persons of the opposite sex.)
(7) Influence of religious, educational, social, and economic factors upon role concepts.

b. Actual marital roles:
(1) Self-roles.
(2) Spouse-roles.

c. Differences between anticipated and actual roles:
(1) Specific areas of difference and how developed.
(2) Reactions to differences.

d. Need satisfactions:
(1) Dependent needs.
(2) Aggressive needs.
(3) Reciprocal affectional needs:
(a) Trust.
(b) Respect.
(c) Admiration.
(d) Sex.
(e) Companionship.
(f) Tender affection.
(4) Need for self-investment in:
(a) Work.
(b) Play.
(c) Hobbies and special interests.
(d) Nonhuman objects (property, money, pets, clothes, art, nature, and the like).

3. Marital interaction in:
a. Handling family finances.
b. Rearing children.
c. Social activities and recreation.
d. In-law relationships.
e. Religion.
f. Friendships.
g. Sexual relations.
h. Maintaining marriage equilibrium.

4. Summary of negative aspects of marital interaction.
5. Summary of positive aspects of marital interaction.
6. Patterns of family interaction:
   a. Dominance patterns.
   b. Valence patterns.
   c. Family ritual patterns.
   d. Happiness maintenance patterns.
   e. Conflict patterns.
   f. Conflict resolution patterns (including adaptive endeavors of each spouse).

D. Estimate of client's need and motivation for accepting further help.

E. Estimate of the validity of counseling as the indicated helping method.

F. Brief resumé of counseling process to date, including any emotional aspects of the client-counselor relationship.

G. Brief resumé of progress in counseling to date.

H. Disposition (plans for further counseling, plans for referral, or for termination).

Progress Notes

Many agencies and clinics request that their staff counselors prepare a monthly or weekly report of progress in each case being carried. Such reports usually are called *progress notes.* They are brief, concise estimates of the use a client has been able to make of his counseling sessions to date. Evidences of case movement are presented along with significant changes in the client's attitudes, life situation, and family interaction.

Ordinarily, progress notes cover interviews which occur after a rather thorough study, marriage assessment summary, or psychiatric consultation has indicated the advisability of continued counseling. The following notes constitute an example of the concise manner in which progress can be indicated.

Mr. and Mrs. L. G.

Individual interviews with Mrs. G. were on June 4, 11, 18, 25.

In contrast to her original concerns with feelings of jealousy and the conviction that her husband did not love her, Mrs. G. has, in the past two interviews, become increasingly aware of evidences of her husband's love. Her tendency to blame her husband for the couple's difficulties has lessened markedly. For example, in her most recent hour, she said that she had begun to understand some of the factors in their relationship that had been separating them. She expressed the belief that she had precipitated many of their crises through her lack of faith in her husband. She recognized that her lack of security in her job at the office had been reflected in her attitudes toward Mr. G. She thought this was unfair to her husband. She has found a more satisfying position and feels now that she "counts for something" and is doing an important job. She has decided to drop divorce proceedings and thinks she will return to her husband although she does not feel ready to do so just yet.

July 3, 195__, R.M., Counselor

Individual interviews with Mr. L. G., June 5, 12, 19, 26.

The client has, until his most recent interviews, constantly struggled with the question of whether he really wants to go back to his wife and live with her. His resentment over her demanding, controlling attitudes is recognized by him as the major deterrent to his return to her. "I love her, but I have to have some life of my own, too."

In his most recent hour, the client began speaking of his wife in a positive manner. He admired her and respected her, but he wondered if she would still attempt to "stifle" him. Obviously he wants to return to his wife but cannot yet be sure that the old troubles will not recur. He concluded that he and his wife should work on their problems for a while yet before any decision is made.

July 4, 195__, R.M., Counselor

Individual interviews with Mrs. L. G.—July 8, 15, 22, 29.

The client has become increasingly positive in her attitudes toward her husband. At the beginning of the month she experienced renewed doubt about the wisdom of having dropped the divorce action but has not mentioned any doubts in the past three weeks. She has increased her social activities and has been elected to official positions in two of the social and service groups to which she belongs. She seems to have developed a much greater (and more realistic) sense of self-esteem than she had a month ago.

She and her husband have spent a great deal of time together in the past two weeks, and she speaks glowingly of these events.

He now comes to her apartment each morning for breakfast and frequently takes her out evenings to dinner, dances, and movies.

Two weeks ago she stated that she had definitely decided to return to her husband and broached the subject of termination. In her latest hour, she stated that she and her husband were now living together and that they had agreed that further appointments for counseling were not necessary. She seemed to be quite happy and satisfied that she had made the right decision. She laughingly said that she "just hoped nothing would happen to spoil it." She asked if she could return if she needed to do so, but she appeared quite confident that she and her husband would be able to continue on their own.

August 4, 195__, R.M., Counselor

Individual interviews with Mr. L. G.—July 9, 16, 23, 30.

Mr. G. continued questioning the wisdom of returning to live with his wife until about the middle of the month. He then began recognizing that neither he nor his wife could be absolutely certain that their aspirations for the marriage would work out as they hoped. He recognized that he was now doubting her motives as she previously had doubted his. He began evaluating the progress each of them had made and concluded that they had every reason to believe that they could now go back together and have a much better relationship than ever before.

About two weeks ago his wife broached the subject of their going back together. He was glad that she made this move, and he thought they would start living together again within the next few days.

In his latest interview, Mr. G. reported that he and his wife were living together and that they were both happy about their decision. He thought both were being very careful not to say or do anything that would hurt the other person. He hoped they would be able to learn to express their feelings without conflict because he was finding this mutual endeavor to avoid tension something of a strain. However, he expressed confidence that he and his wife would be able to cope with any problems that might arise.

August 4, 195__, R.M., Counselor

October 3, 195__. Two months after termination of counseling, Mr. and Mrs. G. approached the counselor in a casual meeting in a local department store to express appreciation for the help they had received. They appeared quite happy and spoke with humor about their "little spats." Mr. G. said that they had discovered that they can have differences of opinion "without the world coming to an end." Mrs. G. laughingly commented, "Well, it took us a long time to find out we're both just human and we both have feelings." Mr. G. remarked that they had, on two or three occasions, considered returning for additional counseling, but "things worked out all right."

R.M., Counselor

Learning Through Studying Case Records

Occasionally one hears experienced counselors say that they no longer write interview records. The reason usually given is that the time pressure is too great when one is seeing a large number of clients. While this attitude is easily understandable —particularly to those who have worked in clinics and agencies with very heavy case loads—some striking disadvantages should be noted.

In the first place, a counselor who keeps little if any record of his interviews may easily fall into the error of being concerned only with what is currently being said or done by the client. Just as the continuity in human behavior becomes understandable when one collects this data in an orderly fashion, so, too, the significance of one interview in the middle phase of counseling may be more clearly recognized if one keeps in mind what has happened in preceding interview hours.

A second difficulty with failure to keep adequate records becomes apparent when one needs material concerning a case for the use of other professional persons. For example, a psychiatric consultant can scarcely be expected to be of very much assistance unless he is given the facts concerning a case.

Then, too, clients may request that information concerning their counseling interviews be provided for the use of a physician, psychiatrist, or other professional person. Such a request should always be signed by the client and witnessed by a doctor or other professional person who needs the information for the benefit of the client's treatment program.

Unfortunately, counselors who have heavy case loads are

frequently the ones who stand in greatest need of records since no one could be expected to keep clearly in mind a large number of cases. Both counselors and clients would benefit if the busiest of counselors would habitually and consistently use a ten-minute interval between interviews to write or dictate cogent and meaningful notes on the hour just ended.

But dictation of records is only one part of the process if records are to be of maximum help in counseling. The second step is to use the records. Several methods for utilizing records to better understand clients have already received our attention.

We come now to a different use of records. Most counselors who consistently adhere to the procedure suggested below will find assurance and a sense of security in the knowledge that they are exerting efforts to do their best not just in any one interview but also in a continued series of counseling sessions.

Each morning before he begins his counseling sessions, a counselor can carefully go over the records of each client he is scheduled to see that day. He can read through the notes for a client and then ask himself some questions concerning the case. What is the problem? In asking for help, what does the client say he really wants? Have doubts and fears about getting help been resolved at this point? What has the client tried to do about his problem, and how have his efforts worked or failed? Has he made any steps toward resolution of his difficulties since he began counseling? Has the counselor adequately estimated the strengths of the client, and has he utilized this estimation by suiting techniques to the level of ego strength of the client? What evidence is there that some movement has taken place in the case? If there is none, how does the counselor account for the lack of movement, and how can he help the client to accelerate progress?

While this list of questions certainly is not exhaustive, it can serve the purpose of helping a counselor keep a much-needed perspective in each case. Once the suggested procedure becomes habitual, the benefits both for the counselor's certainty and for the client's progress far outweigh the expenditure of time involved in the process.

Problems of Isolated Practice

A few counselors are somewhat isolated in their practice. They do not have the professional growth advantages available to those who work in agency or clinical settings in which the team approach is used. In a clinical setting one may present to the staff any case about which questions may arise. Staff consideration provides stimulation and critical evaluation of one's work. The result can be a constant, gradual growth and development of the professional self.

The isolated counselor, on the other hand, is in danger of becoming self-satisfied with a resultant stagnation insofar as professional growth is concerned. Another danger is that such a counselor may try some spur-of-the-moment technique which seems to work well with one client and become so enamored with that technique that he will use it with all clients. This is far less likely to happen if one is constantly reviewing his work with a clinic team.

The isolated counselor needs to seek out other professional persons in his community in order to share some of his thinking and methods. If other counselors are not available, surely some other professional persons will be. Practically every community large enough to use counseling services has social workers, psychologists, or psychiatrists. If not, many physicians will be interested in participating in regular meetings designed to share thinking and experiences in working with people on a counseling basis. Every counselor will do well to consult regularly with a psychiatrist, but in those communities in which this is not possible, one can at least avail himself of the thinking of other professional persons.

Whatever the situation may be concerning sources of consultation, every counselor can make certain that he is carefully studying his case records in some systematic and productive fashion as a safeguard against the dangers cited and as a method for maintaining a dynamic approach to his work. Counseling is a task that demands one's best knowledge, skills, and efforts. Moreover, it is a task where learning and new insight never ceases. We have much to learn and much improvement to make, and our clients deserve the very best counseling we can provide. But we cannot provide it if we become content with acquired skills and competencies.

Ethical Considerations in the Use of Case Records

Few indeed are the individuals who would be able to speak frankly enough to gain help if they did not believe that their counseling sessions were confidential. This is a matter that is ordinarily taken for granted both by counselor and client. Confidentialness is a premise upon which practically all counselors regularly base their work. If clients voice concern about confidentialness they are soon reassured. Most counselors are as concerned about this matter as are their clients.

Unfortunately, however, the counselor does not yet have a legal right to withhold confidential material in what is termed "privileged communication." Few of the helping professions do have such privilege. Case records can be supoenaed by the courts, and counselors can be required to testify in a court trial. However, such an occurrence is unlikely, and if it should happen, most courts would listen carefully to a counselor's request for the maintenance of confidence. In other words, if a counselor states his preferred position in the matter with reason and with concern for the protection of others, he has every reason to hope that he will not have to divulge what has been spoken to him in confidence.

Nevertheless, he can be required to testify, and records can be used. This fact alone suggests that extremely revealing material should not be put into a case record. The counselor does not need such material for his records anyway.

For example, there is no need to put into a case record the

fact that a client has homosexual phantasies. Nor is anything helpful added when one inserts in the record the name of a person with whom a client had an affair. No useful purpose is served by putting such material in the record, and a counselor should exert every reasonable effort to protect his clients against the possibility of material being brought to light that would be highly revealing, remote as that possibility may be.

Counselor training programs should include extensive practice in writing adequate case records. Inexperienced counselors who have recently learned to recognize some of the psychiatric syndromes tend to put psychiatric labels in their records. The notion that such a display of knowledge is good practice ought quickly to be dispelled.

In the first place, for a counselor to label a client "paranoid," "obsessive-compulsive," or "schizophrenic" is to assume a function which is outside his province. Moreover, absolutely nothing worthwhile is added when such appellations are used. To describe is always better than to label.

For example, to say that a client states that he believes someone is trying to poison him or that everybody is against him and that he is constantly being watched is to record important data. Any well-trained person immediately sees in such data a description of possible paranoid reactions, but the "paranoid" label is unnecessary. Descriptions of reactions and behavior are far more appropriate and helpful in understanding the client than are labels which are very easy to put on and extremely hard to wipe off.

Nothing is more important in counseling than to keep constantly in mind the welfare of the client. This principle applies as fully to the construction and use of case records as it does to the techniques of counseling. The welfare of the client demands that appropriate and meaningful records be kept. It also requires that records be carefully guarded as confidential material. Locked files are, of course, a necessity. Equally important are safeguards concerning access to the files. Better one person as, for example, a loyal, trustworthy secretary, have complete charge of files than allow even the counseling staff to go to the files at will. No one person can really be responsible for the records if a number of persons constantly open the files. In the interest of orderliness and responsibility one person may be assigned the task of keeping and guarding the use of the files.

The question of whether case records should be used for teaching or other more or less public purposes is one that is frequently asked by counselors. We believe the best answer to this is that records should never be used except when needed for specific purposes which cannot be adequately served otherwise. It is inexcusable for a teacher of family living or preparation for marriage classes to say such an inane thing as, "I have a case now of a young man and a young woman who are both well known on this campus. He is 20, she is 19, . . ."

Far preferable in teaching is to recall some situation frequently encountered in counseling, pose a hypothetical question or problem situation, and have students react to it. For example, one may say: "Today let's visualize a situation that many young people may encounter and see if we can arrive at some possible methods of dealing with it. I think we can see the problems more clearly if we do some role-playing to depict the situation. The basic problem is that the young man (we'll call him John) and the young woman (we'll call her Mary) are college freshmen, want to be married, but somehow have to deal with the fact that Mary's parents object to the marriage on the ground that she is too young and that John will have to quit school in order to earn a livelihood. Complicating the situation is the fact that John has, for several years, planned to become a physician. We'll need a person to play the part of John and one to play the part of Mary."

This procedure can be quite stimulating and thought-provoking for the entire class. It is far more effective than the "I have a case" approach. It centers attention upon common problems rather than upon curiosity as to the identity of the individuals in a case.

If case records are used verbally or in writing for the benefit of professional workers in the field of counseling, great care should be exercised to eliminate any possibility that the persons involved might be identified. Dates, names of persons, cities, and states should be changed or completely deleted. Again, the welfare of the client should take precedence over all other considerations. Adherence to this principle will answer most of one's questions concerning the use of case material. If one has any doubt about being able adequately to disguise the material, he should secure the client's permission to use the records.

11 THE USE OF PSYCHIATRIC CONSULTATION

The helping professions need one another. No one approach to helping people in trouble can possibly meet all of the needs. Human beings, their internal and external problems, their social and cultural environment are far too complex for one approach to be adequate in all instances.

Professional megalomania is a luxury too costly—both to the helper and to those who seek help—for anyone to afford. What is needed is more adequate cooperation and teamwork among the various disciplines dedicated to the assistance of persons who turn to them for help in time of trouble. Objections to the team approach usually come from those who have never really participated in any realistic attempt to share experiences and methods of procedure with representatives of other disciplines or to learn from them. The principle of putting the welfare of the applicant for help above all other considerations is pertinent here.

Counseling as a Preventive Measure

A well-trained and experienced counselor recognizes that no matter how competent he may be in his field, he will need to refer some individuals for psychiatric evaluation. Indeed, the higher the degree of professional competence one acquires, the more able he will be to recognize the need for consultation. He should also recognize that marriage and family counseling can, in many instances, be a preventive measure in helping some persons to accept psychiatric assistance before an impending, severe emotional break occurs. Conservative estimates indicate that one in every sixteen Americans is suffering from some form of mental or emotional disorder.

A large number of emotionally disturbed persons go first to clergymen, physicians, social workers, psychologists, or counselors for help. Individuals in these professions are in strategic positions to aid those who need psychiatric help to accept it. For many emotionally ill persons, it is less threatening—and therefore more acceptable to them—to consider their difficulty as a marital problem than to concede that the real problem is within themselves, their own reactions, fears, guilts, hostilities, and distortions of reality. Although some emotionally ill persons cannot recognize the severity of their disturbances, for others the problem lies in their inability to accept their problems as psychiatric ones.

Still others have problems associated with procedures for obtaining the appropriate kind of help. Many individuals have a vague recognition of their need for psychiatric treatment but do not know how to obtain it. Such persons may find their way to a clergyman, counselor, or other helping person. The counseling task in these instances is to assist the emotionally disturbed individual in getting to a psychiatrist, hospital, or clinic for the kind of help needed. Undoubtedly many severe mental illnesses could be avoided if psychiatric aid could be obtained before the stresses and strains become overwhelming and incapacitating.

Marriage counseling may be considered a preventive measure in another sense. Many emotionally ill persons have a long history of life dissatisfactions and frustrations. Although foundations for possible illness may have been laid in early childhood, large numbers of emotionally disturbed persons probably would not have become ill had they been helped early enough to cope with stressful life situations. And since marriage constitutes one of the most significant and intimate of all human relationships, it is also laden with a high potential for frustration, disappointment, and anxiety. No other relationship in life provides so much opportunity for gratification or for frustration. In this long-range relationship a couple shares joys and disappointments and suffers through trials of all sorts together.

These experiences can be strengthening for an individual, or the marriage can become a sounding board for one's frustrations.

Individuals who are helped to find adequate means for resolving their marital difficulties are, at the same time, helped to find greater—and more realistic—life satisfactions. A concomitant benefit for the individual is that if help for the marital relationship is sought soon enough, severe stress which might end in emotional damage may be avoided.

Moreover, for most people, participation in adequate counseling serves as a learning experience in which they acquire a clearer (less distorted) view of themselves, the marriage partner, and the marital situation. It is also an experience in which one is helped to draw upon strengths within himself in his endeavor to discover paths leading toward a more satisfactory relationship. If, through counseling, one learns more adequately to cope with the frustrations and stresses in his marital situation, the lesson should carry over when coping with future problems, although, at present, research is insufficient on this point to justify conclusive statements.

Psychiatrists who are aware of these preventive aspects of counseling are usually glad to work cooperatively with competent counselors who seek their professional assistance. Obviously, many psychiatrists have had no contact with marriage counselors and do not know their aims, methods, or even their roles as helping persons. The burden of proof is, therefore, on the counselor. If he knows what he is doing and why he is doing it, and if he can reveal himself without defensiveness, he should be able to form a working relationship with some psychiatrist who will welcome the opportunity to serve as the counselor's consultant. Obviously, this can be done only if a competent psychiatrist is available.

The Purpose of Psychiatric Consultation

A counselor should be aware of five primary responsibilities as he goes about his professional work: (1) his responsibility to his client, (2) his responsibility to himself, (3) his responsibility to his clinic, agency, or sponsoring body, (4) his responsibility to his colleagues, and (5) his responsibility to society. Wise use of psychiatric consultation can be extremely helpful in adequately meeting all of these responsibilities.

The major concern of a counselor must always be the welfare of the client. This will also be the focus of the psychiatrist's concern. What are the needs and desires of the client? What sort of help does he want and how synonymous are his desires and needs? From what kind of help is he most likely to benefit? Is the counselor competent enough to provide this kind of help? If not, he cannot ethically attempt to do so. Rather, his role will be that of helping the client to accept a different kind of assistance. A psychiatric consultant can be of tremendous help in this task as we shall presently see.

A counselor's responsibility to himself involves, among other things, recognition of his limitations. Referral of clients who need medical, legal, or psychiatric help is imperative for the welfare not only of the client but also of the counselor. Uncertainty concerning a client's state of mental health, for example, will tend to weigh heavily upon the counselor's mind—provided, of course, he is not so foolhardy or insensitive as to be unconcerned—and inhibit efforts to be helpful. Here, again, a psychiatric consultant can be of invaluable assistance.

Almost every clinic and agency is limited in terms of the types of service provided. Neither counselor nor agency do everything. Counselors need always to remember that they are working within a certain structure and that they can offer only the kinds of service approved by their agency as part of its work. The psychiatric consultant can make a valuable contribution to the agency by helping to clarify the emotional aspects of the difficulties being experienced by the client. The agency's decision to accept an applicant for continued counseling or to refer for a different kind of help may frequently depend upon the consultant's estimate of the client's ability to use profitably the services afforded by the agency and the suitability of these services to the needs of the client.

A counselor who consistently utilizes psychiatric consultation tends not only to serve his clients and his agency more adequately but also to contribute to the professional status of his colleagues at large. Use of consultation is one indication of a counselor's acknowledgment of the limitations of his skills and of the function of his professional activities. It is also one evidence of a sincere desire to be of maximum help to those who seek his assistance. Consistent and purposeful use of consultation by all counselors would further engender the respect and cooperation of the various professional persons who are endeavoring to help people in trouble.

The Structure and Methods of Consultation

Although consultative processes vary somewhat, depending upon the agreement between the agency and/or counselor and the psychiatrist, the following patterns have been used with good results.

1. Group or staff consultation. Many agencies employ a psychiatrist as consultant to the entire staff. As agency consultant, the psychiatrist meets with the counseling staff for group discussion of cases. Ordinarily time limitations prohibit discussion of all agency cases. Therefore, cases presented for discussion are usually those posing questions concerning the client's state of mental health, difficult problems of procedure, disposition, or counseling process.

Group consultation can provide an atmosphere which is uniquely conducive to the professional growth and development of staff members. When the group and the psychiatrist become well acquainted and mutually respected, group members tend to relax and drop defensive and tense attitudes. Attention then becomes focused upon (1) gaining a better understanding of the client(s); (2) examining the process of counseling in the case with a view to increasing counselor skills; (3) understanding the dynamics of the client-counselor relationship; and (4) planning a suitable course for the future in accordance with the needs of the client, the policies of the agency, and the competencies of the counselor.

Many psychiatrists welcome the opportunity to serve as agency consultants because they recognize the worth and desirability of counseling service for couples and families. They often view the consultation sessions as staff learning situations. Under these circumstances, the consultant's teaching role can become extremely effective within the context of the agency's total in-service training program.

Material to be presented in a consultation conference should be prepared with the aim of creating a crystal clear picture of the client, his marriage and family interaction patterns, the problems presented, the circumstances that precipitated the request for help, the counselor's impression of the problem, a brief resumé of the counseling process and progress thus far, and any questions the counselor may have concerning the case. The marriage assessment summary (page 159) may be used as a guide for the counselor's thinking about the case as he prepares material for presentation.

A typical two-hour weekly group consultation session with a psychiatrist may involve the following considerations after a case presentation has been made by a staff counselor: (Many agencies give priority to certain cases by agreement among case supervisors. Priority is usually established on the basis of evaluation of urgency concerning the apparent state of a client's mental health, questions regarding referral, or crises in the handling of counseling situations.)

(1) Clarification of factual material, including data presented through discussion of questions asked by group members and by the consultant.

(2) Clarification by the consultant of personal character-

istics of the client and their significance and operation in his marital and family relationships.

(3) Clarification of the basic problems presented by the client and of his request for help, including factors related to his seeking help at this time and the kind of help he seems to be seeking.

(4) Discussion of dynamics of the marital and family interpersonal relationships.

(5) Examination of the counseling process to date.

(6) Examination of dynamics of the client-counselor relationship.

(7) Discussion of disposition of the case, including the question of what kind of help seems indicated.

(8) Discussion of appropriate aims and goals for future counseling, including long-term and immediate goals.

(9) Discussion of methods and techniques calculated to aid client movement toward resolution of difficulties, or toward referral for a different kind of help, if indicated.

While the recognition of psychopathological states is an important function of psychiatric consultation, the use of a psychiatrist's time need not—and in the author's opinion should not—be restricted to that function. In an atmosphere of teamwork, mutual respect, and understanding conducive to free-flowing communication between consultant and staff members, the resultant interchange of ideas and concepts as well as the sharing of technical problems and principles can contribute a great deal to agency effectiveness and to the professional development of staff members.

2. Consultation with an individual counselor. As Miller [1] has pointed out, the chief advantage of psychiatric consultation on an individual basis lies in the additional opportunities afforded by this method for discussion of specific elements

---

[1] Arthur A. Miller, M.D., "The Psychiatric Consultant in Family Counseling," *Marriage and Family Living,* Vol. XVIII, no. 3 (August, 1956), pp. 254-58.

in the counselor-client relationship. This is not to imply that consultation hours should be psychotherapy sessions. It does mean, however, that the counselor who wishes to increase his counseling efficiency through a gradually developing understanding of the ways in which he uses himself in various kinds of counselor-client relationships probably can do so more effectively in individual consultation than in group sessions.

Then, too, not all counselors are members of a clinic or agency staff. If they are to use the services of a consultant, they will have to do so on an individual basis. The parish minister to whom so many persons come with their problems ordinarily has no access to psychiatric consultation except through his own initiative in making an individual arrangement for consultation appointments.

Referral for Psychiatric Consultation

To this point, consultation has been discussed in terms of a process in which a psychiatrist is consulted *about* a client. Another process emerges when a client is referred directly for consultation *with* the psychiatrist. This procedure is used when a counselor believes that the welfare of the client will best be served by having a psychiatrist interview the client directly. This kind of consultation is especially helpful in those instances in which apparent organic impairment, regressive processes, depressive reactions, or destructive trends are difficult to evaluate without direct psychiatric appraisal.

A counselor who regularly presents his cases in consultation sessions will have an established relationship with a psychiatrist who can help him to assess the need for direct consultation in a given instance. If his schedule permits, the consultant may offer an appointment time which can be suggested to the client by the counselor.

The method by which appointments are to be made should be explicit and clearly understood by the counselor so that the referral can be smooth and effective. In some instances the most desirable procedure may be to place responsibility for appointment making upon the client. The counselor's task, then, is to help the client prepare for and accept referral to the consultant. In other cases, initiative must be taken by the counselor to the extent that a specific time is offered the client for a prearranged appointment with the psychiatrist.

The latter procedure is applicable when a client seems so confused that he probably will not use his own initiative to call a psychiatrist's office for an appointment. It may also be used when a client appears rather immobilized by depression or when his reasoning ability is obviously impaired.

> Mr. O. was unable to specify his marital dissatisfactions. He was "just miserable" and said he "couldn't stand it any longer." He intended to resign his position the following morning and leave for the West Coast. He was not clear as to just what he would do there. He might find a job, but he was tired of working at a job he did not like in order to keep the rent paid and groceries in the house. He planned to find a girl somewhere who would "keep him." He had heard of such arrangements. His wife and children could look out for themselves.
>
> The counselor explored Mr. O.'s thoughts about this plan and discovered that Mr. O. considered the plan entirely reasonable. However, inquiry into the client's past behavior indicated that his current ideas were entirely antithetical to his previous behavior. Apparently, he had been throughout his adult life a steady, hardworking, responsible person.
>
> The counselor pointed out the radical change and the seriousness of the client's proposed plan. He stated that perhaps the client could benefit by a thorough study of the meaning of these changes before taking such a serious step as the one he proposed. Mr. O. thought his decision had been made, but he was willing to consider it further. The counselor discussed psychiatric consultation with Mr. O. and suggested that he would be glad to call a local clinic for an appointment. The clinic was able to offer an immediate appointment which was accepted by the client.

Referral of Mr. O. for psychiatric consultation was considered imperative by the counselor. His judgment of the client's need was based on the fact that Mr. O's thought processes seemed to be disturbed, as manifested by the following factors that are frequently observed in prepsychotic persons:

(1) Radical changes in thinking concerning morals. The client had not merely fantasied becoming a "kept" man but had plans for doing so.

(2) Radical changes in sense of responsibility. The client's plans indicated a more serious disturbance than is ordinarily manifested by a dissatisfied husband who has reached a point of desperation. He was ready to disclaim any responsibility for his family: They would have to get along as best they could.

(3) Radical changes in reasoning ability. The client was ready to leave home, family, and position without questioning the wisdom of such a move.

Referral for psychiatric consultation may be made in the course of continued counseling when counselor and client recognize that emotional conflicts are seriously impeding the client's progress in counseling.

> After ten interviews each with Mr. and Mrs. Q., progress in overcoming conflicts in the interpersonal relationship was at a standstill. Mr. Q. had been able to recognize his contributions to the marital difficulties and had made tremendous improvement in attitudes and behavior toward his wife and children. But Mrs. Q. could neither forget nor forgive him for his past neglect and self-centeredness. Apparently she wanted to do so but could not. "I don't know why," she said, "but something in me just won't let me forgive him and go on as I know I ought. I can't forget how he has acted. I try to push it out of my mind, but it keeps coming back. I can't stand for him to even touch me. It's me: It isn't him anymore. I'm to blame now, but I can't help it."
>
> Five weeks later, the situation remained unchanged, aside from the fact that Mrs. Q. was becoming discouraged and doubting that her relationship with her husband could ever become any better. She had begun having severe headaches, insomnia, and difficulty in concentration. Two interviews were used to help her recognize the need for psychiatric consultation and to accept referral for that purpose. When Mrs. Q. spoke constantly of her symptoms, the counselor pointed out that her chief concerns now centered around herself and her own emotional and physical

problems. He wondered if she were really saying that she would like to have help for these difficulties. She stated that she felt she must get some relief from her tensions and that she would welcome any opportunity to do so. The counselor said that perhaps she would like an opportunity to talk these matters over with a psychiatrist. She replied that she would like to do that, inasmuch as she could not help thinking that the real trouble was not now in the marriage but in herself.

This kind of referral does not always mean that the client needs psychiatric evaluation and treatment. After seeing the client, the psychiatrist may be convinced that the symptoms result from the client's struggle with the marital problems and that they do not represent severe enough emotional disturbance to warrant a change in the helping method.

If, on the other hand, the psychiatrist concludes that psychiatric evaluation and/or treatment is indicated, he will be able to help the client accept the recommendation. In some instances the spouse may continue counseling; in others both spouses may move into psychiatric treatment; in still others, the psychiatrist may recommend that one spouse be seen regularly by a social worker while the other is in psychiatric treatment.

12 THE USE OF REFERRAL RESOURCES

One of the distinguishing characteristics of a professionally trained counselor is his ability to use wisely and effectively the referral resources that are available in his community.

Competence in referral is a most important but difficult goal for a counselor to achieve. It is largely the outgrowth of experience based upon three primary factors: (1) a clear definition of one's role and function as a counselor; (2) adequate understanding of the client and his problems; and (3) skill in helping clients to accept referral.

The Counselor's Role and Function

For whatever reason—and it is frequently an unrecognized one—insufficiently trained counselors sometimes expect too much of themselves and of their clients. To believe that one ought to be able to provide help for everyone who seeks it is unrealistic. But to attempt to do so without frequent recourse to other professional persons and agencies is far worse. To hold on to a client who should be referred for a diferent kind of help is, under all except the rarest of circumstances, unethical. While it is certainly appropriate to continue working with a client to help him reach an acceptance of another kind of assistance (if this does not involve danger to the client or to other persons), it is *not* appropriate to continue with him merely because the counselor feels he ought to be able to provide the necessary help.

If a counselor is quite clear concerning the exact nature of his role and function, problems around referral will be minimized. The task of a marriage counselor is to aid the client in delineating his problems, to assess the appropriateness of counseling as the preferred kind of help, to enter into and continue work with the client toward adequate resolution of his marital or premarital problems, or (if a different kind of help is believed to be more appropriate for resolution of the problems) to help the client accept referral.

The counselor's role should, at all times, be clearly consonant with his conscious task. The above definition of task implies a consistent, dependable, helping role. If the counselor is clearly perceived in this role by the client, referral, if necessary, is far more readily accepted as part of the helping process. If, on the other hand, the counselor sees himself at one time as history-taker, at another time as diagnostician, and at still another time as referrer, the client's perception of the counselor's role will likewise be confused and fragmented.

While part of the counselor's task may, at one period in counseling, involve securing and clarifying facts about the client and his history, the role of the counselor need not shift but should remain consistent. In other words, this part of the counseling process and every other part of it, should be perceived by the client as an aid to helping him reach toward resolution of his quandary. The fundamental structure of the counseling process remains the same whether counselor and client are attempting to understand historical material in the client's life or attempting to resolve the client's conflict over his (partial) recognition of his need for a different kind of help and his resistance to its acceptance.

Understanding the Client and his Problems

In Chapter Three, considerable attention was given to the matter of the assessment of the client's ego strength. Chapter Ten provided an outline for the assembling of data pertinent to a marriage assessment. If appropriate study is accorded these two items, a counselor should achieve a reasonably accurate picture of his clients and their problems.

A further step may now be taken in the matter of attempting to achieve the kind of understanding of the client and his problems that will enable the counselor to make an appropriate decision to continue counseling with the person or to refer him for a different kind of help. A key question for the counselor is whether the necessary data for the resolution of the difficulty are available to the client's conscious awareness.

If, for example, a male client cannot allow himself to succeed in his marriage, profession, or social life because, unconsciously, he equates such success with "overcoming" or "superseding" his father, any form of help that does not aid the client in the resolution or amelioration of oedipal conflicts will not be likely to be of very great assistance. Since these kinds of conflicts are almost always unconscious, the client's conscious problem-solving capacities are insufficient to cope with the problems. Referral is indicated here. Counseling is a method of helping individuals and couples to utilize their problem-solving capacities in reaching solutions to their interpersonal difficulties; it does not attempt to uncover or deal with the unconscious conflicts. It is, therefore, an appropriate mode of help for some persons but not for others.

Most marriage counselors are not lawyers and should not attempt to give legal advice. Nor should the nonmedical counselor attempt to provide medical counsel. This is not merely a matter of avoiding "professional union" complications or legal entanglements: It is also a matter of professional ethics.

Achieving an understanding of the client and his problems and a perspective on the role of counseling in the case at hand, then, is a task of high importance if the counselor is to be of assistance to those who seek his help.

Referral Resources

In contradistinction to the American family of fifty years ago, today's family is dependent upon a myriad of resources outside the home. Recognition of the family's increasing dependence upon the larger social structure, as a result of such social changes as industrialization and urbanization, is evidenced in national and community provisions for family assistance. National programs such as Social Security have, by their general acceptance by the public, served to alleviate the American family's traditional reluctance to seek extra-familial aid. One reason for this is that the family shares the expense of the program and hence does not need to feel that charity is involved. So, too, United Fund supported clinics and agencies are now far more widely used than they were formerly. Not only is referral to public agencies and professional persons a frequently desirable procedure for the marriage and family counselor to follow; it is also an increasingly acceptable procedure from the public's viewpoint.

Social work agencies constitute some of the most helpful and available referral resources. Public welfare agencies, such as county welfare departments, provide financial help to individuals and families who are in need of public assistance. Many county boards of social welfare administer Federal programs of Old Age Assistance, Aid to Dependent Children, Aid to the Blind, and Aid to the Disabled, in addition to state and local assistance programs, which may include medical care and hospitalization, foster care for children, adoptive home placement and assistance for unmarried mothers.

Member agencies of The Family Service Association of America are readily accessible in more than one hundred cities and are an important referral resource. They provide social casework services for individuals and families,[1] usually on an ability-to-pay, fee basis. Most of these agencies are largely financed by Community Chest funds and, in large cities, maintain a number of district offices to facilitate accessibility to the public.[2]

Medical resources are, of course, readily available in prac-

---

[1] For an illuminating study of casework with persons who seek social agency help for marital problems, see Florence Hollis, *Women in Marital Conflict* (New York: Family Service Association of America, 1949).

[2] Vide Arthur E. Fink, *The Field of Social Work* (New York: Henry Holt & Co., 1942).

tically every community. Unfortunately, however, large numbers of persons still do not make optimum use of medical facilities. Despite the fact that in recent years people have become generally aware of the advisability of having periodic preventive medical examinations, counselors need to be alert to the possibility of ill health as a contributor to marital difficulties. "When did you last consult your physician?" should be a routine question put to new clients.

Strangely enough, a common discovery is that a couple who seek counseling because the wife has seemed disinterested and cold toward her husband since the birth of a child eight or ten months ago did not return to the physician for her six-weeks' check-up following delivery. Obviously, one of the counselor's first tasks in such cases must be to encourage the couple in the use of medical facilities.

Listless, constantly tired, apathetic persons may be exhibiting reactions to environmental stress or to emotional conflicts, but they may also be physically ill. If so, elimination or amelioration of the physical problems may serve to dissipate the marital trouble. Many individuals, when ill, react to their spouses and children in an irritable—and, frequently, irritating—manner. Others become clingingly dependent, demanding, or touchy to the exasperation of the spouse.

Astute counselors quickly pick up such clues as, "I don't know what's come over her recently: Everything I do is wrong. Nothing ever pleases her any more." When a counselor hears this, he knows something has changed in the relationship of the couple. What has changed? When did the change come about? How? Why? While there are many possible explanations, one that should not be overlooked is the possibility of some alteration in the health of one of the partners.

Most marriage counselors are not medical doctors and do not diagnose illness. But they should take note of the generally recognized signs of health or illness in clients. It is far better for a client to be referred unnecessarily to a physician than for a needed referral to be long delayed.

Moreover, physicians have always been counselors to their patients and are becoming increasingly aware of the importance of their counseling function, particularly in general practice and in obstetrics.

Religious resources for help in conquering doubt, disillusionment, and disappointment in life's crises are well known to those persons who consistently utilize such resources *before* some crisis arises. To them, turning to religion is automatic and habitual not only in difficulty but also in day-to-day living. To others, of course, religion means little or nothing. Still others turn to religion only when they are in trouble and attempt to use it as a crutch until the crisis is past, then discard it as an unwanted intruder. In such instances, the means usually determine the end, and results are disappointing. Other persons react to their religious heritage with such strong rebellion that they reveal by the very strength of their protests how much they wish religion could mean to them.

Whatever form one's reaction to his religious heritage may take, of one thing we may be certain: the vast majority of Americans have some elements of their culture ingrained in their personalities. To overlook this fact in counseling is not merely unrealistic: it is not in the best interests of the client. Ignoring a client's religious convictions (or lack of them, for that matter) is as serious an omission as ignoring his feelings toward his father, mother, or wife. For this, too, is part of life, and to assume that it is unimportant or irrelevant is, in most cases, to omit consideration of a vital aspect of life.

To carry this thought a step farther, consider the relation between the way one treats others, as for example, one's wife and children, and the concept and convictions one holds about himself. With the exception, perhaps, of the seriously emotionally disturbed person whose conflictual thoughts and feelings serve to grossly distort his self-concept as well as his perception of others, one's behavior toward other persons directly reflects the view one has of himself. If a man genuinely perceives himself as a loved creation of God and therefore as a person of dignity, worth, responsibility, and integrity, that concept of self will help to activate him in his relationship with others. Psychologically, we know that he can love others who feels himself to be loved and that the concept of one's self as a loving person emerges first out of the percept that one is loved. And when that perception of the self as loved and loving, as worthwhile and contributing to the worthiness of others, as worthy of respect and respecting others comes of age and is consistent and satisfying, one loves fully, unreservedly, and without demanding to be loved in return; for now loving is more gratifying than being loved, though that, too, is satisfying and important. This is not only healthy religion: It is also the essence of emotional health.

Today, some of the greatest minds in the psychiatric world are studiously scrutinizing the relation of religion and psychiatry.[3] Karl A. Menninger has described the daily work of the psychiatrist as a "ministry of care to the most miserable, the most unloved, the most pitiable, and at times the most offensive and even dangerous of human beings." He sees the proper role of the psychiatrist as "that of the friend, the guide, the protector, the helper, the lover of these unhappy people. 'Passing through the valley of weeping, they make it a place of springs' (Psalm 84)."[4] The good psychiatrist meets such manifestations of hate as "stubbornness, anger, spitefulness, silliness, sulkiness, belligerency, desperateness, unreasonableness, maliciousness . . . with an attitude he is not ashamed to call love. We can live, he tells them, if we can love."[5]

This is, of course, the teaching of great religion. Love is the essence and loving behavior toward one's fellows is the inevitable result of one's realization and acceptance of the love of God, according to the New Testament. The emptiness, the

---

[3] For an illuminating account of the attention being given to religion in the work of The Menninger Foundation, see Paul W. Pruyser, "Religion and Psychiatry," *Menninger Quarterly*, Vol. XI, no. 3 (September, 1957), pp. 2-5.

[4] Karl A. Menninger, "Religio Psychiatrici," *Menninger Quarterly*, Vol. V, no. 3 (July, 1951), pp. 21-22.

[5] *Ibid.*, p. 22.

nothingness described by St. Paul as an epitome of the non-loving personality is observed every day by psychiatrists. So is the constructive-destructive dualistic nature of man so clearly discerned by St. Paul and so carefully elaborated in different language and from a different viewpoint by Freud and Menninger.[6]

Whatever else a healthy religion does in the life of a person, it helps make life more meaningful and purposeful and points life in the direction of (love-derived) constructiveness. The goal may frequently be missed, but the direction is unmistakable.

Viewed in this light, religious convictions, far from being extraneous to counseling, are directly relevant to any consideration of interpersonal relationships in marriage and family living. While the author's own belief is that the counselor should be so conversant and unprejudiced as to be able to understand and to accept the client's religious feelings and to support the healthy aspects of them, for some counselors this will not be possible. If it is not possible, and if the counselor cannot be comfortable in dealing with this area of the client's life and personality, surely he can encourage the client to seek spiritual guidance from his minister, priest, or rabbi when, in the counseling sessions, religious matters come into focus.

Worthy also of consideration are the opportunities for education, group participation, and worthwhile social action provided by organized religious groups. Many of the persons who seek counseling lead socially impoverished lives. Some of them are so isolated and unrelated to the life of their community that they easily become overly concerned with themselves and the circumstances that contribute to this unhappiness.

In counseling, one frequently has opportunity to support a client or a couple in some move toward self-investment in group activities. Especially valuable are activities that provide

---

[6] Karl A. Menninger, *Love Against Hate* (New York: Harcourt, Brace & Co., 1942).

opportunity for the participants to acquire a greater feeling of belonging and of contributing their ideas, actions, and other means to a worthwhile task. Church couples groups that are action-oriented can be of significant help to couples who need the support of a group if they are to gain appropriate gratification through self-investment in something other than self. In addition, obvious satisfactions are to be found in new friendships, particularly among people who are in approximately the same stage of the family life cycle. Sharing similar interests, concerns, and endeavors may help to relieve some of the worries, doubts, and often over-concerns a couple may be experiencing.

Psychiatric resources are more readily available than most people think. There are yet far too few psychiatrists to meet the public need, but more and more physicians are being trained in the specialty, and referral is not as difficult as many counselors believe. One of the most difficult problems, from the standpoint of the counselor, is that of finding a psychiatrist who utilizes psychotherapy and who can accept the counselor's referrals at the time when clients are prepared to accept psychiatric help.

Every marriage counselor should be well acquainted with the competent psychiatrists and psychiatric clinics in his community or vicinity. Child guidance and mental hygiene clinics are now established in numerous smaller cities, and many of them operate under city or county auspices with Community Fund support. A marriage counselor who is not fully aware of available psychiatric resources and who does not use them is rightly suspect among his colleagues as well as among other professional persons. For unquestionably, he will see some persons who need psychiatric study and care.

Helping Clients to Accept Referral

Frequently the decision to refer is a tentative decision that may be modified if the client begins to evidence ability to make good use of counseling and if no manifestations of decompensation or of some incipient process going on in the client occur. Usually, however, the factors that indicate referral remain even if the client attempts to cover them when the counselor speaks of referral.

Some principles to keep in mind concerning referral for psychiatric help are stated here as a guide for the counselor's thinking:

1. Be certain that you are quite clear in your own mind concerning the reasons for your decision to refer the client. A well-known maxim in the field of medicine is that the doctor never makes a referral before he examines the patient. While counselors are not psychiatric diagnosticians, they should be well aware of the indications for psychiatric help or study for which the client is being referred.
2. Use the client's own words, thoughts, expressed feelings, and behavior to illustrate his need for a different kind of help. (Also advisable in some cases is to help the client to recognize that he has not been able to make use of the counseling process owing to some process which is evidently going on in him that he does not understand.)

Frequently, the thoughts of the client who is embroiled in intrapsychic conflict simply cannot remain on the marital (interpersonal) problems but are drawn as by a magnet again and again to his own mixed feelings, insecurities, fears, suspicions, and inadequacies. When the counselor is certain that referral is indicated, he may respond to the client's preoccupation with self by saying: "It seems that your thoughts come again and again to these personal feelings and that they are among your greatest concerns. Perhaps it is your difficulty in dealing with your own feelings and reactions rather than the marital problems, as such, for which you feel a need for help."

Facing frankly with the client his most bothersome concerns will usually elicit one of two general responses. A client who is anxious and rather desperate may quickly agree that the counselor has sized up the matter correctly. He may say: "I guess that's right. It's not really the marriage, it's me. It's my feelings that I know are senseless, but that I can't control."

A client who is more constricted may vigorously deny the implications of what he is saying and may muster his protective defenses with renewed vigor. He may deny that he is in any way involved in the marital problems and contend that the spouse is the one who needs help. Projections may run rampant through the client's productions, even to the extent of casting some kind of blame on the counselor.

When this happens, beware of entering into an argument with the client. Instead, meet the projections and the anger and the unreasoning attitudes with firm but kind reiterations of what the client has really conveyed concerning his own personal difficulties. The other spouse may need help, too, but at the moment the counselor is communicating with this particular person and must, therefore, help him to recognize the need for the kind of assistance that seems to be indicated.

If resistance to referral is strong, and if delay involves no apparent danger to the client or others, the counselor may say, "Well, why don't you give it some more thought and we can discuss it again next time." Referral should be considered as a process, not as an interview. It may take one interview or several, depending to a considerable degree upon the actual discomfort being experienced by the client. Some people need psychiatric help but are not motivated to seek it or to accept it. Some are so rigid that denial and projection are constantly and consistently utilized to protect against even the idea that something may be wrong mentally. Therefore, counselors will not always be able to make successful referrals, even with the greatest of skill and tactfulness.

3. Follow through on a referral. The decision to refer is not enough. Nor will tactful mustering of evidence for referral be sufficient unless the counselor follows through with some kind of facilitation of the recommendation. Many persons still fear the implications in psychiatric referral. Some may even ask if

you think they are losing their minds. Others will be concerned about what the spouse, parents, children, or neighbors will think.

These fears can be met with a counteracting spirit of interest and helpfulness as evidenced by such remarks as: "Well, now, aren't you rather jumping to conclusions? You see, what I am suggesting is simply that the nature and complexity of your problems deserve the thorough study that a psychiatrist, who is a physician especially trained to help people with emotional problems, can give them. To secure this kind of study or evaluation you could go the __________ clinic or to one of the psychiatrists in private practice. I'll be glad to give you their names if you'd like."

Knowing just what psychiatric facilities are available in the vicinity is important, and it is wise to be personally acquainted with clinic personnel and with private practitioners. Referrals needing immediate attention may be given appointment precedence, when that is possible, if the counselor's clinical judgment is respected.

The counselor may need to continue seeing the referred client to provide support in a "holding action" until he can be seen by the psychiatrist or some member of the psychiatric team. He can be of supportive assistance as the client expresses fears and doubts concerning the referral. He may appropriately reassure the client that he understands how difficult it is for the client but that he knows, too, how uncomfortable the client has been in his emotional turmoil. His attitude should constantly support the client's positive feelings toward securing the recommended help. After all, everything in the client that is reasonable and capable of forming accurate judgments is on the side of taking positive, appropriate action.

13 PROFESSIONAL TRAINING IN MARRIAGE COUNSELING

In its present state of development, marriage counseling is part of the work of several different professional groups. Chief among them are social work, psychology, theology, sociology, medicine and psychiatry, and law.

Recognition of the marriage counselor's need for special training beyond that afforded by generic training in these professions has stimulated the development of several specific graduate and postgraduate training programs in marriage counseling. Basic standards for such training programs have evolved through the efforts of the American Association of Marriage Counselors' Committee on Standards for Training Programs. The programs are of two general types: (1) those that are included in the curricula of educational institutions as part of the work toward a graduate degree (usually in an interdivisional program in marriage and family living but sometimes in psychology and sociology); and, (2) postgraduate training programs that operate in nonuniversity settings (usually under medical or psychiatric auspices or in close cooperation with these groups). The training program to be described in some detail here is an example of the latter type.[1]

Stemming from the observation that, in its present state, marriage counseling is a professional activity rather than a full-fledged profession in itself, persons accepted for admission to the Menninger Foundation program are already fully trained and well-experienced in their stated profession, such as social

---

[1] Training Program in Marriage Counseling, Department of Education, The Menninger Foundation, Topeka, Kansas. The program and the concomitant materials here described were worked out largely by Robert G. Foster, Ph.D., and the present author, and were utilized during the period of their directorship of the program.

work, law, medicine, psychology, sociology, or theology. Counselor training attempts to provide didactic and clinical experiences that increase proficiency in marriage counseling. These experiences sharpen the trainee's knowledge and understanding of people (particularly of interpersonal relationships in marriage and family living), his use of himself in counseling, and his application of counseling principles and techniques. All parts of the program are integrated into this one concerted effort. In the interest of clarity, they are considered here under two general headings, the didactic and the clinical emphases.

Such a training program aims at helping the trainee, whatever his previous professional training and experience, to acquire the fundamental understandings and competencies requisite for effective counseling of persons experiencing difficulty in marital, premarital, or family interaction. The author believes that these fundamentals are: (1) an adequate understanding of the development, function, and structure of personality (dynamic psychology); (2) knowledge of social and cultural factors that make an impact on marital, family, and personal functioning; (3) a good grasp of the knowledge that is rapidly accumulating in the field of marriage and family-life education and research; (4) an understanding of the process of interpersonal interaction and the factors involved in its contribution to personal, marital, and family stability or instability; (5) knowledge and practice of techniques applicable in marriage counseling; (6) awareness of referral resources and of various professional approaches to the task of helping people who have problems; and (7) a growing awareness of the self as the primary counseling implement and an increasing ability to use one's self in a genuinely helpful manner (development of a professional self).

Didactic Training

Because it operates in a psychiatric training center, the Menninger program utilizes part of the teaching talent and the seminars that are conducted for training in psychiatry and allied professions. Elements of psychiatric training that contribute directly to counselor training are incorporated into the integrated program. Medical information and legal aspects of counseling are also included in the curriculum. In addition, seminars are used to increase the trainee's understanding of the vast body of knowledge now available concerning marriage and family interaction, including pertinent research studies. Counseling principles and techniques are discussed and illustrated in seminars as well as in group and individual case supervision.

The following transcript of a tape-recorded session of the seminar in principles and techniques of marriage counseling is illustrative of both the content of the course and the teaching methods employed in it by the author: [2]

Instructor: Confronting comments or confronting questions certainly have a place in marriage counseling, but a good rule is to proceed with caution. If we use confrontation too quickly with a client, he may assume that we are not listening to the rest of what he wants to say—even if the rest of what he wants to say is the same thing that he has been saying, for example, casting the blame on the spouse—and that we don't really understand him or that we are not attempting to understand him. Not only that, but he undoubtedly comes with considerable fear that we may cast blame on him. And this may be one of the reasons he has to act defensively and place the blame onto the spouse in the beginning. I think what we ordinarily see is spouse-blame in the beginning, but after some ventilation of feelings, then we usually see a lessening of it. Now where we don't see a lessening of it after several interviews and more consideration of the client's own involvement in the difficulty, I think we have to say to ourselves, "What's gone wrong?"

Our task is to help the client find a solution to his problem. We are, in a sense, listeners, but our job is greater than that. And, so, if we simply keep on listening to what's wrong with the spouse we haven't accomplished our task. We need to listen, we need to understand the defenses, we need to accept these feelings, but I think we also need to go on from there. Again, cautiously, not too

[2] See also Chapter IX, "Confronting Comments."

rapidly. Now if we don't listen enough and if we get too quickly in front of us this goal of helping the person to see his own involvement in his difficulties, then what's likely to happen is that we fail to hear because we become impatient. We want to go on and help this person to see his own involvement in the difficulty, and if we become too impatient, we tend not really to listen. We may not hear what the client is really expressing, and when that happens the client knows it.

Now, one of the places in which confrontation may help is at the point that we recognize that the client seems to be stubbornly avoiding any recognition of his own involvement in the difficulty. But, again, proceed with caution. Here is an illustration of what I mean by confrontation.

A woman client, throughout her first three interviews, consistently blamed her husband for all of their marital troubles. She exonerated herself completely and assumed a demanding attitude toward the counselor—at times she asserted that the counselor should tell her husband to treat her differently. She seemed to believe that she was always completely right in her views and behavior and that her husband was completely wrong. This is not really too unusual in the very beginning. I think we have to say to ourselves, "Why? Why can she not move from this point of projecting all the blame? Why can't she move from that on to recognizing her own involvement?" We know that she does this defensively, and we have to let her do it because she has these feelings—not only feelings of hostility but feelings that she must defend herself.

But after a while we need to begin to help her to move on from this point. Now, confrontation can help, but I think it needs to be a gentle kind of confrontation for most people. Otherwise, you may destroy the rapport which largely consists of the client's perception of the counselor as an understanding person who is genuinely interested in helping her with her problem. You can very easily destroy this by being too confronting or by using confrontation too soon, but you can also lessen rapport by not letting the client know that you recognize that he, too, must enter into the problem. There is one way in which the client can be confronted gently. This client, for example, that I've used as an illustration, consistently blamed her husband and kept asking—indeed almost demanding—that the counselor tell her husband that he was wrong. The client says, "Well, I'll tell you this, I've just put up with him about as long as I can. You know what he does. I think someone ought to tell him what's right and what isn't."

Student A: Hadn't she told him?

Instructor: Yes, undoubtedly she's told him. Now, there are several comments or questions that the counselor might make, at this point. What would you say?

Student B: "Haven't you already told him this?" Or something like that.

Instructor: "Haven't you already told him this?" How might the client perceive this?

Student B: Would it seem the counselor is putting her on the defensive?

Instructor: Now the client is pounding at the counselor, really, saying, I think somebody (and you know who that somebody is that she means) ought to tell him to do differently. Now you say, "Haven't you told him?" What we're always interested in is how will the client perceive our response.

Student B: The counselor might seem to be just saying, well, it's your job, not mine, something like that?

Instructor: Perhaps, and isn't it almost like saying, well, maybe you've told him too many times.

Student A: I think I said to one client when she told me this same thing, "You seem to think this is very important—that he should be told."

Instructor: There are two angles that you can take here, it seems to me. One is to pick up the client's expressed feeling. Now this is A's answer, "You feel that's real important." Another way would be picking up the client's feeling in a little different way—"I guess you wish that the problem could be solved by somebody telling him what to do." This would be a reflective kind of comment, you see—reflection of the client's feeling. Now, I think you would ordinarily do this sort of thing—the reflective and clarifying techniques—unless you had reached a point at which you had questioned in yourself, "Why am I getting this constant distortion and lack of involvement so far as the client is concerned?"

Student C: That would be a very good time to really structure. She has as much as told you, you go ahead and tell him off, and you say, "I know, but it would really be a useless thing."

Instructor: Well, this gets us into another topic, which is structure. It also raises the question of how the client becomes aware of the structure. And, obviously, there are two ways. One is the way that you suggest—the counselor tells them what the structure is. This is what you indicate—no, you don't feel that you can work in the way that they've suggested.

Student C: The counselor has had quite a number of interviews, now, and if she still doesn't . . .

Instructor: But isn't there another way for the client to become aware of structure?

Student C: But have other ways been unsuccessful so far?

Student D: Structuring has evidently been done for three sessions.

Student C: She's still off the beaten path. She's not producing at all. Now, you've got to sooner or later come in there with something. Three times and she's still doing nothing but the same old thing.

Instructor: One way to clarify structure is by telling them how you counsel. The other way is by counseling—isn't it?

Student C: Um-huh.

Instructor: And we can say to ourselves, well, this other way hasn't worked. Then we get to the technical question of when it doesn't work, is it better to really lay out the structure for them or is it better to use some confrontation?

Student C: Well, this is confrontation in a sense, isn't it? And you're kind of off in the blue saying what you dare not do if you want to do him any good. Look, if she's got any awareness at all she ought to . . . this could be my client, too.

Instructor: Well, one counselor I know does something like this once in a while. He will say, if somebody keeps pressing him with what do you think I should do or what do you think about this or that, he'll say, "Well, now you keep asking me this. I don't have any faith in my being able to be of any help by answering it, but if you want me to answer, I'll tell you what my opinion is," which sort of softens the effect a bit.

Student D: But he does the other thing, too, by saying that if he were to tell them this would not work or solve the problem.

Instructor: Well, these are all ways of getting at it, and this is where clinical judgment enters in. Always, regardless of the situation at hand, you are the one who is in it at that moment and you have to use your best judgment at that moment. Now, there is another way to do it, and that's by beginning confrontation. And this I would see as something like this. The counselor could answer with a question, "Do you think he doesn't know?" If you have in mind that what you ask at this stage is designed to get her more involved in the counseling situation itself in a different way than simply blaming her spouse, then you may take a little different tack than being only concerned with structure. There are always combinations of these things.

Student E: You don't want to leave yourself with just one road out, is that it?

Instructor: Let's not think in terms of roads out. Let's think of how you help this client.

Student E: Or approaches to, whichever way you want to take it.

Instructor: You use your clinical judgment as to what is best in a particular situation. You see, if you have only the thought in mind that you've got to get this structure business settled with this client—after all, just blaming and blaming and blaming, and you know you're never going to get anywhere this way—you will probably get centered on structure. Then usually what you do is one of two things. You verbalize the structure directly or you pick up the client's expressed feelings about structure. But, if you feel that this is not simply the problem but that the larger problem is not so much structure as it is this client's inability at this point to see her own involvement in the problem, then you may not be quite as concerned with structure as you are with the client's involvement.

Student D: Well, what's the counselor been doing for the first three interviews, assuming this is the fourth? Hasn't he picked up any of these expressed feelings, and if he has, has this been rejected by the client so that she still does this or he does that?

Instructor: This brings up another interesting point. Frequently we assume that, well, we've already dealt with these feelings. But the thing we always need to remember in counseling is that once dealt with doesn't mean finally dealt with, that we have to constantly deal with these feelings, and that repetition is always going to be a part of counseling, because they don't hear at first and they may not hear after a number of times. And, of course, to get us a little humble about this, we don't hear at first either, that is, a lot of things. Sometimes they have to repeat and repeat in order for us finally to get what they're talking about. You see the point that I'm emphasizing, though, is that you can get off your task by getting too concerned with one aspect of what's going on in counseling. But you can also join these two, and I think you do this when you say to her, "Do you think he doesn't know?" because you've given her again what the structure is—not by saying it in so many words but by the way you counsel, by the process. And you've also made a first step toward helping her to see more of her own involvement in the problem. In other words, you have to cut through the stand she is taking bit by bit. One way to do this is to show her the improbability of her thesis. Her thesis is that if only someone would tell him, then the problem would be solved. At another level this means, I don't want to get involved in this, I don't want to have to do anything about it, and at a still deeper level it means, I'm afraid to look at my part in this, I'm afraid to see myself as I really am operating. So we help cut through the projection by helping the client to begin looking at her part in the problem. Now this is only a first step, of course.

Her reply is: "Oh, of course, he knows. Anybody knows. But he goes right on, just as if he didn't know. That's what I told our minister. I said, 'You lay the law down to him.'" Now how would you meet this? What would you say here, bearing in mind what your task is at this stage?

Student E: Well, you could go ahead with the same approach you did there, you could say to her, "Was he effective?"

Instructor: What you'd be doing, then, is . . .

Student E: Throw it right back to her—not in an absolutely confronting way but let her see just what this effect was—the lack of it was.

Instructor: Again you would be really challenging the improbability of this same approach. She has told you that she has already used this approach before.

Student E: Ask her how effective it was when the minister used it. Just be a little curious.

Student C: And nine times out of ten she'd answer that the minister didn't do what I told him to do, he wouldn't even see him, or he saw him for about ten minutes and that was it, and then you'd be off to the races . . . about the minister. Wouldn't you?

Instructor: Well, I think a little gentler way of saying the same thing that E_____ says, and I think that's a good tack E_____, a little gentler way is to say, "And how did that turn out?"

Student D: Then she'd blast the minister, probably.

Instructor: Well, let's see what she responded to that.

Student E: You used that tactic? Go ahead.

Instructor: She said, "Oh, the minister told him, I guess, but it didn't do a bit of good." Now, what do you say?

Student B: Then you could say, "Well, what good do you see in someone's repeating a process that failed?"

Instructor: That you could do, but how might the client perceive this?

Student E: That's a rejection of the idea. So you might say there, okay, he's been told, he's been told by the minister, have you any idea of any more effective way we might approach him in this subject.

Student C: Or, "I wonder why?"

Student E: Or, "I wonder why this hasn't had any effect?"

Student D: "This puzzles me," or something to that effect. I don't know just how you would word it, but . . . she doesn't see her involvement in it.

Student E: Or another thing here, I wonder if we aren't getting sort of afield. 'Course, she's still casting blame, and I guess you have to go along with that. You're getting off on the husband whereas, uh, you're beating the saddle instead of the donkey. Of course, that's probably the picture from the word go in this. She's taken the heat off of herself.

Instructor: Isn't the question, how do we make this transition from all this spouse-blame to the client's recognition of her own involvement?

Student B: Can you ask, "How do you see yourself involved in this?"

Instructor: Yes, but then she has to react defensively. We know she's going to react defensively before we ever say it, so there's little use to say it really. So, instead, we take it by stages.

Student E: How about lighting a cigarette and thinking it over. Giving her time to think.

Student A: A little silence, huh.

Instructor: A little silence? Well, silence is okay if it develops pretty naturally. But I don't think we want to impose silence.

Student E: That, too, would be kind of confronting, I suppose.

Instructor: In terms of the perception of the client, it could be rejection, unless it develops naturally. Unless the client grows silent in a natural sort of way, I don't think silence helps much. Where we impose a silence simply by not responding at all when there isn't quite good evidence that the client will be able to use the silence as a chance to think, then it seems to me it is very likely to be interpreted as rejection.

Student E: Otherwise, I think she's about to get the counselor up a stump here, isn't she?

Student A: What I'm thinking now is that I would almost answer, "Well, this poses a real problem here, doesn't it?"

Instructor: Well, now that raises another question, A______, as to whether you can go in a fairly straight line or whether you're going to let this go around in a kind of vicious circle again, because if you say that at this point, then her next step is to cast blame again. It poses a real problem—"Yes," she might say. "It's a problem but if he would only do the way he ought to do, why, you know he's doing wrong. Somebody ought to tell him, set him straight, lay it on the line to him"—and here we go again, you see. Now that would mean that we'd have to try to break into it somewhere again. Probably by this time, by the third or fourth interview you've probably gone around that circle a number of times. One of you came up with something I thought was pretty close to it a while ago. When the client says, "Oh, why the minister told him all right, I guess, but it didn't do a bit of good," now her own words have said, this doesn't work. This thing I'm asking you to do doesn't work. So I think what you do is to reinforce her own statement and you say, "Well, it kind of looks as if having someone tell him doesn't work out so well."

Student E: Or would you say that you feel that this is not a successful approach to it?

Student B: The client is asking you to believe that this solution will work and you say, well, maybe I don't believe the thing will work, but do you believe it will work. Because, actually, she is talking so much and she actually is not convinced that this will do any good anyway in reality.

Instructor: My own preference is to try to reinforce what the client has said to you right here. She's said it. Now if you reinforce this, there can hardly be an objection to it because these are her words. Actually, she's said this doesn't work, it didn't do a bit of good, and I think perhaps you could improve on the suggestion I made by saying: "It didn't do a bit of good. Looks as if having somebody tell him just doesn't work out well." Since those are her own words, she's either got to refute her own words or else begin to take a closer look at the way she's tried to approach this. Her reply is: "Well, no, I guess not. But what else is there to do? You tell me. I've done everything I know to do." Now how would you meet this?

Student D: Could you summarize just briefly what has just preceded this by saying that these other factors didn't work and would you run into the same difficulty if you repeated the same process, this also wouldn't work? This is the idea—how you would say it would probably be much briefer than that.

Instructor: I think you decide what of this you're going to pick up. She's given you four things, really. She says: "No (reluctantly), I guess not. No, I guess this doesn't work." She says it rather reluctantly because she hates to admit it, but she can't refute her own words. Then a second thing that she gives you that you could pick up is, "But what else is there to do?" You could pick up the third thing, "You tell me," which would be picking up the structure. Or, you could pick up the fourth thing, which is, "I've done everything I know to do." Now, you have at least four choices. Which would you pick up? In terms of your task here, to help her get more involved, see more of her own involvement, what would you select?

Student E: It's obvious that everything hasn't been done, or there possibly might be some changes made.

Instructor: Would you pick this last thing?

Student E: So, I would say, "Are you certain that everything has been done?"

Instructor: Well, now how will the client receive this?

Student E: Then, of course, she'd go back, "Well, what else is there to do?"

Student A: "I've said it and you don't believe me."

Instructor: She might have to be defensive again if she thinks you're accusing her of not having done everything she could. You're saying, you're a bad girl, aren't you? Let's look at this from the client's point of view.

Student E: It's just like a person saying, well, I've done everything in my power I know to do, and my child has still gone wrong. I've done my best, whereas actually none of us, very few of us do our very best.

Instructor: That's true, but again ask yourself why does the client have to say this? She's saying it defensively. "I've done everything I know to do," you see.

Student A: And that could be true, too, and that's why he's the way he is.

Student D: Yes, except what she says as being true for her . . .

Student E: You could drop back to the question, "I accept that but do you?"

Instructor: Well, would she think this is accusing her of lying? Can we think of this in terms of how the client perceives it? I think this is part of the real essence of empathy. How can you help her to move without making it necessary for her to again be defensive?

Student E: Well, of course, you can say, well, let's see if everything's been done, and you can recapitulate all that she's done and then you end up where you'd have to tell her what to do, if you realize everything hasn't been done, and that's something that goes contrary to procedure. The thought that runs through my mind is in helping a person, to really help them and, of course, possibly keep before their mind the idea that you're on their side and not against them, do you have to do like the centipede, which foot follows which, and find itself in the ditch, or try to figure out which foot follows which. It seems to me if you have to spend all your time mulling over in your own mind all the words that you say or whatever approach that you take, where are you going to end up in this thing? If you can do it as second nature . . .

Instructor: It becomes second nature after a while.

Student E: I mean, we're in this stream of events right now of . . .

Student B: Developing a first nature.

Student E: Developing a first nature, that's right.

Instructor: The question again is how do you help people.

Student E: Well, by listening, by making, asking questions, and making comments.

Student B: Boy, that's a real reflective comment.

Student A: That was real confronting.

Instructor: Isn't your first step in making a comment, in listening and so on, to try to sense what is likely to be the client's perception of this.

Student E: Come on, C____, give forth here.

Student A: (Laughing) The wheels are turning.

Student C: That's a good idea. You're asking the kind of thing that you know the answer to before you ask it . . . or to get the client to keep moving along . . .

Student B: She has some idea that you think you know, too, uh, so she's . . .

Student A: Playing games.

Instructor: It seems to me that at a certain stage we have, as a counselor, certain tasks and the client has certain needs at this stage. And here I would believe that the counselor's task is to center upon this one thing, to help the client begin to recognize her own involvement in her problem. Well, let's carry this a bit farther. The counselor has made a beginning confrontation way back here. He says, "You think he doesn't know?" His next confrontation is a little stronger. Well, no, not the next one, it's about the same, "And how did that turn out?" that is, about the minister. Now leading on, "It looks as if having someone tell him doesn't work out so well," clinching what she has already said. And so she says, "Well, no, I guess not. Well, what else is there to do? You tell me. I've done everything I know to do." Counselor says, "How do you see that?" Now this is not saying, no, you haven't done everything. It isn't quite saying, well, now let's take a look at what you've done. We know that she's going to be defensive if she gets any stimulation for her defenses. We want to avoid that because we know this gets to be a vicious circle. When her defensiveness is necessary in order to protect herself, then she is going to use it. And this only gets us into a vicious circle again. So the client says, "Oh, I've pleaded with him, I've begged him, I've threatened to leave him, everything." Now what would you say here?"

Student A: You've really nagged him, huh?

(Laughter)

Instructor: Well, that would be lowering the boom, wouldn't it. Incidentally, there are probably clients with whom you could do this, but not with one who is so defensive. If you do, she assumes you're just like her husband because he's undoubtedly accused her of this.

Student A: I think I could have said that to Mrs. M.

Instructor: And, of course, a lot depends on how you say it.

Student A: I don't think she would have—she would have recoiled a little bit . . .

Student E: The relative level of empathy, too . . .

Student C: I think I'd just use silence there, nod my head, stare off into space.

Instructor: Why would you do that?

Student C: So that she herself can begin to feel that naturally you understand that she has done the nagging and so on but to what avail? Rather than say in so many words, to what avail?

Instructor: Well, you have a lot of faith in your client's ability, and this certainly shouldn't be overlooked. How else might you approach this?

Student B: You could say, "This is very disturbing to you, is it not?"

Student A: And it hasn't worked out.

Student B: Yes, in other words, "You have done what you have thought has been everything but still . . ."

Student E: Uh, yes, very empathic and say, "And this hasn't worked out."

Student A: You're going into her feelings again.

Instructor: Are there other possibilities?

Student D: What was her last comment? How did she end it?

Student E: "Begged, pleaded, threatened, . . ."

Instructor: "Everything."

Student E: Say, "How do you see this?"

Student A: (Laugh) Oh, I'd really confirm it, I'm afraid.

Student E: Or, could you take up, uh, . . . could you take up with her the effects of any one of these things?

Student B: You could say, "What did he do . . ."

Student E: "Let's, uh, dissect one of these approaches that you take and see what . . ."

Instructor: You would want her to specify?

Student E: Yes, specify or recapitulate or give an example of some of this.

Student A: Why would you do that?

Student E: Well, so that she could see just what was involved in the thing. She might also see her own involvement in it.

Student D: Is this a little early to do this?

Student A: I was just wondering—she has already seen that this is not working.

Student D: I think you'd do that eventually.

Instructor: I wonder if you can't help the client to see it more specifically in a little different way.

Student E: I was thinking about, unless you get down to specifics—she's made a great number of generalizations here, and you can go on into the night on things like that, or until the hour is gone, but until you can be a little more specific and see just what is actually happening, the mechanics of it, it seems to me that sometime you're going to have to call a halt on this.

Instructor: I agree with you. I think that this is the better method at this point. But my question is how you do it. And again I would prefer to remember her defenses. I would be inclined to say, "And how does he take all this?"

Student E: "He just rubs it off," she'd say. Well, what is this—that's what I'm trying to get at, what's actually going on?

Instructor: She's told you, essentially. She hasn't given you an illustration of it, but she's told you that she's begged, she's pleaded with him, she's threatened to leave him, everything. Now . . .

Student E: Did you ask her how he took all this and what came out of it?

Student A: How he responded to this.

Instructor: I think the question that's involved here is what is another way of breaking into this impasse. One way is to get her to thinking through—get her to look a little bit through the eyes of the spouse. Can you say in order to do this, "How does he seem to take all this?" "Well," she says, "It doesn't mean a thing to him. He just says, oh, stop nagging me." That's what A_____ was after a while ago.

Student D: "Nagging?"

Student E: O.K., you've got A_____'s reflective question there.

Instructor: Yes. You could pick up on this one, as A_____ did. You could pick up her last word in a questioning way. What else could you do?

Student A: That would be still rough, though. I think that would blast her in the face.

Instructor: Is it very blasting? She's said it. These are her words, not yours.

Student A: This is what her husband said. But she's on the defensive. What she's saying is that this is what my husband says, and I don't see it that way.

Instructor: But isn't this a step? She's come now to the point where she says, "Well, the way he responds is by saying, oh, . . ."

Student E: "Knock off the nagging."

Instructor: "Stop nagging." Now at least you've got her talking about some involvement here. She's talking about some involvement of herself as her husband sees it.

Student A: "I wonder what he's saying here, I wonder what he's trying to convey?"

Instructor: Then, you would try to help her to take another look, maybe a little deeper look into how her husband's seeing this. So, you'd say, "I wonder what he is trying to tell you?"

Student A: "What he's really saying."

Instructor: Well, how else could you do it?

Student D: Would it be inappropriate to use just the reflective word, "nagging," here, or would this say enough to keep her focusing now as she has on what takes place between herself and her husband?

Instructor: You could use either one of these, and aren't there still others that you could use and still be appropriate? Now that she has taken this step you want again to try to clinch it in her thinking.

Student C: Well, if you want to try to clinch it then, I wouldn't just say the word, "nagging?"

(Chorus of voices saying, "No, she'd have to defend it," and the like.)

Instructor: She'd deny it, you think.

Student D: That would be too direct.

Student C: Well, she answers, "No." You just wait for her to stew that over a little bit.

Student E: Or would you say, "Why do you think he responds like this?" That's another way of saying what A_____ said that second time.

Instructor: You'd say, "Why do you think he responds this way?"

Student C: It seems to me you're dealing too much with what the husband thinks there rather than what she's thinking.

Student E: No. She's trying to figure out for herself what the husband's thinking, see.

Student A: "Why does he feel that way?"

Student E: "What makes him feel that way?"

Student A: Because of the way she's handling it.

Instructor: Well, it seems to me that you've reached a point here with this client in which she has said, "He says, oh, stop nagging me." Now you're pretty sure that this is part of the problem, so I think you'd clinch this. You could become a little more pointed about it.

Student A: It certainly doesn't seem to be effectual. "It doesn't seem to solve the problem by doing it this way, does it?" or, "How do you see that this handles it?"

Instructor: My own inclination is to look at this feeling that her husband has, though, so that she gets this more out in the open. Because she probably hasn't thought too much about this. She's been too defensive. You've set up a situation in which she doesn't have to be defensive, because you have avoided stimulating her defensiveness. So I think you can clinch it now by saying something like, "He feels you're nagging him?" This is what she said.

Student E: That's just an empathic statement.

Instructor: It's only a reflection of her . . .

Student E: I mean . . . what she says he says. In other words . . .

Student C: Historical content.

Student E: Yes, that's right.

Student A: The idea is still the same, but it's more gentle.

Instructor: Now I think this is confrontation, but this is a leading up, step-by-step kind of confrontation, and it's still the same confrontation, incidentally.

Student A: Well, when is she going to come to learn that these tactics that she's using are not worthwhile, they're not achieving what she wants?

Student E: Well, did you use this, what did she say there when you told her that?

Instructor: Counselor says, "He feels you're nagging him." "Oh, definitely. 'Just stop nagging me,' he says. Like yesterday, he started to leave and I said, 'Now, John, promise me you won't do anything like you have done, just promise me,' and he got mad and swore and said that if I didn't talk about it all the time, he probably wouldn't do it. So there it was again. You can't depend on him any more than a four-year-old." Now what do you do?

Student E: Well, she's taking the attitude toward him, I mean, that he is just about a four-year-old and probably treating him as such, trying to treat him as a child, mother him.

Instructor: And what do you do?

Student E: Well, I'm trying to get straightened out what she's doing.

Instructor: There's no question about that, is there? She tells you this, really.

Student A: "You kind of wish he'd grow up."

Instructor: She tells you this in terms of what he says.

Student E: Yes, that's true.

Instructor: Which is still, in a sense, warding off the reality of this so far as she's concerned.

Student E: Well, I'd probably have been a little directive and said, "Can you deal with an adult in the same way you deal with a child?"

Instructor: What do you think of that one?

Student A: Sounds good.

Student B: I don't think I'd say that but I need to have time to reflect here.

Student C: You could say, "How far do you trust four-year-olds?"

Student D: It seems to me that she's just trying to evade the very thing that you've just begun to focus on, and now she's coming back and treating him the way that she's done, you've got to get back somehow to the very thing that you've covered in the two previous comments and try to stay on that tack instead of getting off on something else.

Student A: How are you going to focus on—I'm still with this thing—are we attempting here to focus on the way she's handling this situation? That's what I would focus on. Just put it on the table now. "Are you satisfied, do you think this is handling the situation properly? Do you think that you are successful in doing it?" And she has told us that it isn't successful.

Instructor: Well, I wonder if you're a little bit impatient with her. Aren't you trying to move her too quickly?

Student E: You could be just puzzling with her on this thing. "How would you feel if you were treated as a child, being an adult?"

Instructor: Would she be liable to hear that as an accusation?

Student E: No, I'm trying to—no, I'm not trying to accuse her. I'm just trying to ask, to find out what her feeling would be if she found herself in a like situation.

Student A: In your mind you're not accusing her.

Student E: How could you say this to her without accusing her?

Instructor: Again, we don't want to arouse too much of her defensiveness because she's got so much of it.

Student E: Somewhere along the line she needs to put herself in the same position of her husband, if the tables were turned. Suppose she was going out here and doing what he was doing even and he didn't trust her—how would she feel about not being trusted. What you get in this thing—what he's doing—if he gets the blame, he might as well have the game.

Instructor: You see, for some reason she has found it necessary to treat him this way . . .

Student A: "You kind of wish he'd grow up, don't you?"

Instructor: Well, I think you can do this rather easily and simply, without arousing her defensiveness too much. You've been pretty successful so far with clinching what she says, and if you'd rather say gently, "You think maybe he feels that you treat him like a four year old?" You're again helping her to see through her husband's eyes, aren't you?

Student E: His feelings.

Instructor: You're trying to arouse some empathic response in her, which I think is a first step in her seeing her own involvement in the problem.

Student E: That's a bit confronting, though, isn't it?

Instructor: Yes, it is. It is confrontation. You've been leading up to this, step by step, little by little. This is the line that you've been going on. You've had this as your goal all the time, and you've been progressive in this. Again, there's hardly a refutation to this because this is what she has said. Her reply to this was, "What? Oh, I see what you mean. Why, no, no, I don't think so. Well, how else can you treat a grown man that acts the way he does. I don't know. Sometimes I feel like I've got three children instead of two and a husband." Now I've used this as an illustration of what I mean by confrontation. I think it's the same confrontation that you make all the way through. But this one confrontation may be made up of steps. I don't think you confront in one direction and then confront in another direction in the same interview. Now, there are some questions that I would raise about this technique, particularly as we've illustrated it. The first one is how do you gauge the necessity for confrontation as over against the necessity for the other kinds of techniques, like the clarifying, reflecting types?

Student E: Is confrontation sort of a last resort?

Instructor: There's a lot of disagreement on this. I find, though, that where you can use the kinds of techniques that are less defense-arousing and more empathic, you tend to get farther in the long run and that where you attempt confrontation too quickly or too vigorously, with a lot of clients you tend to destroy the positive feelings that the client has toward the counselor and the counseling situation. And this is something we want to preserve, because if it's destroyed or if it's pared down in any way, there is likely to be a resistive attitude on the part of the client or some defensiveness which you have to deal with before you can go on. What you want to have is as clean a situation as you can so that it isn't cluttered with having to go off here and deal with this or off there and deal with that. And if you get a resistive attitude, then you have to deal with that, or it will cling to the whole counseling process. It seems to me one way that you can validly use confrontation in the way I've outlined it is at those points when after several interviews the client continues to place all the blame on the spouse, refusing defensively to recognize his own involvement in the problem. There are certainly other places that you can use it.

Student A: What about a counselor who uses confrontation excessively?

Instructor: Well, what would you say about that, A____? That's a good point to raise here.

Student A: I would say he was pretty aggressive in his own feelings about this—probably some feelings of hostility there.

Instructor: Aggressive and hostile feelings. Well, why would he have feelings of hostility?

Student A: Countertransference.

Instructor: How do you see that?

Student A: He's identifying too much with the situation. Probably he's involved in it himself.

Student D: Client irritates him.

Instructor: Client irritates him, because—because?

Student E: It strikes home.

Student A: It's too personal, maybe.

Student D: May be many reasons.

Instructor: This seems a bit vague. "Strikes home," "too personal."

Student E: Well, what A____ said, maybe, if I understood him correctly, that he might be having problems along the same line or . . .

Student A: You mean unconsciously . . .

Student E: Yes, unconsciously.

Student A: Might remind him of his own wife.

Student E: Or, he might be identifying with, say, the husband or something like that, taking sides in the situation regardless of whether it's a reflection on his home situation or his own personal difficulty.

Instructor: You mean, then, this kind of irritation or hostility would be displaced.

Student E: How would that be?

Instructor: It would be displaced from the object toward whom the hostility actually is felt to another object, is that right?

Student E: Oh, yes, if it was something in his own life he'd be displacing it over on this poor client.

Student A: He doesn't have too much investment in this client anyway so it's easy to take it out on the client rather than taking it out on his wife.

Student D: I think this raises one of the problems that all of us are facing as learners and it's different from the role that we have assumed before. In a sense this possible displacement becomes a little easier in counseling than maybe it would in a different situation. A_____ and I were talking about this the other night.

Student A: I would say it was being punitive.

Student E: Well, the important thing, I suppose, is for him to see or understand what may be taking place. If he can see this in his own counseling.

Student B: Is all this clearly saying that if a counselor uses confrontation too much, it indicates the counselor is irritated at the client because he dislikes his wife and displaces the irritation from hs wife on to the client? Suppose he doesn't have a wife?

Instructor: This has been suggested by A_____ as a possibility. He raised the question first of all, . . .

Student B: He could be angry at the client.

Student A: But why should he be angry at the client? That's the thing. Why should you be mad at the client?

Student B: Because he's not seeing himself involved in the situation.

Student A: I know, but that's not your problem, though, that's the client's problem. So why should you be mad. I went through this thing. I—I—this one man I had in counseling. I wondered why. Why was I so impatient with him? Why did I get so angry with him? And I brought this . . .

Student B: Because you were mad at your wife?

Student A: Could be. I couldn't get anywhere with him. Maybe I can't get anywhere with my wife or maybe with this course or something like that, I don't know.

Instructor: You've suggested some possibilities now. You suggested that if the counselor is too confronting, there may be some answers to this and that one may be that he is taking out on the client some hostility that he feels toward some other important person in his life because there is somehow a chain of connection between these two. It may be very easy to see some connection, and it may be very difficult.

Student E: That doesn't have to be, does it? I mean a doctor who has cancer may still operate on somebody else who has cancer, if he . . .

Student A: That's not getting into feelings though.

Student D: Some surgeons never even want to know their patients because this would interfere with their capacity as a surgeon.

Student B: Well, some psychotherapists are mixed up in their own feelings and yet they help out. I know one . . .

Student A: Sure. Sure.

Student E: That's what I was getting at. There's no reason why he necessarily has to displace it on the client.

Student D: I think A_____'s right. It is a possibility.

Instructor: I think this is suggested as one possible answer to why the counselor may use confrontation excessively. It's only one possibility. Why else might he use confrontation excessively?

Student D: Well, just the impatience after several interviews —a very natural, simple explanation is that the counselor has certain ideas about this, he has certain objectives . . .

Student E: Let's get going, huh?

Student D: Yes, and he just becomes impatient and says, let's move.

Student A: Then he's doing the very same thing that the client is doing. He's not involved in his own problem of being a counselor.

Student D: But I'm saying, this is one possible reason why he . . .

Instructor: This is what B_____ suggested while ago, isn't it? Wasn't it the same thing? Maybe he really is irritated with the client because this client doesn't move, which means because the client doesn't react as the counselor . . .

Student A: Wants him to.

Instructor: Yes, as he expects the client to react. Now let's get below that a little. What's involved in that? What might be involved in it?

Student B: Be involved in what?

Instructor: In the counselor's feelings of impatience and irritation because the client doesn't react as he expects the client to react.

Student A: I'm not a very good counselor.

Student B: Yes, precisely. (Laughter)

Student D: No. What I'm saying is that the . . .

Student B: I think it can be an explanation to this. I mean, we're seeing, A_____ and I are suggesting possible explanations, not exclusive ones.

Student D: Well, what I was going to suggest was another possibility, that counselors have certain goals and models and assumptions, morally and otherwise, and because this person doesn't perceive this, because we perceive it, then this gets involved in the counseling because we so easily think why can't she or he see it.

Student E: But actually isn't that based on fear, that is, the counselor feels he should react this way, but if he doesn't react this way then the next question in the counselor's mind is what do I do next—what other way can he react, and I don't know how to go after that.

Student A: Why is it that the counselor is so disturbed about this? Why is it he wants the client to respond the way he expects?

Student E: Insecurity.

Student B: Because he wants the client to be helped.

Student A: Or does he want to help himself?

Student B: He wants the client to be helped. Like the doctor who tells the man to . . .

Student A: I think there's a vicarious relationship here. I can't be what I ought to be and I want this person to be what I want to be . . .

Student D: That's just what I was saying. What we want to be . . .

Instructor: Now, we've come to two things here. One is if the counselor is acting out impatience; at a deeper level, this may be his own insecurity—he wants to help but he is being frustrated. The way he sees himself as a helping person isn't working. And he doesn't know what else to do. You've suggested that one may be insecure in his role: Can insecurity within himself raise his anxiety about himself as a worthy person?

Student E: In other words, if he fails here, "Gee, I've failed. I might as well get out of this business."

Student D: I'm dubious.

Student A: I think his projection is really . . .

Student D: I'm not sure that I see the relationship between the specific insecurity of the counselor and actual insecurity of the counselor. He may feel insecure insofar as what to do next because his model and his convictions have failed, but because he has these particular convictions and he doesn't know what to do next, I do not see this as necessarily following out of his own insecurity.

Student A: I've got my subject for my paper now.

Student D: It may imply inability in terms of techniques and methods that he should use, but I don't necessarily see this as implying an insecurity basically on the part of the counselor.

Instructor: Why is it so important to him, D_____, that the client react in accordance with the counselor's own ideas? The counselor has certain models, ideals, ideas that he believes in. He has these convictions. But the client doesn't react in this way. The question I would raise here is, is it possible that part of his insecurity is that he needs to be very sure within himself that what he is relying on is really reliable?

Student D: I don't think this necessarily follows.

Instructor: If the counselor is in this situation and if, as you indicate, part of this insecurity has some relation to the counselor's basic convictions, I'm not quite sure how you see this relation.

Student D: I think we'd raise questions about the adequacy of his convictions becoming relevant to the immediate situation and the methods he uses to implement what his convictions are. Why should we say the other? Now it may be in some instances that this would be true. But I think it raises a question of, the question of methodology, of how we use ourselves and the degree to which we are able to get the client at this stage to see what we hold as the basic fundamental convictions.

Instructor: You feel it's necessary to get him to see?

Student D: Well, I think, I think that . . .

Student B: If you believe that one way will lead to happiness, then I think that, sure, it's necessary for them to see this.

Student D: And we can't separate this fundamental conviction that we have from our personality or what we do. This is . . .

Student B: May I offer another suggestion. It might be that the fundamental conviction itself is insecure, but it might be that the fundamental perfection which we are supposed to have we haven't obtained, and we might be insecure in that.

Instructor: Now, is this a third possibility? That is, that when we become impatient with the client, there may be a possibility that we are reacting to that part of the client which reminds us of our own imperfection, our own defenses, our own reactions in one way or another. In other words, we are seeing in the client something of ourselves that we don't like; we, therefore, become impatient with the client because we are equally impatient with ourselves.

Student D: This is one possibility. Let's leave this as a possibility also. That's all I'm saying. This might very well be true, as it undoubtedly is in some situations.

Instructor: Maybe the most important thing is not precisely what the motivation of the counselor is but that whatever it is he be able to recognize, at least in part, when he is confronting excessively or doing anything else excessively in the counseling situation, and that he question this within himself. Why is he doing this? So that he will gradually develop a better use of himself, so that gradually he develops the ability to get himself off his hands and not get in the way of the counseling.

Clinical Aspects of Training

Theoretical formulations concerning counseling are of little value unless and until their relevance to the actual practice of counseling becomes apparent to the learner through practical, personal application in the helping process itself. There is no substitute for supervised practice. Role-playing or socio-drama and similar devices, while of some value in the creation of "group feeling" among trainees and in easing their apprehension about accepting their first clients for counseling, can never really bridge the gap between theory and practice. For theory becomes real only as one demonstrates its validity for himself in actual counseling. Moreover, supervised practice offers one of the best means to recognize how one may be limiting or short-circuiting his counseling effectiveness. It offers, therefore, a practical approach to the development of a "professional self" based largely upon increased self-awareness and the integration of theoretical knowledge and practical experience.

Established agencies and clinics which include marriage and family counseling in the services offered to the public provide excellent opportunities for the acquisition of supervised counseling experience. The agency's policies, setting and status in the community, its established procedures, its range and scope of services, its personnel and their sense of teamwork and group responsibility, its use of psychiatric and other consultants, its use of fees, its clientele and the status accorded trainees by its administrators and personnel, all can elicit trainee reactions that an astute supervisor can direct toward the trainee's increased awareness and use of himself in the work of counseling.

The following principles of individual case supervision have evolved through many years of experience in supervising marriage counseling trainees. While this is not, in any sense, a complete list of supervisory principles and certainly not a thorough analysis of the supervisory task, it does include some of the most important issues to be faced in the process of supervision.

1. *The primary focus of supervision should be upon the professional growth and development of the counselor.* A supervisor must, of course, remain constantly aware of his responsibility to his agency and to the clients of the supervised counselor. But these responsibilities need not shift his focus and should not distract his attention from his primary task.
2. *The teaching role of the supervisor should be quite clear to him and easily discernible to his counselors-in-training.* Supervision involves the need for especially skillful teaching. It is a kind of teaching that is not likely to be experienced in other types of learning situations, for it is concentrated on the development of self-awareness in the interest of professional growth. This means, in practice, that the appeal to and support of the counselor's ego strength becomes the primary method by which the trainee's integration of theoretical concepts into his own system of perceiving, thinking, feeling, organizing, and adapting takes place.
3. *Supervisory hours in which the central focus is upon the development of counselor self-awareness and professional growth, rather than wholly upon the client and his problem, offer the most rewarding experience in learning.* Real understanding of the client and his problems is dependent upon the extent to which the counselor is freely able to use himself for that purpose in the counseling session. Therefore, the supervisor's task is to help the counselor learn to so use himself that the client can be understood and helped.

If a supervisor centers all of his attention upon the client and his difficulties, the trainee being supervised almost inevitably comes to view the supervision process as one in which he secures a blueprint for future counseling hours. The supervisor can appropriately help the counselor to become more fully aware of the dynamic factors involved in the counseling process—and that includes the client's personality and his mode of interpersonal interaction—provided that the method the supervisor uses to do this really stimulates learning. Our experience indicates that going over the counselor's case records and pointing out how he might better have responded at this point or that is a relatively sterile process. Blunt explanations of how a client may be reacting or possible meanings the reactions may have are also unprofitable.

In supervision, the most effective learning seems to take place when the supervisor skillfully applies the same principles and techniques that are effective in the counseling process, but with a different focus and goal. In counseling the focus is upon the client and his marital interaction. The goal is to help him perceive his situation, himself, and his spouse more clearly and to provide stimulation and support to his ego strengths as he learns to use himself more effectively and satisfactorily.

Similarly, the supervisor's goal is to help the counselor clarify and sharpen his perceptive powers to the end that his analysis of clients and their problems may become more accurate. The supervisor's goal also includes helping the counselor to learn to use himself more fully and appropriately in the counseling process. The focus is upon how the counselor perceives his task and his clients and their problems and how he attempts to provide help. The supervisor enables the counselor to stimulate his perceptive functions and provides ego support as the counselor applies his perceptive, organizing, and calculating powers toward appropriate execution of his counseling task.

4. *Essentially the same problems that are encountered in the process of counseling may be expected to arise also in the process of supervision.* After all, some of the same basic factors

are present in both processes. One person is attempting to help another person who is trying to learn more effective methods of coping with some aspects of interpersonal relationships.

Resistive attitudes [3] are frequently present in both processes. Missing appointments or being late for them, overly compliant attitudes, belligerence, asking others for supervisory assistance, and many other manifestations of resistance on the part of the counselor-in-training are reminiscent of client resistance. Moreover, they can be handled in much the same manner and with essentially the same approaches one would use in counseling.

5. *Anxiety associated with a counselor's student status can be a useful stimulus to the learning process.* Unless it is quite extreme, the student's wish to do well and to strive for success in his tasks can be helpful in training in much the same manner that some degree of anxiety or discomfort can stimulate a client toward working at the problem-solving task. Therefore, justifiable attempts to relieve extreme discomfort should not be overdone by a supervisor but should be tempered by the realization that some degree of discomfort can be correlated with the supervisor's "pull" upon the ego strength of the trainee.

6. *Structure is useful in supervision in the same way and for the same reasons that it is in counseling.* Changes in the structure, such as changes in appointment hours, should be made with careful consideration and agreement of the trainee. Capriciousness on the part of the supervisor can be damaging to the trainee-supervisor relationship and to the supervisor's effectiveness. Consistent attitudes toward the trainee of respect for his dignity and integrity, his right to freedom of choice and action within the recognized structural limits imposed by the training situation, his right to self-determination and self-actualization, and respect for and understanding of factors within the trainee and the training environment that may limit or block professional growth provide enabling support for him.

---

[3] Vide Arthur L. Leader, "The Problem of Resistance in Social Work," *Social Work,* Vol. III, no. 2 (April, 1958), pp. 19-23.

To be effective these attitudes must be constant: vacillation is confusing and disabling to the trainee.

Supervision may properly help the trainee to understand the reasons for his assignment to work with a certain kind of client and problem. If, for example, the assignment is made in order to further the counselor's understanding of a person who has quite different personal characteristics from those of his former clients, giving information to the trainee supports his feeling that he is being treated with respect and purposeful consideration. The information and the counselor's subjective response to his perception of its meaning tends to promote positive anticipation of the new task.

Similarly, the supervisor may help to allay a counselor's apprehension about beginning counseling with a new client by considering with him any available information concerning the client and his difficulties. Care should be taken, however, to prevent the development of preconceived notions concerning these factors.

Counselors-in-training need to know what to put in their case records and what to bring to the supervision hours. An effective way of teaching this latter aspect of the counseling task (in addition to seminar work, and the like) is to provide some kind of guide for the counselor's thinking as he prepares for his supervision hours. He, then, enters the sessions after giving careful consideration to the crucial factors to be discussed. The following suggestions have been used effectively as an aid to counselor's preparation for supervision hours.

SUGGESTIONS FOR USE OF INDIVIDUAL CASE SUPERVISION HOURS. The primary purpose of supervision is to help you to increase your counseling knowledge and skills. To this end, consideration of the following factors in preparation for supervision sessions is suggested.

a. *The client(s).* What are they like as persons? What is their appearance, and how would you describe them so that your hearer may gain a correct image of them? How do they behave toward each other (if you see them jointly)? What are their actions in the interview hour? How clearly do you understand the personality structure and functioning of the client? How do they cope with stress? What defenses are evident? What other adaptive measures do they use? How resilient and flexible are they? What does this mean in terms of their marital interaction? What additional information would shed further light on the personality and interaction factors? How does each client seem to see himself and his spouse?

b. *The problem(s).* What do the clients present as the problem(s) in their interpersonal relationships? How do they approach the problem(s) in telling you about it? How did it start? What (in the general life of the couple) was happening at that time? What has happened since that time? How have they tried to cope with it? What prevented their coping with the problem? Have they ever consulted anyone else about it? With what results? When? For how long? How do they seem to view that experience? What do the clients want to do about the difficulty? Do both want to work it out? Is one reluctant and one ready to try to better the situation, or just how do they view it?

c. *The counselor-client relationship.* How do the clients approach you in their attempt to get help? With what attitude? Do they seem fearful? Anxious? Desperate? Resentful? Compliant? Dependent? Or in just what manner do they approach counseling? How do they seem to perceive you (as evidenced by the way they relate to you)? How do you see yourself in this relationship?

d. *The counselor's use of himself.* What was your feeling about this counseling hour? How secure and how comfortable did you feel? If uncomfortable, have you considered what may have stimulated your discomfort? Did you enjoy working with this client? If so—or if not—have you considered what may have stimulated your reaction? Are there specific questions you asked or responses you made about which you later had misgivings or wished you had not used? Did you have moments in the counseling hour when you felt you did not know what really was happening between you and the client? If so, have you considered why? Did you feel that you knew *why* you asked what you asked or said what you said? Or did you feel that you were going about your task rather blindly?

e. *The counseling process.* What was the process by which counseling proceeded (this is directly related to *d* above)? What did you see as your task as counselor? How did you attempt to help the client? What movement (if any) do you believe the client made toward resolution of his difficulty (through acquiring a better understanding of self, spouse, their interpersonal interaction, ability to do something about the difficulty, and the like)? Which of your attempts to help the client seemed most helpful? Which of your attempts were not helpful? Which of your attempts seemed to hinder the client's progress rather than to help?

f. *Plans for future appointments.* What do you see as your counseling task with this client (immediate; long-range)? Why? How do you hope to accomplish this task?

7. *Supervision is a training process, not a treatment process.* While the goal in supervision is to help the counselor to attain greater understanding and more effective professional use of himself, this is not a treatment process. Therefore, when a trainee's need and desire for therapy becomes evident to him and to his supervisor, the matter should be openly discussed, and he should be referred to some other qualified person for the necessary help. Ordinarily his training can continue in the usual manner. He may mention his therapy from time to time, but the supervisor is not responsible in any sense for the treatment program.

8. *In supervision, learning is facilitated far more by positive approaches than by negative ones.* Constant criticism of a trainee or his methods may cause him to become discouraged and to stop trying to improve his counseling. Then, too, constant criticism will tend to arouse his defenses for protective maneuvers to meet any felt danger to his self-esteem.

Cruser and his colleagues, reporting results of a 1956–57 study of supervisory practice conducted by the Committee on Social Work Practice for the Western New York Chapter of the National Association of Social Workers, stated that the most helpful aspects of supervision, according to survey respondents, were "stimulation of thinking, support and encouragement, and appreciation of efforts." [4] In this kind of positive supervisory climate, a counselor-in-training can feel free enough to examine thoughtfully and candidly his counseling methods and his interaction with his clients. Professional growth and development can flourish only in an atmosphere that is conducive to this kind of self-scrutiny.

The author's experience in supervising the counseling of counselors-in-training for many years indicates that the supervisory process as experienced by the counselor-in-training typically proceeds by stages. The accompanying chart (see Figure 13–1) delineates these stages in terms of the counselor's perception of the process and of the supervisor in each of the several stages.

Integration of Didactic and Clinical Training

Training in marriage counseling, as presented here, involves educational endeavors and the concerted, intensive efforts of many professional persons.

A skilled psychiatrist, meeting regularly in case conferences with counselors-in-training, can be of inestimable value in helping trainees to see the clinical significance of didactic material. He can effectively reinforce students' didactic training by using their own case material to elaborate and illustrate theoretical formulations of dynamic psychology.

The following outline of didactic and clinical activities and their contributions to counselor training in The Menninger Foundation program provides some indication of the scope and

---

[4] Robert W. Cruser, *et al.*, "Chapter Study on Supervision," *Social Work*, Vol. III, no. 1 (January, 1958), p. 25.

Figure 13–1

Stages in Counselor-Supervisor Relationship

Counselor's Perception of Supervision	Counselor's Perception of Self	Counselor's Resultant Behavior	Meaning of Counselor's Reaction
1. Judge–evaluator.	1. Dependent–learner.	1. Conformity. "Best foot forward". Suggestions used without discrimination.	1. Wish for approval.
2. Evaluator–helper.	2. Dependent–learner (Being helped).	2. Conformity – unrecognized rebellion (disappointment). Revealed by outward conformity and practical nonconformity, *e.g.* records written too late for supervision hour.	2. Frustrated wish for complete help which would mean complete approval.
3. Evaluator–helper–confronter.	3. Dependent–learner–resists (righteously) attack.	3. Anger–revealed by lessened adherence to "rules of the game," covert conflict with supervisor.	3. Defense against self-recognition and against passive wishes.
4. Unjust judge–withholding "father."	4. Persecuted and unfairly treated person whose rights are violated (learning suspended).	4. Undisguised hostility–"do as I please" –reversion in practice to presupervisory level.	4. Defense against dependency wishes. Protection of ego. SE. Allows open anger because "it is justified." (Sour grapes.)
5. Fallible person like all others–faded omnipotence and omniscience.	5. Ambivalent. Attempts at reconciliation on plane of acceptance of own responsibility–clearer (less distorted and less dependent) use of help.	5. Wiser use of help. Greater discrimination in use of suggestions. (Better, more effective counseling.) (Reality principle.)	5. Reorganization in homeostatic balance. Clearer perception of self and supervisor.
6. Teacher–helper rather than judge or all-giving object of dependency longings.	6. Learner–friend with certain clearer personality needs which are more clearly seen and handled.	6. Increase in wish to understand self and others and to counsel more effectively. (Balance between dependence–independence.) Subjectively, greater feeling of wish to take responsibility for actions and ideas.	6. Stabilization of homeostatic pattern with resultant emergence of gratification on the level of mature helper.

intensity of a postgraduate training program in marriage counseling:

SUMMARY OF THE RELATION OF SPECIFIC COURSES IN THE MARRIAGE COUNSELING TRAINING PROGRAM CURRICULUM TO THE GOALS OF MARRIAGE COUNSELING TRAINING

1. *Psychiatric Case Study*

a. To provide the marriage counseling trainee with an orientation to the kind of study a psychiatrist makes in the course of psychiatric evalution.

b. To provide understanding of the methodological approach of the psychiatrist to an adequate understanding of patients.

c. To provide orientation to the basic philosophy underlying the psychiatric approach to an evaluative study of individuals.

d. To provide opportunity for trainees to become better acquainted with the instructor and to observe interviews conducted by a well-trained psychiatrist.

2. *Normal Development of the Individual in the Family*

a. To provide a basic understanding of the normal growth and development of the individual from the prenatal stage through the period of adolescence.

b. To provide orientation to the increasingly large body of research being accumulated in the attempt to better understand maturation and emotional development of the individual.

3. *Marriage and Family Literature and Research*

a. To provide a basic background of familiarity with the body of knowledge now available in the field of marriage and the family.

b. To sensitize trainees to the influences upon the individual from social and cultural as well as from psychological factors.

c. To encourage familiarity with past and current research materials in this field and to examine their implications for counseling.

4. *Seminar in Principles and Techniques of Marriage Counseling*

a. To encourage delineation of basic principles and philosophy underlying the use of technical methods and procedures in counseling.

b. To provide an orientation to the aims and techniques of social casework and of psychotherapy and to aid the trainee in acquiring an understanding of similarities and differences in these approaches and in the approach of marriage counseling.

c. To encourage the acquisition of adequate marriage counseling skills and techniques through the use of such teaching devices as role playing, tape recordings, and clinical case materials.

5. *Research Seminar*

a. To provide opportunity for professional growth through intensive study, survey of the literature, and consequent writing of papers on specific subjects pertinent to the field of marriage and family counseling or to the field of marriage and family living.

b. To encourage in the trainee the development of scholarly pursuits in the interest of personal professional growth and contributions to the field of counseling.

6. *Legal Aspects of Domestic Relations*

a. To provide orientation to the legal profession in relation to the practice of marriage counseling.

b. To provide basic knowledge of laws and legal matters related to marriage, annulment, divorce, and responsibility for children.

c. To provide an understanding of the legal responsibility of the counselor.

7. *Psychotherapy*

a. To provide for the trainee an understanding of the approach of psychoanalytic psychotherapy to helping emotionally disturbed persons.

b. To provide opportunity for trainees to delineate similarities and differences in psychotherapy and counseling.

c. To encourage increased understanding of those elements of the psychotherapeutic approach which are validly applicable in the field of marriage counseling.

8. *Psychopathology*

a. To provide opportunity for trainees to acquire some understanding of the symptomatology and psychodynamics of mental illness and severe emotional disturbance.

b. To enhance the trainee's ability to distinguish between manifestations of severe intrapsychic conflict and manifestations of situational distress normally encountered in marital difficulties.

c. To provide additional understanding of individual psychodynamics.

9. *Application of Adjunctive Therapies to Family Mental Hygiene*

a. To provide trainees with a background of theory underlying the use of adjunctive therapy in psychiatry.

b. To provide for trainees a laboratory experience in personal use of crafts and activities used in adjunctive therapy.

c. To encourage the development of hobbies and interests conducive to the mental health of the trainee and his family.

10. *Seminar in the Application of Dynamic Psychology to Marriage Counseling*

a. To provide basic understandings of psychosexual development and dynamic psychology in the interest of the trainee's enhanced understanding of clients and of himself.

b. To provide opportunity for clarification and discussion of concepts and theories concerning personality with which he may have been unfamiliar prior to coming for advanced study.

c. To provide opportunity for the consideration of current clinical material in the light of concepts basic to dynamic psychology.

11. *The Application of Psychological Tests to Marital Problems*

a. To orient the trainee to some of the major tests used by clinical psychologists such as the Rorschach, the Thematic Apperception Test, the Wechsler, and the Minnesota Multiphasic Personality Inventory.

b. To provide opportuniy for an evaluation of the possibility of professional relationships between counselors and clinical psychologists who are trained in the use of psychological tests.

12. *Medical Information for Counselors*

a. To provide for the trainee some understanding of the viewpoint and terminology of the practicing physician.

b. To acquaint the trainee with physical symptoms which may indicate the advisability of referral to the medical doctor.

13. *Orientation to Neurological Diagnosis*

a. To broaden the trainee's knowledge of medical specialties.

b. To provide a brief explanation of neurological examination and diagnosis so that the trainee may acquire a better understanding of how organic neurological problems are differentiated from emotional disturbances.

c. To help the trainee become aware of some evidences of neurological difficulties in the interest of adequate referral.

14. *Psychiatric Approach to Parent-Child Interaction*

a. To broaden the trainee's understanding of interaction factors in the family.

b. To broaden the trainee's understanding of the behavior of seriously disturbed children.

15. *Seminar in Psychiatry and Religion*

a. To aid the trainee in broadening his understanding of the relation of psychiatry and religion.

b. To provide opportunity for open discussion of similarities and differences in viewpoint concerning the role of religion in the life of the individual.

c. To broaden the trainee's understanding of the role religion may play in the lives of seriously emotionally disturbed individuals.

16. *Seminar in Economics of the Family*

a. To broaden the trainee's understanding of the role of economic factors in marital and family interaction.

b. To sensitize the trainee to the relation of financial problems to marital conflict.

c. To help the trainee to deal more adequately with budgetary and financial matters in counseling.

17. *Classical Psychiatric Syndromes*

a. To enhance the trainee's understanding of the psychodynamics of severe emotional disturbances.

b. To aid the trainee in recognizing manifestations of emotional disturbances that necessitate referral.

18. *History of Dynamic Psychiatry*

a. To aid the trainee in an acquisition of an adequate perspective concerning the psychiatric field.

b. To provide opportunity for consolidation of material related to psychiatric concepts.

19. *Orientation to Psychiatric Social Work*

a. To provide further understanding of the role of the psychiatric social worker in psychiatric out-patient and hospital settings.

b. To provide opportunity for the examination of principal skills and techniques of social casework and to evaluate their application to the field of marriage counseling.

20. *Clinical Field Trip*

a. To broaden the trainee's understanding of the various approaches to helping people in trouble.

b. To provide opportunity for discussions with outstanding leaders in counseling, casework, and psychotherapy.

21. *Children's Out-Patient Department Case Conference Observation*

a. To provide observation of the team approach to diagnosis and treatment recommendations in the problems of disturbed children.

b. To enhance the trainee's understanding of the values and methods of study employed by each of the disciplines represented in the team.

c. To broaden the trainee's understanding of the dynamics and etiology of the various difficulties of disturbed children as seen by the clinic team.

22. *Diagnostic and Appraisal Conference Observation*

a. To acquaint the trainee with policies and procedures of the psychiatric hospital in diagnosis and treatment.

b. To broaden the trainee's knowledge of the kinds of difficulties brought to psychiatric hospitals.

23. *Clinical Practice in Counseling*

a. To provide opportunity for the trainee to develop professional skills based on principles, techniques, and theoretical considerations learned in the didactic courses.

b. To aid the trainee in sharpening his clinical perceptiveness.

c. To help the trainee better distinguish cases in which marriage counseling is indicated from those in which a different kind of help is needed.

d. To provide a most effective setting for the trainee's development of greater self-understanding for the purpose of increasing his effectiveness as a professional helping person.

24. *Individual Case Supervision*

a. To encourage the professional growth of the trainee through a regular appraisal of skills and techniques employed.

b. To provide opportunity for the trainee's enlarged understanding of individuals and of himself and of his use of himself in counseling.

c. To provide for the trainee interpretation of policies and procedures of the various placement agencies.

d. To aid the counselor in meeting his responsibilities to himself, his agency, his clients, and society.

25. *Psychiatric Consultation and Supervision*

a. To provide safeguards in the clinical practice of trainees in the best interests of clients, trainees, and the placement agencies.

b. To provide psychiatric appraisal of the advisability of continuing with certain cases or of referring them for psychiatric evaluation.

c. To enhance the trainee's development of skills and techniques in counseling.

d. To enhance the trainee's understanding of psychodynamics and manifestations of psychopathology.

26. *Case Conferences*

a. To provide trainee experience in preparing for and in presenting clinical material before professional staffs.

b. To aid the trainee in evaluating skills and techniques in counseling.

c. To provide opportunity for the trainee's increased understanding of clients, their problems, their approaches to seeking help, their use of counseling time, and the client-counselor relationship.

d. To provide stimulation for the trainee's development of greater ability in appraisal of difficulties and in the counseling process.

Integration of the various aspects of the didactic and clinical elements in a counselor training program of this kind depends largely upon how clearly the faculty and other professional persons who contribute to the program view their roles and the degree of dedication with which they pursue their common goal. Clear vision of one's role, firm belief in the value of the purposes to which one gives himself, and zestful dedication to those purposes are nowhere more rewarding than in education. And, no educational field of training surpasses marriage counseling in providing needed help for so many or, as yet, in being available to so few.

BIBLIOGRAPHY

Chapter I. MARRIAGE COUNSELING–ITS AIM AND DEVELOPMENT

Foster, Robert G., "Marriage Counseling in a Psychiatric Setting," *Marriage and Family Living*, XII (Spring, 1950), 41-43.

Kerckhoff, Richard K., "The Profession of Marriage Counseling as Viewed by Members of Four Allied Professions: A Study in the Sociology of Occupations," *Marriage and Family Living*, XV (November, 1953), 340-344.

Laidlaw, Robert W., "The Psychiatrist as Marriage Counselor," *The American Journal of Psychiatry*, 106 (April, 1950), 732-36.

Mace, David R., "What Is a Marriage Counselor?" *Marriage and Family Living*, XVI (May, 1954), 135-38.

Mudd, Emily H., *The Practice of Marriage Counseling*. New York: Association Press, 1951.

———, "Psychiatry and Marital Problems," *Eugenics Quarterly*, II (June, 1955), 110-17.

Chapter II. WHO SEEKS MARRIAGE COUNSELING?

Flügel, J. C., *The Psycho-Analytic Study of the Family*. London: Hogarth Press, 1921.

Hollis, Florence, *Women in Marital Conflict*. New York: Family Service Association of America, 1949.

McLean, Helen, "The Emotional Background of Marital Difficulties," *American Sociological Review*, VI (1941), 384-88.

Sirjamaki, John, *The American Family in the Twentieth Century*. Cambridge: The Harvard University Press, 1955.

Skidmore, Rex A., Hulda Van Steeter Garrett, and C. Jay Skidmore, *Marriage Consulting*. New York: Harper and Brothers, 1956.

Vincent, Clark E., *Readings in Marriage Counseling*. New York: Thomas Y. Crowell Company, 1957.

Chapter III. THE CLIENT

Angyal, Andras, *Foundations for a Science of Personality*. New York: The Commonwealth Fund, 1941.

Bordin, Edward S., "A Counseling Psychologist Views Personality Development," *Journal of Counseling Psychology,* IV (Spring, 1957), 3-8.

Brenner, Charles, *An Elementary Textbook of Psychoanalysis.* New York: International Universities Press, Inc., 1955.

English, O. Spurgeon, and G. H. J. Pearson, *Emotional Problems of Living.* New York: W. W. Norton and Company, 1945.

Erikson, Erik H., *Childhood and Society.* New York: W. W. Norton, 1950.

Freud, Sigmund, *The Basic Writings of Sigmund Freud,* A. A. Brill, ed. New York: The Modern Library, 1938.

Hunt, J. McV., ed., *Personality and the Behavior Disorders.* New York: Ronald Press Company, 1944.

Josselyn, Irene M., *Psychosocial Development of Children.* New York: Family Service Association of America, 1949.

Kluckhohn, Florence, and Henry Murray, *Personality in Nature, Society, and Culture.* New York: Knopf, 1953.

Menninger, Karl A., *The Human Mind.* New York: Knopf, 1946.

Parsons, Talcott, "Certain Primary Sources and Patterns of Aggression in the Western World," *Psychiatry,* X (1947).

Winch, Robert F., *Mate-Selection: A Study of Complementary Needs.* New York: Harper and Brothers, 1958.

———, *The Modern Family.* New York: Holt, 1952.

Chapter IV. THE COUNSELOR

Danskin, D. G., "Roles Played by Counselors in their Interviews," *Journal of Counseling Psychology,* II (1955), 22-27.

Foster, Robert G., "Counseling Is the Counselor." Unpublished manuscript, The Menninger Foundation, 1955.

Hiltner, Seward, *The Counselor In Counseling.* Nashville: Abingdon-Cokesbury Press, 1952.

Johnson, Dean, "Understanding and Use of the Self in Counseling," *Bulletin of the Menninger Clinic,* XVII (1953), 29-35.

Robinson, Francis P., "The Dynamics of Communication in Counseling," *Journal of Counseling Psychology,* Vol. II, no. 3 (Fall, 1955), pp. 163-69.

Chapter V. CREATING AN EFFECTIVE COUNSELING RELATIONSHIP

Biestek, Felix P., *The Casework Relationship.* Chicago: Loyola University Press, 1957.

Colby, Kenneth M., *A Primer for Psychotherapists.* New York: The Ronald Press Company, 1951.

Curran, Charles A., *Personality Factors in Counseling.* New York: Grune and Stratton, 1945.

Irvine, May, "Communication and Relationship in Social Casework," *Journal of Social Casework,* Vol. XXXIV, no. 1 (January, 1955), pp. 13-21.

Wolberg, Lewis R., *The Technique of Psychotherapy.* New York: Grune and Stratton, 1954.

Chapter VI. THE BEGINNING INTERVIEW

Blenkner, M., J. McV. Hunt, and L. S. Kogan, "A Study of Interrelated Factors in the Initial Interview with New Clients," *Journal of Social Casework,* XXXII (1951), 23-20.

Bordin, E. S., "The Implications of Client Expectations for the Counseling Process," *Journal of Counseling Psychology,* I (1954), 17-21.

Fenlason, Anne F., *Essentials in Interviewing.* New York: Harper and Brothers, 1952.

Garrett, Annette, *Interviewing–Its Principles and Methods.* New York: Family Welfare Association of America, 1942.

Hamilton, Gordon, *Theory and Practice of Social Case Work.* New York: Columbia University Press, 1951.

Scherz, Frances S., "Intake: Concept and Process," *Journal of Social Casework,* Vol. XXXIII, no. 6 (June, 1952), pp. 233-240.

Chapter VII. EARLY PHASES OF COUNSELING

Bibring, Grete, "Psychiatric Principles in Casework," *Journal of Social Casework,* XXX (1949), 230-35.

Curran, Charles A., *Personality Factors in Counseling.* New York: Grune and Stratton, 1945.

Foster, Robert G., "A Point of View on Marriage Counseling," *Journal Of Consulting Psychology,* III (Fall, 1956), 212-15.

Gomberg, M. Robert, and Frances T. Levinson, *Diagnosis and Process in Family Counseling.* New York: Family Service Association of America, 1951.

Skidmore, Rex A., and Hulda Van Steeter Garrett, "The Joint Interview in Marriage Counseling," *Marriage and Family Living,* XVII (November, 1955), 349-54.

Chapter VIII. COUNSELING ON A CONTINUING BASIS

Duvall, Evelyn Millis, *Family Development.* New York: Lippincott, 1957.

Fishbein, Morris, and Ruby Jo Reeves Kennedy, *Modern Marriage and Family Living.* New York: Oxford University Press, 1957.

Foote, Nelson, and Leonard J. Cottrell, *Identity and Interpersonal Competence.* Chicago: University of Chicago Press, 1955.

Franzblau, Abraham, *The Road to Sexual Maturity.* New York: Simon and Schuster, 1954.

Parsons, Talcott, and Robert F. Bales, *Family, Socialization and Interaction Process.* Glencoe: Free Press, 1955.

Perlman, Helen Harris, *Social Casework: A Problem-Solving Process.* Chicago: The University of Chicago Press, 1957.

Walker, Donald E., and Herbert C. Peiffer, Jr., "The Goals of Counseling," *Journal of Consulting Psychology,* IV (Fall, 1957), 204-209.

Chapter IX. COUNSELING SKILLS AND TECHNIQUES

Gomberg, M. Robert, "Family-Oriented Treatment of Marital Problems," *Social Casework,* XXXVII (January, 1956), 3-10.

Parsons, Talcott, and E. A. Shils, eds., *Toward a General Theory of Action.* Cambridge: Harvard University Press, 1951.

Porter, E. H., Jr., *An Introduction to Therapeutic Counseling.* Boston: Houghton-Mifflin, 1950.

Reik, Theodore, *Listening with the Third Ear.* New York: Farrar, Straus, 1952.

Rogers, Carl R., *Client-Centered Therapy.* Boston: Houghton-Mifflin, 1951.

Ruesch, Jurgen, and Gregory Bateson, *Communication.* New York: W. W. Norton, 1951.

Chapter X. CASE RECORDING

Hamilton, Gordon, *Theory and Practice of Social Case Work*, Rev. Ed. New York: Columbia University Press, 1951.

Kogan, L. S., L. H. Arfa, and E. J. Heilbrunn, "Validation of Caseworker's Impression by Verbatim Interviews Recording," *Journal of Social Casework*, XXXII (1951), 376-81.

Menninger, Karl A., *A Manual for Psychiatric Case Study*. New York: Grune and Stratton, 1952.

Sprafkin, Benjamin R., "A New Look At Confidentiality," *Social Casework*, XL, no. 2 (February, 1959), pp. 87-90.

Chapter XI. THE USE OF PSYCHIATRIC CONSULTATION IN COUNSELING

Eisenstein, Victor W., ed., *Neurotic Interaction in Marriage*. New York: Basic Books, 1956.

Miller, Arthur A., "The Psychiatric Consultant in Family Counseling," *Marriage and Family Living*, Vol. XVIII, no. 3 (August, 1956), pp. 254-58.

Chapter XII. THE USE OF REFERRAL RESOURCES

Flügel, J. C., *Man, Morals, and Society*. New York: International Universities Press, 1945.

Freud, Anna, *The Ego and the Mechanisms of Defense*. New York: International Universities Press, 1946.

Hiltner, Seward S., *Religion and Health*. New York: Macmillan, 1943.

Maslow, A. H., and Béla Mittleman, *Principles of Abnormal Psychology*. New York: Harper and Brothers, 1951.

Menninger, Karl A., "Religious Applications of Psychiatry," *Pastoral Counseling*, I (1950), 13-22.

Menninger, William C., "Psychiatry and Religion," *Pastoral Psychology*, I (1950), 14-16.

Weiss, Edoardo, *Principles of Psychodynamics*. New York: Grune and Stratton, 1950.

INDEX

A

Abnormal psychology, 2, 4
Acceptance of client, counselor, 58, 62, 87 (*see also* Counseling relationship)
Accepting client for counseling, 83-87
Ackerman, Nathan, 23-24
Adoptive home placement, 185
Advice-giving, 130, 158
Agencies, counseling:
- client acceptance, 83-87
- counselor's responsibility, 174-175
- environmental structure, 51-53, 113-114
- intake interview, 61
- psychiatric consultation, 175-178
- record-keeping, 152-170
- referral, 15-16, 182, 184
- services, types of, 11-12
- supervised training, 218
- time, use of, 53-54

Aid to Dependent Children, 185
Aid to the Blind, 185
Aid to the Disabled, 185
Alexander and French studies, 4
American Association of Marriage Counselors, 2, 7, 10, 34, 194
Anger at termination, 126
Anxiety:
- client, 97, 114-115, 150
- learning stimulus, 221
- tolerance, 86

Appointments, making, 53-54, 114-117, 178-179, 221
Attitudes:
- client, 104-109, 111-112
- counselor, 35-50, 87-88, 102, 104-109
- social learning, 7

B

Behavior in counseling, 58-60 (*see also* Counseling relationship)
Biological personality forces, 21, 22-24
Biology, training in, 3

C

Cannon, Walter, 22
Capacity, counselor faith in, 48
Case conference course, 232
Case records:
- recording, 152-164
- training guide, 222
- use, 164-170

Case studies:
- beneficial counseling reactions, 102-103
- both spouses, counseling, 122-124
- clarifying question, 135
- clients, types of, 13-15
- confronting comments, 142-143, 145-146
- confronting question, 138
- connecting comments, 141-142
- connecting questions, 136
- didactic training, 196-218
- empathic comment, 139
- enabling comments, 140-141
- fears, client, 18-20
- information-gathering question, 137
- informative comment, 147-148
- interview summary, 154-156
- joint initial interview, 73-79
- metaphor, use of, 118-119
- misuse of counseling, 128
- premarital initial interview, 63-72

Case studies (*Cont.*):
progress notes, 161-164
psychiatric referral, 179, 180-181
purposeful listening, 90-92
puzzling comments, 140
reflective comment, 139
reflective question, 135-136
silence, use of, 121, 150, 151
structure problems, 57, 115-117
verbalization, facilitating, 92-94, 95
Chairs, counseling use of, 52-53, 118-119
Child guidance clinics, 190
Child psychology, 4-5
Children's out-patient observation, 231
Clarifying question technique, 135, 198, 212
Clergymen, 10, 172, 178, 189
Client:
accepting for counseling, 83-87
assessing, 25-33
bio-psycho-social composition, 21-25
case records, 152-170
causes for counseling, 11-15
consciousness of material, 8-9
consultation considerations, 176-178
counseling, view of, 101-109
counselor relationship, 51-60 (*see also* Counseling relationship)
counselor's responsibility, 174
counselor training, role in, 219-220
definition, 2
ego assessment, 26-33
evaluation (*see* Evaluation of client)
expectations and fears, 16-20
initial interview, 61-82
marriage assessment, 159-161
metaphor, use of, 117-119
problems (*see* Problems, client)
psychiatric referral, 178-181
rapport, 87-89, 104, 105, 106, 140, 197
readiness for help, 131
referent reactions, 109-113
referral, 15-16, 182-193
religious convictions, 187
role, 41-42
Client (*Cont.*):
tardiness and appointment breaking, 54
techniques, response to, 133-151
termination, 125-127 (*see also* Termination)
training guide, 222-223
types, 10-11
Clinical judgment, 199, 200
Clinical psychology, 2, 4
Clinical training, 195, 218-232
Clinics, counseling (*see* Agencies, counseling)
Commenting technique, 89, 92-94, 138-149
Communication in counseling, 55-58 (*see also* Counseling relationship)
Community Chest agencies, 185, 190
Comparative psychology, 4
Compulsive reactions, 85
Conference observation, 231
Confidence, assurance of, 124, 167-168
Conflict, client, 6, 191
Confrontation, 97-98, 137-138, 139-140, 142-146, 196-218
Confronting comment technique, 142-146, 196-218
Confronting question technique, 137-138, 196-218
Connecting comments technique, 141-142
Connecting question technique, 136
Conscience, client's, 32, 86
Consciousness as counseling criteria, 184
Constancy, principle of, 23
Consultation, psychiatric, 171-181
Counseling (*see* Marriage counseling)
Counseling relationship:
both spouses, 122-125
client's role, 41-42
client's view, 101-109
early phases, 83-98
individual consultation, 177-178
metaphor, use of, 117-119
personal structure, 55-60
physical structure, 51-53, 113-114
quiet stages, 120-122
rapport, 87-89
recording, 152-170

Counseling relationship (*Cont.*):
staff consultation benefits, 176
stages, 104-109
testing, 99-101
time structure, 53-54, 114-117
training guide, 223-224
withholding information, 119-120, 150
Counseling room, 52-53
Counseling techniques (*see* Techniques, counseling)
Counselor (*see* Marriage counselor)
Countertransference, 40, 41, 213
Crises, meeting, 32-33
Cruser, Robert, 225
Cuber, John, 36
Cultural anthropology, 2, 4
Cultural aspects of personality, 46, 195
Cultural training of the counselor, 49-50
Cumulative confrontation, 143-144
Decompensation, 191
Desk, counseling use of, 53
Deterrents in counseling, 96-98

D

Developmental psychology, 4-5
Didactic training, 49, 195-218, 225-232
Displacement, 213-214
Disposition of cases, 177 (*see also* Referral; Termination)
Divorce, problems of, 13, 81
Drives, study of, 4-5
Dynamic psychiatry course, 230
Dynamic psychology, 195, 225, 229

E

Economic assistance, 147-148
Economics of the family course, 230
Economic study, 2
Educational institution training programs, 194
Educators as counselors, 10
Ego, 27, 28, 29-33 (*see also* Ego strength)
Ego defenses, 29-30, 33, 85, 86, 192
Ego strength:
assessing client, 26-33, 81, 86, 183
Ego strength (*Cont.*):
confrontation basis, 145
counselor, 195, 219, 220, 221
intake evaluation, 81
tentative assessment, 86
v. unconscious technique, 9
Emotional health and disorders, 171-173, 180, 188
Emotions:
evaluating reactions, 85, 87-88
studies, 4
Empathic comment technique, 139
Empathy, counselor, 45, 47, 139
Enabling comment technique, 140-141
Environment, counseling, 51-54, 113-114
Ethics:
case records, 167-170
counselor, 48
referral, 182, 184
Ethnic values, 5
Evaluation of client:
accepting for continued counseling, 83-87
ego strength, 26-33, 183
intake interview, 80-82
marriage assessment summary, 158-161
recording, 152-164
Experimental psychology, 2, 4

F

Faith, counselor, 48
Family assistance, 2, 184-190, 195
Family mental hygiene course, 229
Family Service Association of America, 185
Fears, client, 18-20, 87-88, 124, 192-193
Fechner's principle of constancy, 23
Feelings, studies of, 4
Fenichel, Otto, 23*n*
Files, access to, 168-169
Financial assistance, 26
Fink, Arthur E., 185*n*
Flexibility of client, 86
Forms for case recording, 152-156
Foster care for children, 185
Foster, Robert, 9*n*, 194*n*
French, psychotherapeutic views of, 4

Freud, Sigmund, 3, 23, 27, 37, 40, 43, 189
Frustration in marriage, 172-173
Frustration tolerance, 32

G

Garrett, Annette, 40
General semantics, 2
Genetic psychology, 2, 4
Genetics, 3
Gestalt psychology, 4
Graduate training programs, 194
Group consultation, 175-177
Guilt feelings, 32, 86, 146

H

Head-on confronting comment, 143-144
Holding action of referral, 193
Hollis, Florence, 185*n*
Homeostasis, 22-24
Horney, psychotherapeutic view of, 4
Hostility, client, 120
Human behavior (*see also* Personality):
- assessing, 21-33
- counselor understanding, 3-6
- psychotherapy value, 38

Humor, client's sense of, 33
Husband-wife role:
- cause of counseling, 12, 13, 14
- cultural definition, 5
- marriage assessment, 160
- religious influence, 5-6

Hysterical reactions, 44, 85

I

Id, 27-28, 30
Individual case supervision, 222-224, 231-232
Individual consultation, 177-178
Individual development course, 227
Information-gathering question technique, 136-137
Information-giving function, 6, 147-149
Informative comment technique, 147-149
Initial interview:
- case record form, 154
- summarizing, 158-159
- techniques, 61-82

Intake interviewer, 61 (*see also* Initial interview)
Interests, client, 32
Interpersonal relationships:
- assessment, 31-33, 86, 183
- both spouses, counseling of, 122-125
- client-counselor, 55-60 (*see also* Counseling relationship)
- conflict, 6, 191
- consultation clarification, 177
- counseling carryover, 102
- deterrents, 96-98
- marriage assessment summary, 159-161
- personality formation, 4
- rapport, 87-89
- spouse reactions, 8
- training fundamental, 3, 195, 223

Interpretation technique, 146
Interviews:
- both spouses, counseling, 122-125
- counseling definition, 3
- early phases, 83, 87-98
- initial, 61-82
- physical aspects, 51-53
- recording, 152-164
- referral, 192
- silence, use of, 149-151
- structuring, 113-122
- techniques, 132-151
- terminating (*see* Termination)
- time, use of, 53-54, 114-117

Intrapsychic conflict, 191
Isolated practice, problems of, 166-167

J

Joint counseling, 122-125
Joint interviews, 52, 73-79 (*see also* Interviews)
Jones, Ernest, 23*n*

L

Leader, Arthur, 221*n*
Legal assistance, 26, 147, 184, 228

Legal information in counselor training, 3, 196
Lighting in counseling environment, 53
Limitations, principle of, 131-132
Listening technique:
  development, 133-134
  early counseling, 89-95
  intake interview, 79
Lower-class groups, 11

M

Marital conflict, 141
Marital relationships (*see* Interpersonal relationships)
Marital values, 5-6
Marriage assessment summary, 158-161, 176, 183
Marriage counseling:
  agencies (*see* Agencies, counseling)
  aims, 7-9, 60
  case history, use of, 164-170
  case recording, 152-164
  client, 10-33 (*see also* Client)
  continued basis, 99-127
  counselor-client relationship, 51-60 (*see also* Counseling relationship)
  data correlation, 10
  definition, 2-3, 8-9
  early phases, 83-98
  historical development, 1-7
  initial interview, 61-82
  motivation for counseling career, 36
  professional training, 194-232
  psychiatric consultation, 171-181
  referral, 12-15, 182-193
  skill acquisition, 151
  stages, 104-109
  techniques, 128-151 (*see also* Techniques, counseling)
  transference, 41-42
Marriage counselor:
  accepting client for counseling, 83-87
  case history, use of, 164-170
  case recording, 152-164
  client relationship, 41-42, 51-60 (*see also* Counseling relationship)
Marriage counselor (*Cont.*):
  confidential assurance, 124, 167-168
  dangers in counseling, 128-129
  initial interview, 61-82
  principles, 129-132
  psychiatric consultation, 171-181
  rapport, 87-89, 104, 105, 106, 140, 197
  referral resources, 182-193
  responsibilities, 173-175
  role and function, 182-183
  supervision guidance, 222-224, 225, 226
  tasks by counseling stage, 104-109
  techniques (*see* Techniques, counseling)
  termination determination, 125-127
  training, 34-50, 194-232 (*see also* Training, counselor)
  unconscious life, dealing with, 9
  value system, 5, 6
  working knowledge, 2, 6
Marriage education, 3, 6, 147, 195
Medical assistance, 80, 147, 172, 184, 185-187
Medical information in training, 196, 229
Menninger Foundation training program, 194-218, 225-232
Menninger, Karl, 40-41, 188, 189
Menningers' psychotherapeutic views, 4
Mental disorders, 171-173
Mental hygiene clinics, 190
Metaphor in counseling, 117-119
Middle-class clients, 11
Middle-class values, 5
Miller, Arthur, 177
Ministers as counselors, 10, 172, 178, 189
Motivation:
  client, 24-26, 61-62, 63-64, 84-85
  counselor, 6, 45
  intake evaluation, 80
  self-preservation drive, 27
  studies, 4, 5
  time factors, 114
Mudd, Emily, 1*n*, 3*n*, 10*n*
Murray's concept of personology, 1-2

N

National Association of Social Workers, 225
Needs:
  client, 24-26, 104-109, 160
  counselor, 39-40
Nelson, Janet, 2*n*
Neurological diagnosis, 229
Neurology, study of, 2
Nimkoff, Meyer, 5
Note-taking in interviews, 152-153

O

Office, counseling, 52-53
Old Age Assistance, 185
Overcompensation, 30, 46

P

Parent-child interaction course, 230
Parenthood, preparation for, 13
Pathological reactions, 1, 85
Perceptive powers, 29
Permissiveness, counselor, 58, 59, 62, 87
Personality:
  cause of counseling, 13
  client assessment, 21-33
  counseling goal, 95-96
  counselor training, 3, 35-46
  dynamic psychology training, 195
  Freud's contribution, 3, 27-28
  growth and development studies, 1-2
  maladaptive reactions, 7
  psychology, contribution of, 4-5
  spouse reactions, 8
  worth principle, 129
Personology, 1-2 (*see also* Personality)
Philosophy, counselor, 47, 132
Phonographic recordings, use of, 156-158
Physicians, role in counseling, 80, 147, 172, 187
Physiological psychology, 4
Physiology:
  counselor training, 3
  personology basis, 2
Postgraduate training programs, 194
Postmarital counseling, 12 (*see also* Marriage counseling)
Premarital counseling:
  client problems, 12-13
  information-giving comments, 148-149
  initial interview case study, 63-72
  intake evaluation, 81
Principle of constancy, 23
Principles of counseling, 129-132, 220
Privileged communication, 167
Problems, client:
  appraising, 83-87
  both spouses, 122-125
  clarifying, 135
  confrontation, 142 (*see also* Confrontation)
  consultation clarification, 177
  intake evaluation, 80-82
  marriage assessment summary, 159-161
  referral v. counseling, 183-184
  stages in counseling, 105-109
  training, role in, 219-220, 223
Problems, training, 220
Progress notes, 161-164
Projection, 30, 33, 86, 192
Psychiatric case study course, 227
Psychiatric consultation and supervision course, 232
Psychiatric consultation, use of, 171-181
Psychiatric referral, 83-84, 95, 171, 178-181, 190, 191-193 (*see also* Psychotherapy; Referral)
Psychiatric social work course, 230
Psychiatrists:
  counselor's consultant, 166, 173-181
  ministerial role, 188
  referral resource, 190
  training aide, 225
Psychiatry:
  career motivation, 36
  counselor training, 3
  Menninger program, 196, 227, 228, 230, 232
  religion, relation of, 188
  personology basis, 2
  studies, 5
Psychoanalysis as training factor, 37
Psychogenetic studies, 4-5

Psychological personality forces, 22-33, 35-46
Psychological tests, 229
Psychologists, role of, 10, 41, 172
Psychology:
career motivation, 36
counseling contribution, 4-5
counselor training programs, 3, 194, 195, 225
dynamic training, 195
marriage counseling practice, 10
Menninger Foundation program courses, 229
personology basis, 2
Psychopathology course, 228
Psychotherapy:
consultation hours, 178
counseling contribution, 4
counselor training, 38-39, 224
introspection help, 146
learning relationship, 6-7
Menninger course, 228
referral, 190
transference, 40-41, 112-113
v. counseling, 9
Public welfare agencies, 185
Purposeful listening, 90, 133-134 (*see also* Listening technique)
Puzzling comment technique, 139-140

Q

Questioning technique:
early counseling stage, 89-90, 92-94
intake interview, 79-80
types applied, 134-138
Quiet stages in counseling, 120-122, 149-151

R

Rank, psychotherapeutic views of, 4
Rapport, establishing, 87-89, 104, 105, 106, 140, 197
Rationalization, 30
Reaction formation, 30
Record-keeping, 152-170
Referent reaction:
client role, 42
counselor self-understanding, 42-45
identifying, 109-113
Referral:
causes, 11-15
Referral (*Cont.*):
client understanding factor, 158
consultation clarification, 177
counselor training, 224
intake evaluation, 80
limitations principle, 131
necessity, 147-149
other help, 28-29
psychiatric, 83-84, 95, 171, 178-181, 190, 191-193
resource use, 182-193
training fundamental, 195
transfer of case records, 164
types, 15-16
Reflective comment technique, 94-95, 138-139, 198, 212
Reflective question technique, 135-136, 212
Regression, 41
Religion:
husband-wife values, 5-6
Menninger Foundation course, 230
referral resources, 187-190
Repetition compulsion, 40
Resistance to counseling, 59-60, 95-96, 221
Rogers, Carl, 4, 36
Role-playing training, 218

S

Self, concept of, 187-188
Self awareness, counselor, 37-40, 42-46, 195, 219, 220
Self-determination freedom, principle of, 129-131
Self-preservation drive, 27
Self-respect, client, 31-32, 86
Seminars in training program, 196
Separation, marital, 13
Services, counseling (*see* Agencies, counseling)
Sexual relationship, 32
Sharpe, Ella, 118*n*
Silence, technique of, 121, 149-151, 202
Skill, counseling, 151
Social and community participation, client, 86
Social factors of personality, 21-22, 195
Social psychology, 2, 4
Social Security programs, 185

Social work:
agencies, 184
career motivation, 36
counselor training, 6, 194-195, 230
Social workers, counseling role of, 10, 41, 172, 181
Socio-drama training, 218
Sociology:
contributions to counseling, 5-6
counselor training, 3, 194, 195
personology basis, 2
Space, counseling, 51-53
Spouse-blame, 196, 202
Staff consultation, 166, 175-177
Stages in counseling, 104-109
Stages of counselor supervision, 225, 226
Structure:
counseling, 113-117, 122-125, 198-199, 200
training, 221-222
Subpoenaed case records, 167
Sullivan, psychotherapeutic views of, 4
Superego, 27, 28
Supervision of training (*see also* Training, counselor):
professional clinical practice, 218-232
self-understanding aid, 39
skill, attaining, 151

T

Tape recording, counseling use, 156-158
Teaching, case record use in, 169-170
Techniques, counseling (*see also specific technique*):
both spouses, counseling, 125
consultation clarification, 177
didactic training, 196-218
early phases, 87-98
ego strength v. unconscious, 9
interview, 79-82 (*see also* Interviews)
Menninger course, 227-228
metaphorical meaning, recognizing, 119
overview, 132, 151
science and art, 47
training fundamentals, 3, 195, 220
types, 133-151
Termination:
consultation clarification, 177
counseling stage, 109
determining, 125-127
premature, 97-98, 99-101
referral (*see* Referral)
silence-caused, 150
The American Association of Marriage Counselors, 2, 7, 10, 34, 194
The Family Service Association of America, 185
Time, use of in counseling, 53-54, 59, 114-117
Training, counselor:
agency in-service program, 176
basic fields, 3, 6
case records:
use of, 169-170
writing, 168
counseling concept influence, 7-8
personal, 34-46
professional, 34, 47-50, 194-232
selection standards, 48-49
supervised experience, 39, 151, 218-232
tape recorder use, 157
Transference, 40-42, 43-44, 110, 112-113

U

Unconscious, dealing with, 9, 17-18
United Fund clinics and agencies, 185, 190
Unmarried mothers, assistance for, 185
Upper-class clients, 11

V

Value systems, counselor, 5, 37-38, 47, 130
Verbalizing, facilitating, 92-95, 140, 149-150
Verbatim records, 156-158

W

Wish-defense systems, 25, 28
Withholding information, 119-120, 150
Worth of human personality principle, 129